Dreaming Souls

Sleep, Dreams, and the Evolution of the Conscious Mind

Owen Flanagan

OXFORD
UNIVERSITY PRESS

OXFORD
UNIVERSITY PRESS

Oxford   New York
Athens   Auckland   Bangkok   Bogotá   Buenos Aires
Calcutta   Cape Town   Chennai   Dar es Salaam   Delhi
Florence   Hong Kong   Istanbul   Karachi   Kuala Lumpur
Madrid   Melbourne   Mexico City   Mumbai   Nairobi
Paris   São Paulo   Shanghai   Singapore   Taipei   Tokyo   Toronto   Warsaw

and associated companies in

Berlin   Ibadan

First published by Oxford University Press, Inc., 2000
198 Madison Avenue, New York, New York 10016
http://www.oup-usa.org
1-800-334-4249

First issued as an Oxford University Press paperback, 2001

Oxford is a registered trademark of Oxford University Press

Library of Congress Cataloging-in-Publication Data
Flanagan, Owen J.
Dreaming souls : sleep, dreams, and the evolution
of the conscious mind / by Owen Flanagan
p.   cm. — (Philosophy of mind series)
Includes bibliographical references and index.
ISBN 0-19-512687-4 (Cloth)
ISBN 0-19-514235-7 (Pbk.)
1. Dreams. 2. Dream interpretation. 3. Philosophy of mind.
I. Title. II. Series.
BF1091.F58   2000
154.6'3 — DC21

10 9 8 7 6 5 4 3 2 1
Printed in the United States of America
on acid-free paper

Dreaming Souls

DATE DUE

PHILOSOPHY OF MIND SERIES
Series Editor
Owen Flanagan, Duke University

SELF EXPRESSIONS
Mind, Morals, and the Meaning of Life
Owen Flanagan

THE CONSCIOUS MIND
In Search of a Fundamental Theory
David J. Chalmers

DECONSTRUCTING THE MIND
Stephen P. Stich

THE HUMAN ANIMAL
Personal Identity Without Psychology
Eric Olson

MINDS AND BODIES
Philosophers and Their Ideas
Colin McGinn

WHAT'S WITHIN?
Nativism Reconsidered
Fiona Cowie

Other Books by Owen Flanagan

THE SCIENCE OF THE MIND

IDENTITY, CHARACTER, AND MORALITY
(ed. with Amelie Rorty)

VARIETIES OF MORAL PERSONALITY: ETHICS AND
PSYCHOLOGICAL REALISM

CONSCIOUSNESS RECONSIDERED

THE NATURE OF CONSCIOUSNESS
(ed. with Ned Block and Guven Guzeldere)

To

Nancy Zinsser Walworth,

Edward H. Walworth,

and the Walworth Clan

With love, respect, and gratitude

Contents

Acknowledgments

During a memorable summer vacation in 1977 near Bar Harbor on the coast of Maine, I read Freud's *The Interpretation of Dreams* carefully. Time passed. A decade. And then, on a snowy night in 1988, I gobbled up Allan Hobson's first book on dreams, *The Dreaming Brain*, after discovering it at Wordsworth in Harvard Square. I remembered that night that my friend Paul Churchland had written that almost nothing was known about sleep and dreams, and I was pleased to think I had found an illuminating, instructive, and empirically well-grounded theory in Hobson's book—now drenched in melted snow, due to my slow, absorbed, page-turning walk from Harvard to Kendall Square, near MIT. By the next day I was back to teaching, family, and preparing for coaching the upcoming Little League baseball season. But by then thinking about dreams had secured its own room in my head, and I started hesitantly to talk and wonder aloud about dreams in my philosophy of mind courses at Wellesley College and Brandeis University.

Several years later, some combination of my interests, my new colleagues at Duke (where I moved in 1993), and my time on earth took me to worrying about how little we understand about the nature and function of consciousness and of certain everyday and universal kinds of consciousness, such as dreams. I made a first pass at the issue in my Presidential Address to the Society for Philosophy and Psychology in 1994, which was published the next year in *The Journal of Philosophy* under the title "Deconstructing Dreams: The Spandrels of Sleep."

Sometimes, at least in philosophy, you pronounce on a topic, and think you are done with it. Then the conspiracy happens. Others— and you yourself—want to know more about what you are thinking and why. This book is a result of such a conspiracy. It registers, records, and develops my thinking about the nature and function of dreams into—Lord, keep the words from my lips—a full-blown theory. I am extremely lucky to have many acquaintances interested in dreams—good friends and loved ones, as well as conscientious correspondents and tireless critics. Before I throw bouquets, I do want to say that I have been privy to the most intimate dream reports of both friends and strangers. Sometimes, after patient, comforting, and serendipitously wise analyses, I would ask the dreamer to be a dream donor and allow me to use the dream in the book. No one, I repeat, no one, ever gave permission. This is one reason you have suffered more of my dreams and thus more of me than you expected and may have wished.

Now for the flowers. Lindie Bosniak was there at the very beginning when over twenty years ago I read Freud in Maine. Deborah Stalkopf and Gail March were there over a decade later when they helped me explore and then encouraged my heretical views about the nature of dreams. There are those who read the entire manuscript—at some stage—and made valuable comments: Francis Crick, Gillian Einstein, Güven Güzeldere, Valerie Hardcastle, Allan Hobson, Robert Miller, my editor, Thomas Polger, Kevin Sauvé, Steven Stich, and Joyce Walworth.

Joseph Bogen, Robert Brandon, Andy Clark, John Cleary, Leda Cosmides, Peter Godfrey-Smith, Christof Koch, Elizabeth Knoll, Alasdair MacIntyre, James Mahon, Phil Merikle, Eddy Nahmias, Joe Neisser, Dick Neisser, Veronica Poncé, Beth Preston, Bob Richardson, L. D. Russell, David Sanford, Tad Schmaltz, Betty Stanton, and John Tooby asked helpful, difficult questions, offered wise criticism and advice, and in several cases read and commented on parts of the manuscript.

Conversations with Dan Dennett (who I swear admitted the usefulness of a notion such as "spandrels" for dealing with dreams—we were at a drinking emporium in Minnesota, so there is "deniability"), Joel Kupperman (who told me about the Buddhist schism over wet dreams and sent me information about it), and Dave Chalmers (who wins the prize for having heard me speak on this topic more than anyone else) were extremely helpful.

Joellyn Ausanka, the production/copy editor, Mary Ellen Curley, the marketing director who oversaw the design of the cover, and Elissa Morris, Robert Miller's assistant, did yeoman's work in getting the book out expeditiously.

Besides these particular individuals, I am thankful also to have had opportunities in the last five years to have spoken on dreams in a variety of places. Audiences help speakers learn, and I am grateful to the heavenly host of audiences who taught me many things. Abroad, I learned a great deal in Dublin, Kyoto, Melbourne, Oxford, and San Sebastian, Spain. At home, I was helped by audiences in Athens, Ga.; Berkeley, Palo Alto, and Pasadena, Calif.; Birmingham, Ala.; Columbia, S.C.; Durham, N.C.; Memphis and Nashville, Tenn.; New Orleans, La.; New York City; Oxford, Miss.; St. Louis, Mo.; St. Paul, Minn.; Stony Brook and Ithaca, N.Y.; and Tucson, Ariz.

Almost every audience I have spoken to has been filled with its critics. De-meaning dreams was the usual charge. Dreams exist. I have them. As do you. Some are meaningful and worth learning from. Some aren't. One colleague called me a "hermeneutical nihilist," to which I responded that I would have thought I was a "promiscuous hermeneut"—one who believes in the meaningfulness—possibly not worth exploring—of most everything. Dreams have meaning because they contain thoughts, images, and feelings, and these have meaning. Whether all thoughts, images, and feelings strung together, however, have meaning is unclear. And whether, even if meaning is there, it is worth attending to is also unclear. In fact it is doubtful. I think that neither strings made up of meaning nor all meaningful strings are worth the effort of interpretation. There I stand.

I have already thanked Joyce Walworth for her careful reading of the manuscript, but I owe her a special debt of gratitude for her patient love and support during what turned out, for a variety of reasons, to be the most difficult time in our eighteen years together. Then there are our teenagers, Ben and Kate. In the late autumn of 1997, when I first started work on this book, Kate had to choose a topic for her "senior project" (eighth grade). Dreaming was her choice. I discovered this while driving Kate and her friends Emmy and Kaitlin (who was also going to write on dreams) to school one morning, and exclaimed that I too was working on dreams. Kaitlin seemed happy; Kate did not. The school has a rule: Consult experts unless one of the experts is your own parent. Somehow, late in the year, Kate and I snuck in a few conversations, and we shared the merriment of working on overheads for her project presentation in the spring. Ben, my rock star son, does music—and sometimes, school. The high school Ben attends is run by Quakers. Friendly and low-keyed as they are, they do have some rules. So Ben was set the task, in order to pass English, to recite a famous literary passage. He chose Hamlet's "To be, or not to be" speech, which led it to be on my mind. I remember vividly asking Ben what the speech meant. He was shocked that I found it difficult to understand, but then explained its meaning to me, more clearly and deeply than I could have seen. I adore Kate and Ben; they mean more than anything in the world to me, and I am grateful to them for who and what they are, and for the many ways they inspire me.

Gillian Einstein and Güven Güzeldere gave more than collegial support, as did Brook Sadler and Steve Geisz. Thank you.

My greatest debt on this particular voyage is to Thomas Polger. Tom and I talk about mind and consciousness most days. "Polger," as I call him, has read every word in this book, several times. He has talked over every idea in the book with me, many times. He has helped me get clearer on most everything, and he has drawn many of the figures that appear in the book. Words escape me—or perhaps, as I suspect, words cannot do this kind of job—when I try to say what Thomas Polger's thinking and criticism have meant to me. They, and he, mean a great deal to me. More than I can say.

Durham, North Carolina
January 1999

Dreaming Souls

"To Sleep: Perchance to Dream"

To be, or not to be: that is the question:
Whether 'tis nobler in the mind to suffer
The slings and arrows of outrageous fortune,
Or to take arms against a sea of troubles,
And by opposing end them? To die: to sleep;
No more; and, by a sleep to say we end
The heartache and the thousand natural shocks
That flesh is heir to, 'tis a consummation
Devoutly to be wished. To die, to sleep;
To sleep: perchance to dream: ay, there's the rub;
For in that sleep of death what dreams may come
When we have shuffled off this mortal coil,
Must give us pause.

—*William Shakespeare*, Hamlet, *Act III, Scene i*

WHEN HAMLET, THE PRINCE OF Denmark, asks the compelling question "To be, or not to be?," he is, of course, contemplating suicide. Is it worth going on to face "the slings and arrows of outrageous fortune, . . . the heartache and the thousand . . . shocks that flesh is heir to"—when one could just end things? At first the thought of death as eternal rest comforts Hamlet. But he immediately worries "to sleep: perchance to dream: ay, there's the rub"! We know not "what dreams may come when we have shuffled off this mortal coil."

It is this thought, that we might not find eternal rest in "that sleep of death" but instead might have hellish dreams for all eternity, that is "the rub." And it is this thought that "give[s] us pause," "puzzles the will," and ultimately "makes cowards of us all." The "dread of something after death" makes us bear "those ills we have than fly to others we know not of."

This speech, possibly the most famous in all of English literature, gets quickly to the heart of the problem: the problem of consciousness in general and dream consciousness in particular. Hamlet is in anguish. Were he a different sort of person with a different sort of life, he might be happy about how things have gone for him. However, the thought of death and the worry that after death he might continue to exist in some horrible dreamland could just as easily worry a happy Hamlet as it does the actual distraught Hamlet. Indeed, the very same set of concerns arise in a conversation Socrates has with two of his students, Simmias and Cebes, on the very day in 499 B.C.E. that he drinks the hemlock cocktail provided at state expense. Socrates is calm and rational in the "Phaedo," whereas his much younger friends are clearly agitated—fearful both of the prospect of a death that is dreamless and one that is rich in dreams.

It is in virtue of being conscious in the way he is that Hamlet experiences his life as at this choice point. Being the kind of conscious creature he is enables Hamlet both to feel the weight of his past and to contemplate the uncertainty of the future. And it is the progression of conscious thinking that takes him from the brief comforting thought of death as eternal restful sleep to the concern that his woes might continue even after he has been released from his body—even after he has shuffled off "this mortal coil"—so long as he, even though dead, continues to experience things, so long as he continues to dream.

In 1600, when *Hamlet* was written, the word "conscience" meant consciousness. So when Hamlet concludes the speech by announcing that "conscience doth make cowards of us all," he means that consciousness, awareness, our sensitivity to the state of our own hearts and minds, and our wide-ranging capacities to discern future prospects bring with it knowledge that can just as easily immobilize the will as mobilize it.

Hamlet asks the most frightening existential question. And he is able to do so because he is conscious of life and death, of living and dying, in the way human beings are. Philosophically, consciousness warrants attention because so much, indeed essentially everything, depends upon it. Life as we know it, whether it goes well or badly at each moment or over periods of time, possibly over the course of a whole life, depends on how that life is experienced by the individual who lives it. Who has not wondered why experience touches us so deeply—indeed, why it touches us at all? Who has not sought rest in sleep, a sleep we hope will involve pleasant, peaceful dreams, or no dreams at all? The question "to be, or not to be?" is a question for conscious creatures, and even so, only for conscious creatures of a very sophisticated sort.

From a scientific point of view, consciousness presents its own puzzles. First, how is it realized? How does the brain produce consciousness? How is subjective experience possible in an objective, material world? We know that it is possible because we are animals existing in a material world, and we are conscious. But we do not understand how it is that numerous complexly structured, insentient neurons, in virtue of being well connected and living in a sea of exotic, but equally dumb, neurochemicals, generate a subjective life.

The second puzzling aspect of consciousness has to do with its function. What, if anything, is consciousness for? To be sure, you would not be you, nor would I be me, if we did not have the rich conscious lives we in fact have. But it is not clear why Mother Nature endowed us, and many other animals, with consciousness in the first place. What function does consciousness serve that couldn't be equally well but more simply served by being a very intelligent creature that lacks experience altogether?

In the mid 1990s, a computer, "Deep Blue," beat Gary Kasparov, the world champion, at chess. No one thinks Deep Blue experiences anything. Deep Blue has no inner life whatsoever. But Deep Blue plays world class chess. And it does so by processing information, keeping track of patterns, and by being able to adjust its behavior creatively in response to new stimuli on the basis of stored information. Deep Blue is an intelligent, but utterly nonconscious, system.

Deep Blue shows that consciousness and intelligence can come apart. Why, in addition to processing information, storing it, and utilizing it, do we, and probably most other animals, have experiences? What does experience add to being intelligent other than, as it were, experience?

Life would not be the same without consciousness. Joy, love, happiness, sadness, and despair would all be missing. There would be no "thrill of victory" and no "agony of defeat." Life would have no personal meaning or significance if we didn't experience it as meaningful and endow it with meaning. Hamlet's question could not be asked were we not conscious.

This reaction expresses, and in some sense explains, why almost no conscious individual would want to live or relive his life without consciousness—even Hamlet in his moment of despair. However, it does not explain why Mother Nature selected for consciousness, for subjectivity, in the first place. Mother Nature selects traits because they are fitness enhancing—not because she thinks these traits will provide fun and eventually be dear to the hearts of the organisms that have those traits, or because they will give life meaning. It will be good, therefore, if we can explain how it is that consciousness is fitness enhancing independently of whether it is happy making or meaning enhancing.

Intuitively, pain consciousness, visual consciousness, auditory consciousness, sexual pleasure or displeasure, even happiness or sadness, seem like traits that might fit with nature's aims. These kinds of consciousness might lead to rapid detection and utilization of certain kinds of important information if the mind was designed to stamp such information "top priority" and thereby get that information noticed, really noticed, getting it instantaneously onto center stage—bright lights and all—and thus singled out for special attention.

Maybe having the system direct all the bright lights to information that can be credibly tied to chances for continued survival or to reproductive success is an adaptation. However, even if there is some such plausible explanation for the evolution of consciousness in the five sensory modalities, other types of consciousness remain harder to explain in such terms.

Dream consciousness is especially puzzling. Everyone dreams. But unlike conscious sensory experience, which is also universal and which generally yields reliable information about the world, dreams don't seem to track the truth reliably. We entertain the false and the bizarre in dreams. Furthermore, it isn't as if most dreams provide enjoyable fun-filled entertainment suitable for family viewing. More dreams are unpleasant than are pleasant (perhaps Hamlet was aware of this, and perhaps this awareness heightened his worry about the possible nature of his postdeath experiences were he to choose to be released from his "mortal coil"). We often think and behave oddly— even badly—in dreams. And despite anecdotal hype to the contrary, dreams rarely yield directly to creativity in the arts, music, mathematics, science, or philosophy. It is hard to see what fitness-enhancing function dreams might serve. What use are wild-and-crazy nocturnal thoughts? And if they are of no use, why do they exist at all?

What are dreams for? That is the question. Are they an adaptation created by natural selection with some as yet undiscovered fitness-enhancing role? Or are they a mental analog of the appendix, a generally useless but occasionally harmful leftover from the design of ancestral species from whom *Homo sapiens* descended. Or are dreams like the off-white color of bones, which is a side effect of selection for firm and rigid skeletal structures in a calcium-rich environment. Nature's aim was for good hard bones. She cared not one bit about their color. Perhaps dreaming is an expectable side effect of selection for creatures designed to have and utilize experiences while they are awake, and which continue to have experiences after the lights go off—experiences which, during sleep, neither help nor hinder fitness. This I think is the truth, more or less, about dreams.

Even if Mother Nature didn't give high priority, or any priority at all, to the existence of dreaming, virtually every culture ever known has given high priority to the meaning of dreams. Is there anything to this urge to find meaning in dreams? Is there any meaning there? Can we use dreams to understand ourselves? These questions are not crazy. Many cultures, including my own, have engaged in astrological practices based on the belief that there is meaning in the stars; for example, believing that the positions of the heavenly bodies at the time of one's birth can reveal one's personality traits, and that subsequent positions of the stars and planets can yield reliable predictions about how one's day will go. Astrology is the possibility proof that a set of practices of interpretation, a set of widely held beliefs about what is revelatory, can be nearly universal, but utterly misguided. Empty.

For anyone interested in the nature of persons, in consciousness, in how the mind-brain works—and especially for anyone interested in issues of personal identity, self-expression, self-knowledge, and self-transformation—dreams represent an especially hard-to-fit piece of the vast and still largely incomplete puzzle that is the mind. The topic of sleep and dreams is something most everyone likes to talk about. Most ordinary folk as well as most scholars are surprised to find out that mentation goes on during non-rapid-eye-movement (NREM) sleep as well as during rapid-eye-movement (REM) sleep. In fact many books continue to identify periods of dreaming only with periods of REMing. Furthermore, most everyone is surprised to discover that sleepwalking, sleep-talking, nocturnal emissions, and night terrors are NREM phenomena—as is most snoring. And everyone is interested in the topic of dream interpretation. Many of the main theories about the nature and meaning of dreams come from the humanities—there are Hellenistic, Talmudic, Christian views, to name a few. And, of course, there are psychological views, Jungian and Freudian views, which have been extraordinarily influential in humanistic thought. I will not attempt or pretend to deal with all these views in any depth—indeed, some I will not deal with at all beyond mentioning their existence (which I have just now done). My mission will be accomplished by my own lights if I can bring the main interesting issues and credible positions on the nature and meaning of dreams into conversation and show how best, at the turn of the millennium, to think about a phenomenon that has affected and puzzled our species since the first sparks of consciousness and self-consciousness occurred.

It is uncertainty about whether some form of consciousness continues after we die, and if so which kind it is, that immobilizes Hamlet, and thereby keeps the play from ending before intermission. Are these phenomena—consciousness, death, sleep, and dreams—still as mysterious as they were four hundred years ago when Hamlet rightly wondered about them? Are they as mysterious as they were twenty-five hundred years ago when Socrates and his students puzzled over the problem of whether death is like dreamless sleep, nightmarish sleep, or filled with sweet dreams? I think not. Let me explain.

1

Heart
Throbs

We should count time by heart-throbs.

—*Philip James Bailey,"Festus," 1839*

My Dreams

1955: *A pack of wolves was chasing me. I was terrified and couldn't run away fast enough.* I awoke breathless, trying unsuccessfully to scream. Dad heard my feeble cries and arrived bedside to comfort me.

1997: *I was involved in a military maneuver sponsored by the CIA. My unit was badly positioned relative to the enemy, and we were pathetically armed. I was very frightened. I tried to explain to my comrades—between normal trips to get the clutch on my car fixed—that our nonautomatic rifles, a cross between a musket and an M-1 but with no magazines, were losers. Then I gave an antiwar speech insisting that we not obey government orders to do battle. I had some supporters and was subject to some ridicule. The chair of my department appeared in a feathered cap and wearing a tartan-plaid kilt, his weapon pointed as if he did not know what to do with it. He was clearly our leader. I was amused and scared. I picked up my car and was congratulated by the auto mechanics on our victory.* Then I awoke.

Dreaming Souls

What is a dream? Why do we dream? Do dreams mean anything? Do dreams matter to who we are, to our identity, to our personal relations? Do we express ourselves in dreams? Can we use dreams to understand ourselves and our lives? Do we solve personal, philosophical, scientific, or mathematical problems in dreams which we then reenact forgetfully by the light of day? Do dreams yield artistic insight—are they a laboratory where great poetry, paintings, novels, and music are cooked up? If dreams matter to who we are and to what we accomplish, why is memory for them so poor?

These are some of the important questions about dreams. There are further questions: Is dream consciousness a biological adaptation selected for because it contributes to fitness and thus to reproductive success like a well-designed heart? Or is dreaming like the sound the heart makes, which comes as a free-rider with any circulatory system that has at its center a pump in a cavity? Is dream consciousness a biological adaptation like pain consciousness or visual consciousness? Or is dreaming like the prize in the box of Cracker Jacks—a "freebie" that is of no consequence whatsoever to the Cracker Jacks themselves or to how they taste—and which in addition is often a throwaway? Or, to consider yet another possibility, could dream consciousness be maladaptive? No one thinks that the type of consciousness associated with paranoid schizophrenia is a biological adaptation despite the fact that it has a strong genetic component. But it is not uncommon. Dreams share many features with psychoses. Could dreams be a kind of universal psychosis, luckily sequestered to a time and place where it is okay, or at least not harmful, to be crazy?

These are sensible and difficult questions. This book provides some answers. My theory is a neurophilosophical one. I have tried to follow out the implications of recent work in the sciences of the mind on the nature and function of sleep and dreams while at the same time trying to fit dreams into a general philosophical theory of the conscious mind and the nature of persons. What is a general philosophical theory? To paraphrase Wilfred Sellars, it involves "trying to show how things in the broadest possible sense, hang together in the broadest possible sense." I like to think of the philosopher as a free-range chicken rather than a cooped-up one, ideally living in an area where getting to the other side of the road is at least possible, even though, whether you are free-ranged or cooped-up, you probably will be someone's dinner in the end. The ever perceptive Nietzsche notes that although the philosopher normally aims to build an edifice that will withstand every onslaught—Nietzsche calls this the "philosopher's error"—posterity typically finds value, and then only if the philosopher is lucky, in some of the building materials he uses.

The present aim is to provide a theory of the conscious mind, of persons, of self-expression, that takes mind-science seriously and tries in particular to explain the nature and function of dreams. If even a few of the building blocks of the theory prove useful to future enquirers I will consider the pretense of aiming actually to build such a grand theory worth every ounce of effort it has involved. Dreams and dream interpretation have been thought by many to be a rich mine for gaining self-knowledge—"the royal road to the unconscious mind," according to Freud—and by others not to merit much attention—"unmusical fingers wandering over the keys of a piano," as Wilhelm Wundt, a founding father of scientific psychology, put it. On either view, we are dreaming souls.

The fact that we are dreaming souls does not answer the question of what contribution, if any, dreams make to who we are, nor does the fact that we are dreaming souls answer the question of whether dreams express or yield knowledge—in particular, whether they express or yield self-knowledge. Perhaps dreams are just noise, unmelodious tunes the brain generates while we sleep.

What are we to make of my 1955 wolf nightmare and of my bizarre 1997 war dream? Perhaps they say something about me. Perhaps they say nothing and are as unworthy of attention as an occasional gurgling sound emanating from my stomach. How do we tell? How can we find out?

I have my dreams and you have yours. As with conscious mental life generally, I have my thoughts and you have yours. In 1890, William James put the point this way: "My thoughts belong with my other thoughts, and your thoughts with your other thoughts. The only states of consciousness that we naturally deal with are found in particular consciousnesses, minds, selves, concrete particular I's and you's."

The fact that we each have our own thoughts, and no one else's thoughts, keeps things neat and tidy. We can share our thoughts, of course, as I have already done, telling you about two dreams I had forty-two years apart, but we can't actually have each other's thoughts. Happily, neither waking nor dreaming mentation is part of one cosmic glob of thinking. Thoughts belong to particular thinkers.

The question remains: Do my dreams express anything about me or yours about you? The answer to this question is less clear than is the question of who has whose dreams. And it is a central part of our topic. Do dreams have a function, are they identity expressive; do dreams have meaning, and if so what do they mean, and how are they to be interpreted?

Perhaps dreams are a time-suck. Dreaming takes up a lot of time. If you are thirty years old, you have been alive about eleven thousand days. If you sleep eight hours a night and dream as little as two hours each night, then that is about one thousand days' worth of dreaming, approximately two and one-half years. Based on the evidence, I think it possible, even likely, that we dream all night long which, if true, means you have spent about four thousand days' worth, about ten years of your thirty years on earth, under the spell. As a rule, anything that takes up that much time in a life matters, and if it doesn't matter, then it seems worth wondering why it exists. Dreams exist. Do they matter? If so, how? If not, why not?

We are not the only animals that dream. If having experiences while asleep is taken as the criterion for dreaming, then many, possibly most, animals dream. Dreaming itself does not make us unique. It is what we do, or at least what we can do, with dreams that is unique and creative.

Objectifying Dreams

Before the argument that dreams are important and useful can be won, I first need a theory of dreams. But in order to have a theory of dreams that is more than just a riff on how dreams seem to me—a theory of dreams from this man's bedside, as it were—I need to explain how such private, fleeting, and forgettable experiences as dreams can be studied empirically. We need a method, or a set of procedures, for making dreams reveal their objective side. We want to know not only how dreams seem to the dreamer, but how dreams are produced in the brain and what effects dreams have on such things as one's mood and thoughts the morning after, and we want to know how they have whatever effects they have. Ultimately, we need to know what dreams are like from the objective point of view of science, as well as from the subjective point of view of the dreamer.

To get a feeling for the sort of theory I have in mind, consider my two dreams. The 1955 wolf dream seems, to this day, the scariest dream I ever had. But since, like you, I have no way of accurately assessing the relative scariness of all the dreams I have had, I can't know that it was, in fact, the most frightening dream I have ever had. Even if I had such a method of assessment, I would need to remember all my dreams in order to apply it. But I don't now remember all my dreams. Furthermore, there is reason to think that some very scary dreams were never noted upon awakening and thus were never remembered even briefly by the light of day. All this to one side, I do know that I had this particular dream, that it was very frightening, and that my father came to comfort me.

The second dream, the war dream, occurred early in Thanksgiving week of 1997, while I was starting to work on this book. I actually woke up during this dream and was relieved to discover that my experiences were only a dream. I resolved to go back to sleep and to dream about more pleasant things than risking my life in battle. My resolve, unfortunately, was to no avail. The dream continued, as if it had a will of its own, resuming at the point of my antiwar speech and moving on from there.

In telling you how the dreams seemed, I have provided you with the phenomenology. Phenomenology, literally "the study of appearances," is the philosopher's useful jargon for the study of how things seem from the subject's point of view. I have said what the dreams were about and what events and emotions I remember experiencing. From the first person point of view, from the point of view uninformed by theory, this is all we ever know or can say about our dreams. Dreams have a phenomenological surface structure. What, if anything, is behind them psychologically—whether dreams are expressions of unconscious wishes or just noise—is not revealed at the phenomenological surface. If I insist that my dreams express, reveal, or release unconscious wishes, I have said more than how they seem. I have cast how they seem in the mold of a particular psychological theory, one that has only become widely available and accepted over the course of the last century in the West.

Furthermore, not only are the psychological roots of my dreams not revealed by the dreams themselves, neither are any physical properties of dreams—assuming there are any—revealed by or in my dreams. Given all the facts about how dreams seem from the dreamer's point of view, nothing is revealed, one way or the other, about whether they take place in one's incorporeal soul, or in one's knees, liver, heart, or brain. My dreams definitely seem to occur to me, and not in God's mind or on the World Wide Web. My dreams are mine and yours are yours. My dreams occur in and to me. But it remains completely opaque from a first person perspective uninformed by scientific theory about such matters, where it is in me that my dreams occur, and how it is that my dreams work, that is, what physical mechanisms make them happen.

As with theories about the psychology of dreams, theories about the location of mental life have varied widely among cultures. It seems to me (and there is now good evidence that this is so) that my brain is the seat of my consciousness. It did not seem that way to ancient Egyptians, Mesopotamians, Jews, Hindus, Chinese, and Greeks, all of whom privileged the heart as the seat of the soul while occasionally also attributing mental functions to the spleen, bladder, liver, and head. The point is that we need more than phenomenology to understand the nature, function, meaning and location of dreams in general, and my two dreams in particular.

Psychology tells us that we learn, that our selves grow and are enriched by experience. Owen, the boy of five, had learned about wolves. The stories of the Three Little Pigs, terrorized by the huffing and puffing wolf, and of Little Red Riding Hood, who mistook the ferocious, hungry wolf for her grandmother, were everyday fare in my home.

Owen, the man of forty-eight, had experienced and thus remembered more than Owen the boy of five. Among other things, there was coming of age during Vietnam, time spent in antiwar protests and then on active duty in the military, familiarity with getting cars repaired, and years spent as a member of an academic department at a university.

My boyhood dream is simple; my adult dream is complex. Psychology predicts this should be so. As we develop, we gain in experience, memory, and complexity. Dreams are produced in and by individuals with different kinds and amounts of experience, in and by mind-brains with unique raw materials from which dreams can be built. As we age, there is more and more material available in the system to make either elaborate noise and nonsense, if that is what dreams do, or to produce increasingly complex self-expressive and self-revealing narratives, if that is what dreams do. Either way, whether dreams produce noise or knowledge, psychology and cognitive science predict greater complexity in the dreams of adults than in the dreams of young children.

Neuroscience helps fill out the picture further. Sleeping comes in two forms: non-rapid eye-movement (NREM) sleep and rapid-eye-movement (REM) sleep. NREM and REM mean exactly what they say. In NREM, your eyes are relatively stationary beneath the lids. In REM, your eyes are darting around beneath the lids. Dreams occur during both NREM and REM sleep. NREM dreams are more thoughtlike and less imagistic than REM dreams, akin to reading an article in the newspaper about the best time to plant the vegetable garden. REM dreams are more bizarre than NREM dreams, more akin to watching a Fellini motion picture while high on marijuana than reading the tip about tomato planting in the morning paper while drinking orange juice.

At a certain point in the sleep cycle—after an hour or so in NREM sleep—the brainstem, activated by changes in neurochemistry, starts to send pulses to higher brain regions. REMing coincides with pulses going to areas of the cortex that are known to be active when we are having vivid visual experiences while awake. Since both my dreams are rich in visual imagery, it is a reasonable inference that my dreams took place during REM sleep and not during NREM sleep and that they were initiated by the brainstem activation of memories and experiences stored in various parts of my cerebral cortex. In both dreams, my mind appears to have put the activated memories and experiences into a story, into a narrative structure. How exactly this is done, and why, is one puzzle that needs attention.

The emotions experienced, especially the fear, were in all likelihood due to activation of the amygdala, twin almond-shaped organs buried deep beneath my ears. The amygdala were activated by signals received by the thalamus from areas of the visual cortex where pictures of wolves and war were conjured up, as well as from other cortical areas that know, nonimagistically, as it were, that wolves and war are bad, that they are things worth being scared of. Furthermore, the activation of the amygdala by images and thoughts of wolves and war almost certainly caused an adrenaline surge in my bloodstream, which made me, all of me, frightened, with increased heart rate and the like.[1]

The Natural Method

The discussion of my two dreams reveals the strategy I favor for building a robust empirical theory of dreams. The best tactic for understanding consciousness, generally, and dream consciousness in particular requires employing "the natural method," what the philosopher Patricia Smith Churchland calls the "co-evolutionary strategy." The idea is to keep one's eye, as much as is humanly possible, on all the relevant hypotheses and data sources at once in the attempt to construct a credible theory.

The natural method involves seeking consistency and equilibrium among different modes of analysis applied to the study of some mental phenomenon (Fig. 1.1). The method is designed to be perfectly general, applicable to any kind of mental state.[2] In the case of dreams, phenomenology, will supply us with first-person reports about how dreams *seem*, especially how particular dreams seem from the point of view of the person who has the dream. Everything about how the dream seems is grist for the phenomenological mill: what the dream is about, what happened in the dream, emotions experienced, what seems vivid, what seems vague, and so on. Phenomenology will provide us, as it were, with the dream as dreamed or, what is different, the dream as remembered, the dream as it seems by the light of day.

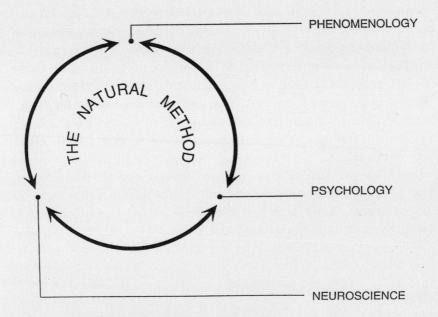

Figure 1.1 The natural method. Adapted from Flanagan, "Deconstructing Dreams," p. 9.

The mental sciences—psychology, cognitive science, and neuroscience—are needed to provide answers to a host of questions that are not answered by how things seem, even if we take how they seem to be as how they really are for the dreamer. The mental sciences will tell us about the objective side of dreams.

To get a sense of the subjective-objective contrast, of how different things might look from the subjective versus the objective perspective, consider the phenomenon of lower back pain. Lower back pain feels a certain way—it aches in one's lower back, and not in one's shoulder or neck—which is why we call it lower back pain, and not shoulder or neck pain. But how the lower back pain feels to the person with the pain tells that person nothing, at least nothing reliable, about what the muscles, tissues, nerves, and blood vessels in her lower back are doing. A person is always right about where she feels pain—in the present case, the pain is *in* her lower back. But she could be wrong about the source of her pain, about where her ache in fact emanates from. Some pain is "referred pain." The source of what seems to be lower back pain is sometimes not strained or knotted muscles in one's back, but a growth or misalignment higher up in the spine, shoulder, neck, even in the brain.

And so it is with sleep and dreams. The phenomenology of sleep and dreams, the subjective side of sleep and dreams, is something about which we can each claim some expertise. But what is going on in the brain and the rest of the body when we sleep and dream is not something introspective attention reveals.

Neuroscience will provide information about the relationship between sleep and dreams. Are we always dreaming while asleep? Or, is some time genuine quiet time where we sleep and no thinking whatsoever occurs? If so, then there are times in which we are alive but not conscious.

Neuroscience will also tell us about which brain areas are active and inactive during sleep and dreaming. Many REM dreams seem to involve almost exclusively vision and motion. What is going on in the olfactory and auditory areas when we dream? Why aren't there more smells and sounds in dreams? Or are there lots of smells and sounds in dreams, but just terrible memory for these things?[3] I sometimes seem to hear things in dreams. Still, despite the fact that many of my dreams involve conversations, they don't seem to involve my hearing what is said. Could this be the way things are in my dreams—conversations without a sound track—or is my impression that I hear no words just a memory problem? What is going on neurochemically during dreams and what function, if any, do changes in neurochemistry associated with different stages of sleep and different types of dreaming serve?

Developmental psychology will tell us how and why the dreams of young children differ from the dreams of adults; for example, why kids' dreams are less bizarre than the dreams of adults. Physiological and behavioral psychology will tell us about motor and eye movement patterns during periods in which people are dreaming. When you are sound asleep, but picturing wild-and-crazy things, your eyes are darting every-which-way-and-that beneath the lids. Paradoxically, during this REM sleep your eyes are aflutter, but the rest of your body is immobilized. During NREM sleep, when your eyes are relatively still and your dreams are both more peaceful and more bland, you may well be tossing and turning, twitching, and grunting, even uttering words and sentences—possibly even walking.

Psychology, in concert with neuroscience, will also inform us about correlations between sleepwalking, sleep-talking, night terrors, teeth-grinding, nocturnal emissions, and different stages of sleep and different types of dreams, for example, dreams rich in visual imagery and dreams that lack imagery.

Cognitive psychology will provide information about changes in mental performance associated with sleep rich in dreams versus nights less blessed with nocturnal mentation. Most people do better at cognitive tasks if they have had a good night's sleep that includes up to two hours of REMing—two hours of having wild and crazy ideas—than if they miss REM sleep altogether. However, the very depressed often feel better, and do better, if they do not have REM dreams. Neurobiologically informed psychiatry and psychopharmacology will need to explain why this is so.

Cognitive ethology and comparative psychology will tell us about sleep and dreams across species, especially closely related species. It may be disheartening, but we sleep and dream more like sewer rats than like dolphins. And, of course, we will need to look to evolutionary biology for insight into the question of the biological function, if any, of dreaming.

Anthropology, sociology, and social psychology are also important in providing a complete picture of dreams. This is because the uses, if any, to which dreams are put depend on local customs and habits.

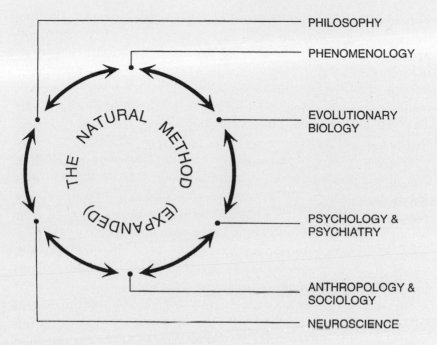

PHILOSOPHY

PHENOMENOLOGY

EVOLUTIONARY
BIOLOGY

PSYCHOLOGY &
PSYCHIATRY

ANTHROPOLOGY &
SOCIOLOGY

NEUROSCIENCE

Figure 1.2   The natural method, expanded. Adapted from Flanagan,
"Deconstructing Dreams," p. 9.

Dreams are the tools of the seer, the fortune-teller, and the shaman
in some cultures. They are grist for the therapeutic mill in others.
And they are considered mere noise, not worthy of any attention
whatsoever, in others.

What the foregoing shows is that even if the natural method is natural, its application to even a single type of consciousness, in the present case dream consciousness, is extraordinarily complex. A robust
theory of the nature and function of dreams will need to bring into
equilibrium insights from philosophy, phenomenology, neuroscience, psychology, psychiatry, evolutionary biology, sociology, and
anthropology (Fig. 1.2).

Sacred texts, literature, and autobiography are further valuable
sources of hypotheses about the nature and function of dreams. One
advantage of the natural method is that it can be expanded indefi-
nitely as needed to bring to bear all the data necessary to explain the
relevant target domain.

Classical Philosophical Problems about Dreams

The natural method provides a strategy for developing an empirically responsible and well-motivated theory of dreams. In addition to being scientifically credible, a good theory of dreams must be able to resolve or dissolve traditional philosophical problems about dreams. The two most famous philosophical problems about dreams are these:

1. *How can I be sure I am not always dreaming?* (René Descartes' problem; also Plato's and Cicero's). It is a notorious fact that while dreaming we do not normally know that we are asleep. Everything seems perfectly real. Given this, what makes us so sure that we are awake when we think we are, and not in some deep dream state? Descartes' solution required a proof for the existence of an all-good God, who would never allow us to make a mistake of such grand proportions as not to be able to distinguish dreaming from being awake or, as I will say for shorthand, not knowing dreams from reality.

2. *Can I be immoral in dreams?* (St. Augustine's problem). In his autobiographical *Confessions*, Augustine recalls registering this complaint with God about his dreams after his transformation, in his early thirties, from philandering pagan to an ascetic Christian:

> You commanded me not to commit fornication. . . . But when I dream [thoughts of fornication] not only give me pleasure but are very much like acquiescence to the act. . . . Yet the difference between waking and sleeping is so great [that] I return to a clear conscience when I wake and realize that, because of this difference, I am not responsible for the act, although I am sorry that by some means or other it happened in me.

Augustine proposed a theory for how dreams might contain sinful content (in his case thoughts of fornication) without being sins. His proposal, in modern terms, is that dreams are happenings, not actions. Whereas one is responsible for what one does or chooses to think about, one is not responsible for thoughts that involuntarily occur in one's mind.

A third problem was formulated in the twentieth century by Norman Malcolm and Daniel Dennett, a worry generated by the fact that the accuracy of dream reports is exceptionally hard to prove or disprove since by everyone's admission memory is uniquely rotten for alleged goings-on during sleep. If we are distrustful of the accuracy of reports of what we dreamed about, then we have equally good reason to be distrustful of the accuracy of reports about when dreams took place. The question is:

3. *Are dreams experiences that occur during sleep?* Or are so-called dreams just reports of experiences we think we had while sleeping but which in fact are, insofar as they are experiences at all, constituted by certain thoughts we have while waking up? Many think that dreamy thoughts, even if they do occur during sleep, occur in a flash, in an instant of time. Immanuel Kant believed this. I was taught that this was so as a small boy. If this sort of confabulation, this sort of elaboration and enrichment of a brief episode of sleeping-mentation, is possible, then the extreme case in which we simply make up the whole thing upon waking is possible, too.

I intend to address directly these three philosophical problems about dreams, but only after I have laid out the general neurophilosophical view of sleep and dreams I favor. Looking at these philosophical puzzles from a perspective informed by good science and a good theory of the nature of identity and self-expression makes them appear very different than they do when addressed with the standard purely philosophical tool kit. For those impatient readers who are especially gripped by the three philosophical questions and are dying to know the answers, here they are:

1. Rest assured, you are not always dreaming. How exactly we distinguish between dreaming and waking thought is, however, an interesting question, philosophically, psychologically, and neurobiologically. But once we have a credible theory of sleep and dreams in view, we will understand that there are telling phenomenological and neurobiological differences between being awake and asleep that can alleviate (but not eliminate—nothing can) even the most extreme skeptical worries.

2. Augustine is right that committing adultery, murder, and so on in dreams normally is not sinful. However, given a certain conception of morality, it may be possible to be immoral while dreaming. Many traditions hold us accountable for our thoughts and characters as well as our actions. On the view I'll be defending, dreams are sometimes, and to varying degrees, identity expressive. To the extent that the shape of our characters is under voluntary control and deformed, then we may express certain bad aspects of ourselves when we dream. Some evidence suggests that for certain individuals—primarily lucid dreamers, that is, dreamers who know they are

dreaming while they are—the plot and content of specific dreams can fall under executive control. If morality is tied to choice and control, then it follows that for such dreamers, their dreams may reasonably be judged as morally revealing, and thus they are to some degree responsible for what they dream about.

3. Dreams *are* experiences that take place during sleep. Dreams are perfectly natural phenomena, as opposed to paranormal phenomena. But dreams are not a natural kind in the sense that dreams are a single, unified type of thing that answers to a unitary set of laws—in the way, for example, water, salt, gold, or protons are natural kinds. NREM mentation and REM mentation differ phenomenologically (along, for example, a bizarreness scale), and they differ neurobiologically (for example, in terms of ratios of different kinds of neurotransmitters and whether the brainstem is sending out powerful waves or is relatively quiet). The unity dreams possess consists in this alone: They comprise the set, or the dominant set, of experiences that take place while a person is asleep.

Two New Philosophical Problems

Supposing that these three answers are correct—that we are not always dreaming, that we sometimes express our character in dreams, and that dreams are experiences that take place while we are asleep—two other interesting philosophical problems remain, problems in the philosophy of mind and biology about the function of dreams.

4. *Is dreaming functional?* And if it is functional, in what sense is it so? What biological end, if any, was dreaming designed to serve? What psychological or cultural end, if any, was dreaming discovered or coopted to serve?

The evolutionary biological concept of functional is tied closely to the concept of inclusive genetic fitness, which is simply the traditional Darwinian notion of fitness as understood from the perspective of modern population genetics. An organism is fit if it passes on its genes. But an organism can contribute to passing on its genes even if it takes vows of celibacy, so long as the celibate does things that help its close relations to pass on their genes. Inclusive genetic fitness is simply a measure of fitness in this broader sense.

A trait's proper biological function is the function that normally enhances fitness. An adaptation is a trait that was selected and maintained because it reliably enhances the fitness of organisms that have the trait.

We also use the language of function and design, even of optimal-function and design-excellence, in a broadly biological sense that has nothing directly or indirectly to do with inclusive genetic fitness. We say, "He has the perfect body for a basketball player—6 feet 8 inches tall, good hand-eye coordination, long arms, great jumper"; or, "She was a born to be a gymnast: incredible coordination, tremendous strength in her arms and legs, and of short stature." Although we don't know much about what brain mechanisms subserve musical or mathematical virtuosity, we do, I think, believe that some brains have the equipment designed to produce such virtuosity. Certain brains have rare design features that endow the individuals who possess the brains with special talents. Such gifts may not contribute to success at dating or mating, but they are gifts of Mother Nature nonetheless.

Finally, we use the concept of functional in a sense that is primarily psychological or cultural. If I say, "Had I not learned to read or write, I would not function very well in the world," I say something true. However, there is no respected evolutionary biologist who thinks that Mother Nature selected for brains that could read and write. We just lucked out. The ability to read and write comes like the prize in the Cracker Jacks; it is part of the package. But unlike the silly Cracker Jack treats, the capacities to read and write are very useful. We picked up on these uses over world historical time, long after our brains were as they are now, and we put them to use. But take any group of humans, fail to socialize them in the relevant literate practices, and these practices will simply not emerge—at least not for many thousands of years until the usefulness of literacy is rediscovered, if it is rediscovered.

My answer to the fourth dream problem, *Is dreaming functional?*, is this: Although there are credible adaptationist accounts for sleep and phases of the sleep cycle itself, there is reason to think that the phenomenal mentation, the dreaming, that occurs during sleep is a good example of a by-product of what the system was designed to do while awake *and* during sleep and sleep-cycling. If this is right, then dreams are not an evolutionary adaptation but, at most, an evolutionary exaptation, something that first appeared as a side effect of an adaptation and which was then coopted to serve some new adaptive biological function. Wing buds on insects are thought to have appeared first as adaptations for keeping warm or cooling off depending on whether they were raised or lowered. A few mutant insects developed larger than normal wing buds, which gave these mutants the ability to hop, skip, and fly a bit. This was a very good thing for an insect to be able to do, especially if there were reptiles and amphibians around who liked to eat them. Wings allowing a bug to become airborne were originally side effects, "exaptations," of wing buds selected to serve thermoregulatory functions that because of the extraordinary advantage they conferred were themselves selected for.

It is possible, indeed I think it is true, that dreams are not even exaptations; that is, they have never been subjected to biological selection pressures themselves. They are free riders that come with sleep. Dreams are the spandrels of sleep. Let me explain briefly in preparation for a more complete argument in a later chapter.

"Spandrel" is an architectural term that refers to the roughly triangular space between the outside of the curve of the arch (called the *extrados*) and the line formed from the top of the keystone (Fig. 1.3).

In many great churches, massive vaulted ceilings or domes are

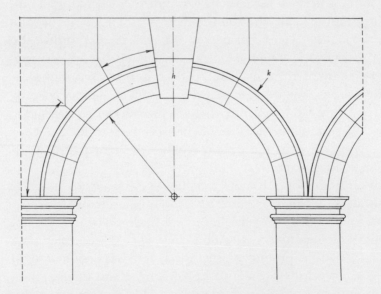

Figure 1.3   A spandrel is a roughly triangular area between the extrados (k) and the line formed from the top of the keystone (h) of an arch, or twice that area if the two arches are placed adjacently, as shown. Adapted from *Classical Architecture* © Adam 1991. Used by permission.

Figure 1.4   Author's children, Kate and Ben, in front of Pont du Gard, summer 1990.

mounted on the arches, either on the frames of the arches lined up in a row or over the frames of arches placed at right angles to form a square of arches over which a round dome is mounted. Usually spandrels are decorated with paint, mosaics, or frescoes. But what makes a spandrel a spandrel is that it is an inevitable architectural side effect of the main design intentions of the architect. You automatically get spandrels as side effects of certain kinds of arch designs.

The most famous Roman aqueduct is the Pont du Gard in the South of France built in the late first century C.E. (see Fig. 1.4). Actually, the top level of the Pont du Gard carried water, and the lower level was a viaduct, a walkway. The series of great arches produces a series of massive spandrels, but unlike those in churches, these are not decorated. The Roman architects and engineers had reasons beyond aesthetic ones to prefer rounded arches to rectangular ones. By 1400 B.C.E., the Egyptians had discovered that wedging stones in a semicircle made it possible to span greater distances than by building a rectangular opening. The reason is simple: The weight of stone is distributed outward in a rounded arch, whereas a single slab mounted on pillars would be exceedingly vulnerable to collapse, given that all its weight is directed downward. Stone is much better at resisting crushing than shearing forces. So rounded arches are ideal for creating large, stable, open spaces that can carry water and human and animal traffic. Spandrels, the triangular spaces where arches meet their frames, are a side effect.

In a famous and controversial paper, "The Spandrels of San Marco and the Panglossian Paradigm," published in 1978, Stephen Jay Gould and Richard Lewontin suggested that some, possibly many, traits and characteristics of natural phenomena are—now speaking metaphorically—side effects of the design intentions of Mother Nature.

Take the design of the heart. The heart is a pump. The function of the heart is to pump blood in a regular and reliable manner throughout the body, thereby keeping the body oxygenated. A pump needs room to expand and contract. At no point in the process of heart design did Mother Nature think that it would be good to make a noisy heart, because making a sound matters not one iota to the design of a well-functioning circulatory system. Heartbeats are simply what you get automatically from a blood pump housed in a body cavity.[4] To be sure, the sound of your heartbeat can be used diagnostically to see if your heart is pumping the way it should, just as spandrels can be filled with beautiful artwork. But neither heart sounds nor triangular spaces at the top of arches were part of the primary design intentions of evolutionary, pagan, or ecclesiastical architecture.

And so it is with dreams. Mother Nature didn't work to make us, or any other animals, dreamers. Mother Nature worked hard on the design of awake cognition and she worked hard on sleep design, in part because of its importance to awake cognition. What she did not care about, or work at designing, was dreaming, thinking-while-asleep. Dreaming came along as a free rider on a system designed to think and to sleep.

I said above that dreaming does not make us unique. Many other animals—almost certainly most mammals—dream. It is what we humans do with dreams that is unique and creative. Dreaming is useless noise for nonhuman animals. The dreams of nonhuman animals, just like our dreams, were not designed by nature to serve any function—not rehearsal of instincts, not release of otherwise unreleasable impulses. Nothing, *nada*, just noise, like the gurgling of the stomach or the sound of the heart. But we, unlike other animals, have discovered and invented functions for our dreams. We have done with dreams what we have done with spandrels and beating hearts. We have learned to use them in a variety of creative, imaginative, and helpful ways.

Once one has discovered a use for something originally useless, it would be silly to give it up. Imagine that architects discover ways to make dome and arch designs without creating spandrels along the way, or suppose manufacturers of artificial hearts find they can make perfectly silent pumps. There would be nothing unreasonable in saying that we want to keep the spandrels after all because we have discovered all sorts of wonderful uses for them. The same with noisy chest pumps. Unless the artificial-heart makers also create a replacement, say a computer chip under the thumbnail that provides the same or better quality heart diagnostics than heart sounds, we don't want silent hearts. We have found too many uses for the serendipitous noises hearts make.

And so it is with dreams. Even if scientists discover ways to turn dreaming off altogether or turn it way down (techniques for the latter already exist, and cases of people who do not have REM dreams exist) while not interfering one bit with the good sleep does, we can easily imagine declining to use their invention. We have over the centuries learned to do certain useful things with our dreams. Plus, sometimes at least, dreams are fun.

If this much is true a fifth dream problem arises:

5. *Can dreams fail to have an adaptationist evolutionary explanation but still make sense, still be identity expressive—possibly even identity constituting—and thus worth attention in the project of seeking self-knowledge?* The answer is yes.

The problem is to explain how this is possible, how, thinking of dreaming in a way consistent with the best scientific research leaves room—as I think it does—for some form of the traditional view that dreams are meaningful, interpretable, identity constitutive, and self-expressive.

Identity, Memory, and Dreams

One can imagine a skeptic suggesting that I am taking dreams much too seriously, especially since I myself don't believe dreams serve any interesting biological function. Leave dreams be, the critic might argue. Dreams are of minimal importance to the philosophy of mind and to cognitive neuroscience because they are just a kind of silly-thinking, the mental analog of a gurgling stomach.

One argument for this view, related to one suggested earlier, would involve trying to marginalize dreams not just on the grounds that they lack a biological function, but also on grounds that they lack any psychological significance—first, most dreams are not remembered; second, those that are remembered often express what is false or nonsensical.

The problems with this dismissive tactic are, first, that something not remembered may still gain a foothold in our psychological economy; second, memories can be false but identity constitutive. The first point is established by a vast literature on implicit learning and subliminal perception that establishes that experiences not remembered, and which cannot be reported, can have significant effects. Recent work by the psychologists Philip Merikle and Meredyth Daneman indicates that even people under general anesthesia remember or, better, show strong signs of remembering, certain things said while they are being operated on.

The second point is that the falsehood of a memory is of no consequence with respect to the question of whether the memory contributes to one's identity. Indeed, one might argue that most memories are false in the sense that they involve either more or less than what in fact happened. If the falsehood of a memory is taken to imply that it cannot, in virtue of being false, or in virtue of not being completely true, have any effects on who one is, then no memories have any effect.

This of course is preposterous. Fortunately, we need not entertain such absurd positions as that all our memories are false or that no false memories can be identity constitutive, since it is easy to point to commonplace exaggerations and confabulations that become identity constitutive. For example, confabulated stories of imaginary friends, or exaggerated narratives involving actual acquaintances from childhood, are common. If carried through life and rehearsed often enough, such memories will not only be thought to be true but can, I am certain, have some effect—sometimes, I think, a positive effect—on the ability to have healthy adult friendships, even to the point of helping one to know how to act in such relationships.

At Thanksgiving dinner in 1985 my mother mentioned to the assembled group that she had worried about my adjustment to first grade in the States since I had grown up in Puerto Rico, where I "had no friends." I was appalled that my beloved and normally attentive mother had forgotten about my best friend, Billy Fletcher, with whom I had played every day. My parents clued me in to the fact that Billy was the son of an American business acquaintance with whom I had played on exactly *one* afternoon! I now believe this to be the truth, but I also believe that my extended notional relationship with Billy, possibly including dreams about our "friendship," contributed some to my adjustment, such as it was, to school. So false memories can contribute positively to identity. In all likelihood, the same is true with bad false memories. Falsely believing that one was abducted by aliens might well have sorry effects on one's personality.

The short version of the point is this: False thoughts of imaginary friends involve the possible. False thoughts of alien abductions involve the extremely unlikely, the nearly impossible. Such thoughts are nonsensical, or close to being nonsensical. But the examples show that the fact that a thought or a story that one sincerely believes to be true is false or that is nonsensical is of no consequence whatsoever when it comes to the question of whether the thought or the story is identity constitutive or self-revealing or both. Some dreams may express what is true and what makes sense. But even if it is rare for dreams to express the true and the sensible, this is no objection to the idea that some dreams, despite being spandrels of sleep, contribute to making me who I am, are self-revealing, and are possibly worth self-exploration.

No wolves chased me in 1955, and the CIA did not call me up to do its dirty work in 1997. But there may be something to these dreams, something worth paying attention to, and this despite the fact that these things didn't really happen.

"Up and At 'Em"

My parents, my father especially, used to try to get us kids out of bed in the morning by barking, "OK, up and at 'em!"—as in "Darling children, it is time to get up and face the world." Until my early teens, I actually thought the expression was "Up and Adam," which makes no sense, except in a religious household. In any case, whatever exactly Dad was saying, I knew it was time to get out of bed and face the world.

The time has come for us, from our waking pose—I hope you are still awake—to get "up and at 'em." However, instead of leaving home to face the cold, cruel outside world, I want to stay here in the bedroom, to look back on those who are still in bed, sleeping and dreaming, to crawl under the covers with them, to enter, as it were, into their heads. What is it that they are doing? Why are they doing it? And how are they doing it?

Notes

1. Whether more complex, socially learned emotions, such as the amusement that occurs in the 1997 dream, can be explained in terms of the amygdala is less clear. Joseph LeDoux of New York University has shown that fear is mediated by the amygdala. But we do not yet know if the other basic emotions, that is, anger, sadness, happiness, disgust, and surprise, are mediated exclusively or primarily by the amygdala. And no one would be surprised if socially acquired emotions, such as amusement, compassion, empathy, and pride, involve processes occurring throughout the limbic system and beyond.

2. It might seem that in cases where the mental phenomena being studied are unconscious or nonconscious, for example, the processes by which language is understood, phenomenology makes no contribution. But actually it does. It is itself a piece of phenomenology to report that I am clueless about how I comprehend the speech of another. I hear sounds and understand what they mean, but I am simply not in touch with what goes on in between. Phenomenology in such cases shows us why and how much we need psychology, cognitive science, and neuroscience to assist in the awesome job of explaining the mind.

3. Joseph Shabala, the lead singer for Ladysmith Black Mambazo (famous to me from Paul Simon's *Graceland*), claimed to hear just the right sounds, ones he could only approximate in his music, in his dreams.

4. Valerie Hardcastle, a philosopher from Virginia Tech, has raised this worry about the example of heart sounds. Noisy hearts might have a derivative natural function. An infant's auditory system develops in part by listening to noisy whooshes in utero and to thumps of the mother's circulatory system, including the heart. An infant is soothed after birth by being placed on the mother's chest so that it can hear the familiar beats again. It might be that hearts were originally selected for because they can pump blood. However, a case can be made that there are additional selection pressures for keeping the hearts noisy. This argument is clever, but it won't work. The reason is this: For there to be selection pressures for noisy hearts or for keeping hearts noisy, there would have to be variation—some creatures with noisy hearts, some with silent ones. But there never was such variation among reproductively success-

ful *Homo sapiens.* The function of a heart and the structure of the cavity it needs to pump mean that all hearts are noisy ones. What the argument shows is that there might have been selection pressures on fetuses and infants to be sensitive to heart sounds. But it does not show that there was—or even might have been—selection for noisy hearts.

2
The Dreaming Mind

Time, like an ever rolling stream,
Bears all its sons away;
They fly forgotten, as a dream
Dies at the opening day.

—*William Croft (1709) and Isaac Watts (1718),*
"O God, our help in ages past," v. 5

The Mind's Design

A mind when functioning well is designed, on most every view, be it theistic or naturalistic, to track reality, to provide reliable information about the world—to yield the truth. The mind's job is to help us live well as "living well" is conceived by the relevant background theory.

If the mind's design is God's doing, and God is good, then He must have provided a reliable knowledge-yielding design, since we are made in His image and He is omniscient. We therefore better have at least some knowledge-yielding capacities. Which ones will we need? According to most traditions, we will need capacities to distinguish what is true and what is good from what is false and evil.

If, on the other hand, the mind's design is the work of evolution behind which stands no God, but only a "blind watchmaker"—that is, even if the world as we know it is the unfolding of a cosmic accident behind which no mind stands—similar design demands apply. Evolution cares about fitness, about reproductive success, which depending on the type of organism under scrutiny, requires survival of a certain duration. Survival requires doing the things required not to die or get killed too quickly after entering the world, at least not so quickly that there is no time to spread some genetic material. For simple organisms, doing the right things can be pretty much preprogrammed: "Where there is light move towards it and divide!" But for creatures that mature gradually, are highly mobile, reproduce sexually, and deal constantly with changing environments, such as reptiles, amphibians, birds, and mammals, nature will need to design them to pick up on what is happening in the surrounding flux. For such creatures, fitness requires quick and reliable detection of the true. The world is filled with dangers—immovable objects in one's path, cliffs, predators, enemies, disease, lightning, freezing cold, broiling heat, assorted vagaries of weather, and a zillion other things worth avoiding. The world is also filled, possibly more niggardly, with good things—nourishing food, reliable shelter, mates and potential friends. Intelligence without reliable on-line information pickup mechanisms will do little good when it comes to achieving inclusive genetic fitness.

On the evolutionary story, as on the theological story, we need to be designed to detect the true, or at least to detect what is going on around us at a level suited to gaining enough information to get by. Whether, on the evolutionary story, we need also to be designed to detect the good is a more complicated issue. Or to put it somewhat differently, even if among social species it is important to know the local conventions—for example, the mores of the red-winged blackbird, vampire bat, chimp, bonobo (formerly, "pygmy chimp"), or human communities to which one belongs—it may be best from the point of view of fitness, at least at certain times, to seem good rather than to *be* good.[1] On the other hand, there is emerging evidence from primate ethology as well as psychology and cognitive science that social species such as bonobos and humans are designed to utilize and display not just what we know but also how we feel; that among the range of emotions we are naturally disposed to experience and display are positive ones such as sympathy and happiness as well as negative ones such as anger and fear; that our compatriots are good detectors of what we are really feeling; and that success in living, be it by the standards of biological fitness or by more socially based criteria involving happiness, flourishing, being well adjusted and the like, involve, indeed require, having both reason and emotion attuned to the world and to each other. Not to put too fine a point on it, it will do no good to know that some attractive individual is a potential mate if one does not also experience attraction and detect that the feeling is mutual.

The first point is that on both the theistic and naturalistic stories, we had better be designed to reliably detect the true or, to be more precise, to detect the relevant set of truths required to survive and live well enough to gain heavenly reward or long enough to enhance our inclusive genetic fitness.[2] But the second point is that the minds of *Homo sapiens,* and probably many other species as well, are not well designed if they are simply efficient epistemic engines. Antonio Damasio calls the privileging of the rational, logical, knowing parts of ourselves "Descartes' Error." Whether Descartes actually committed the error that now bears his name is a matter I leave to Descartes scholars. The key point is that we are not simply knowers, unfeeling automata that track the truth. On both the theistic and naturalistic stories, we are well designed only if we either do or can learn to care and feel appropriately towards the things that we detect, and only if we are differentially interested in and differentially attracted to the things that matter relative to those that don't matter or are worthless or bad for us. Or to put it differently, merely detecting what is good or what matters will not help one bit when it comes to gaining one's heavenly reward or the rewards of being genetically fit if one does not feel, experience, or assess that what one detects *is* good and in fact matters, and thus should be sought for the relevant purposes, whatever these might be. Our sort of rational animal is a thinking-feeling being. If minds are analogous to engines, then we are *epistemic-emotional engines*—knowing-feeling engines—and highly adjustable, plastic and malleable ones at that.

Dreams and Dreaming

Dreams present a problem for the view I have just sketched. The claim so far is that the "designer," be it a divine designer or a natural designer, had to produce epistemically efficient creatures, creatures that can more or less reliably, and at the right level of grain for them, pick up information about the world and that in addition can coordinate their interests, motives, emotions, and feelings to behave aptly towards what they detect is there. No matter what kind of engineering, divine or natural, went into the origin of—to keep things simple—the species *Homo sapiens,* it had better have involved the production of reliable truth-tracking capacities that are coordinated with, and reliably interact with, an attuned and tunable emotional-conative economy.

But dreams, many of them at any rate, are hallucinatory. We imagine things that are not really happening, did not ever happen, or could not conceivably happen. The bizarre content of some dreams involves the violation of natural and moral law—I fly to Saturn and have the time of my life with strange, lovable, and fun-loving extraterrestrials on the famous different-colored rings of Saturn, which are actually amusement park slides surrounding the planet. That sort of thing.

This can't be true; it can't really have happened or be happening. But things seem so *real* while I am dreaming, so real that typically there is no obvious indicator to me while dreaming that I am not tracking the truth but instead thinking crazy and false things and having peculiar feelings about what is happening, about what, in some sense, "I" am doing.

Here in a nutshell is the problem: Why would a well-designed mind spend so much time thinking and emoting about the false and the crazy rather than, as it is supposed to, the true and the good—or at least the valuable—by the lights of the relevant background theory? We spend one-third of our lives sleeping and at least a good portion of that in REM sleep, the kind associated with really weird dreams. But dreaming also occurs during NREM sleep, although there is some residual skepticism about whether there is dreaming during the delta portion of NREM, a small segment of NREM sleep. And even NREM dreams are not cognitively or conatively efficient despite the fact that they do not normally involve the patently false or bizarre. NREM mentation, NREM dreaming, as I'll usually refer to it, often involves worrying and perseverating (persevering in a repetitive thought-loop), but not doing anything to overcome or resolve the worries or anxieties that one is caught up in. Furthermore, many NREM worries are not worth worrying about by ordinary rational standards of what is worth worrying about. As REM dreams share properties with psychotic thought, NREM dreams share properties with neurotic thought. NREM dreams often have obsessive qualities—worrying, for example, about whether one's appointment book, which before going to sleep one has no reason to think is anywhere other than where it always is, say, in one's briefcase, might have been left in the restaurant where one had lunch—and then worrying about this over and over again.

I recently found myself recycling, for no good reason whatsoever and seemingly endlessly, an anxious obsessive worry about whether I had hung my sportsjacket in the hall closet or the bedroom closet. My perseverative rut never involved any sort of reasonable concern such as that I might have tossed it in a heap on the dog's bed. The jacket, according to the dream plot; was always hung up in one of the two closets in which I hang my jackets, but I was very concerned about which closet it was. Furthermore, since I was asleep I did nothing—for example, get up and look—that would have put the worries to rest.

So the problem is that if the mind's design across otherwise incompatible theories is supposed to involve truth detection and attention to what matters, has value, and is relevant, as well as apt feelings and progressive problem-solving rather than spinning in perseverative circles or entertaining bizarre thoughts, then dreams, many of them at any rate, don't involve doing what a well-designed mind should be doing. Or, so it seems.

> October 9th: *I visited an old college friend, P., with a philosopher G. Her parents M. and J. (in fact, at the time of the dream J. was dead) were there, and P., who lives in Silicon Valley and works in the computer business, had a photo of her latest movie appearance with Jane Fonda. P. morphed at some point into a woman, A., who I knew a bit in college and had last seen at my twenty-fifth college reunion in 1995. A. was living in an artists' commune. G. and I agreed that the quality of art produced would be better if there was less marijuana consumption in the commune. I tried to convince G. to leave, which was hard since he had taken a fancy to one of A.'s housemates.*

For reasons that will become clear later, this is likely a REM dream, whereas the sports jacket dream is likely a NREM dream. I'll have more to say about the interpretation of both dreams later. But before I tip my hand and start to reveal my own theory of dream interpretation, it will be best to say a bit more about what dreams are and what dreams might be for, since this has a large impact on what they mean, indeed on whether they mean anything at all.

What Are Dreams For?

The problem that needs addressing is the problem of function. The problem is old. In the *Parva Naturalia*, written almost twenty-five hundred years ago, Aristotle wrote that "we must inquire what dreams are, and from what cause sleepers sometimes dream, and sometimes do not; or whether the truth is that sleepers always dream but do not always remember; and if this occurs, what its explanation is."

If the problem of function has been solved over the centuries, then many very intelligent people have not been clued in. Thus Paul Churchland writes in his 1995 book, *The Engine of Reason, The Seat of the Soul,* that "Consciousness *disappears in deep sleep* [and] *reappears in dreaming* at least in muted or disjointed form. [T]he sort of consciousness one has during dreams is decidedly nonstandard. . . . We would like to know how it differs, and why it should exist at all."

The question of the function of dreams is one of the very oldest, possibly the oldest, asked but still unanswered question about an everyday thing minds do. It is a question raised in some form in every ancient text, dramatic, mythic, sacred, or secular, from the East and from the West. And whereas we have some grasp of the functions of sensation, perception, attention, memory, and learning, the function of dreams is very poorly understood.

There are of course many ways one might respond to the questions and concerns I have raised about the function of dreams, about the question of what, if anything, dreams are for. Here are three interesting responses that provide a sense of some of the main contender views currently afloat.

Dreams Are Noise

This first response concedes that dreaming is not an adaptation and serves no fitness enhancing function. Someone who holds the view that dreams are noise might claim that I have made dreams sound like a special problem and created an unnecessary worry by overstating the degree to which a well-designed mind must at all times function as a reliable truth tracker and apt feeler. This mistake comes from thinking that every capacity we possess must be an adaptation or serve some evolutionary function. This sin is called "panadaptationism." Since I don't believe in panadaptationism, I don't think I am making that mistake in asking the question: What, if anything, are dreams for?

Many capacities we have do not serve and were not selected to serve an evolutionary function. Calculus, quantum physics, playing bocci ball and bridge are things we can do, but they are not adaptations. In all likelihood, they neither enhance nor detract from inclusive genetic fitness. On the other hand, and importantly, these capacities serve functions, have purposes, and are worthwhile. The point, although I will not fuss over it now, is that some capacity or activity can be adaptive, functional, fun, and a host of other good things without being an adaptation in the biological sense.

Perhaps I am guilty of making the different but related mistake of assuming that evolution cares about optimally adaptive mechanisms across the board, when all it really cares about are mechanisms that work pretty well, but not necessarily optimally, for purposes of inclusive genetic fitness, when and where such mechanisms can provide relevant payoffs. Economists and cognitive scientists refer to satisfactory but nonoptimal designs as "satisficers." In the useful jargon of these disciplines, such designs are not optimific but they satisfice. An atomic clock keeps perfect time but costs a fortune, whereas a wristwatch that works just fine for ordinary purposes can be purchased for $10. The claim then is that our rational and emotional capacities satisfice when we are up and about, that is, when utilizing these capacities pays off. And it is of no consequence that they continue to reverberate and serve no purpose whatsoever when they are not on duty.

Furthermore, what the mind does during sleep is at least not disadvantageous. When we are involved in crazy or obsessive thinking we are in bed, not up and about wreaking havoc by acting on our crazy and obsessive beliefs and desires. When it comes to truth-tracking and coordinating thought, feeling, and action, human minds do well enough when they need to, namely, when we are awake and moving around in the real world. The fact that the mind goes bonkers when off duty has no obvious effect on inclusive genetic fitness nor presumably does it offend a good God who cares that we think, act, and feel well when engaged in the part of our life under voluntary control.

Well-designed eyes should provide reliable information about the visible world in which and through which we move with our legs which, if they are well designed, enable us to walk through the potentially dangerous maze of natural and human-made objects, some of which are stationary and some of which are themselves in motion. It is no objection to the terrific adaptiveness of our visual system, of our ambulatory abilities, and the coordination between them, that our eyes and our legs are doing nothing when we sit in an easy chair, eyes closed, listening to music; or when we shut our eyes and assume a yoga position to meditate; or even when we sleep. Adaptiveness of a capacity is, to a first approximation, adaptiveness relative to the times and places the capacity is needed to do its job.

All this seems right. It would be a mistake to assume optimal functioning for any human capacity even at the times and in the places for which such capacities were designed to do their job. And it is an even greater mistake to complain that a capacity is not functioning well when it doesn't need to, as is the case at the moment with my ambulatory capacity, with my legs that are designed for getting around but which are going nowhere as I type these words.

That said, a puzzle still remains with respect to dreams. Even if it is no objection to the idea that the mind is first and foremost a well-designed thinking and feeling device that doesn't give a hoot about the true or the good while we are asleep, the fact remains that unlike the eyes or legs in the examples just mentioned, which do nothing at all, or nothing much, when not needed, the mind keeps doing something while we sleep and that something is odd—"decidedly nonstandard," as Paul Churchland politely puts it.

One wonders why during the time when the system could just shut down and stop caring about tracking the true and the good and take an eight-hour vacation from thinking and feeling anything at all, it is so prone to think of the false, the bizarre, the odd, and the sinful.[3] Why does sleep deliver us to a place where the mind spins out crazy narratives and, when it is not doing that, sets us to whirling in endless spirals going nowhere, to obsessive, anxious perseveration about whether the car has gas in it, or whether the door is locked, or whether the meeting with the boss is tomorrow or the next day or the day after that. The point is that it is one thing for a capacity to turn off when its labor is not needed; it is another thing for a system to stay on and behave oddly when it is not needed. My legs stop moving when I sit to read or watch television or write on my computer. Why doesn't my mind behave as well and just take a break when I sleep?

Aristotle worried about this issue when he tried to explain the function of sleep. He reasoned that all animals need to rest their sense organs: "It is necessary that every creature which wakes must also be capable of sleeping, since it is impossible that it should always be actualizing its powers." Later he adds:

Nature operates for the sake of an end, and this end is a good;

and that to every creature which is endowed by nature with the power to move, but cannot with pleasure to itself move always and continuously, rest is necessary and beneficial; and since, taught by truth itself, men apply to sleep this metaphorical term, calling it a rest: we conclude that its end is the conservation of animals. But the waking state is the goal, since the exercise of sense perception or of thought is the goal for all beings to which either of these appertains; inasmuch as these are best, and the goal is what is best.

Dreams, Aristotle realized, create a serious problem for his account of sleep, since if conservation of movement, sensation, and thought is what sleep is for, then dreams, especially if they occur all night long, don't completely conserve what needs conserving. He suggests the following credible idea: The mentation and movement that takes place during sleep does, at least, provide a rest at the sensory periphery—even if not a complete one. The eyes are closed after all. But deeper in the system various resonances, initiated at the periphery when we were awake, continue like eddies in a river to create waves and thus to produce images and thoughts. These images and thoughts are often "confused," "weird," and "incoherent" and, according to Aristotle, are prone to illusions induced by the emotional state of the individual.

One might sum up Aristotle's view this way: Waking life is the best; we flourish, if we do flourish, in virtue of how we feel, think, and act while awake. But we are animals with limited capacities, and, just as plants need sun and water, we need sleep to allow us to function well while awake. The disturbances involved in dreams are predictable according to the idea that experiences that happen while awake continue to reverberate. Happily, the reverberations are not so disruptive that they prevent the organism's powers from being sufficiently rested and restored.

An account such as this is still held by many people, and certain features of it are almost certainly true. Aristotle was not, of course, right about everything. He tied the function of dreams to digestion. This enabled Aristotle to provide advice about diet as it affects dreams. One ought to avoid eating beans and the head of an octopus if one is prone to bad dreams, and especially if one is prone to the delusion that dreams are messages from the gods.[4] One can only admire Aristotle's brilliance. On the other hand, a research program is not normally considered to be progressive when some of the best ideas in it are two and one-half millennia old.

In any case, the first response to the question of function denies that dreams have a function and points out that this is not a problem for a sophisticated neo-Darwinian theory. The color of blood serves no evolutionary function, nor do certain psychophysical capacities— capacities to play chess, checkers, and backgammon, to write sonnets or philosophical treatises. Even if dreaming is a side effect of selection for a mind that thinks but that doesn't turn off completely during sleep, there is also no problem, since fitness is not compromised, and, in any case, nature doesn't care or need to care about optimizing every capacity, even the ones it selects for. Satisficing will do. If dreaming was maladaptive, then supposing mutants with dream-dampers were born, they would have out-reproduced us and we would all by now have silent nights.

On the first view, either dreams serve no function at all or, compatible with this possibility, they are simply noise left over from the work a mind designed for a day job continues to make on the night shift. Fortunately, this noise, despite not making for optimal efficiency, does not jeopardize inclusive fitness, and thus there were no engineering reasons to work on damping it, even if the mutants who just sleep and don't dream were in fact available for evolutionary tinkering.

Dreams and Deep Thoughts

There is, of course, a well-known view of dreams that vehemently denies that dreams are nonfunctional noise. This view appears in a set of theories known as "depth psychology." On the first view— dreams are noise—the dreaming mind does no harm despite its noisiness and nonstandard character; or it is seen as misbehaving, either a lot or a little, given its job description, normally not creating obstacles to fitness but sometimes coming close. After all, even if some part of the system—audition, for example—is vigilant while we sleep, one is still much more susceptible to predation while asleep than one is when all five senses are in operation and directed at the external world. Furthermore, there are sleepwalkers, as well as individuals with lesions in the pontine brainstem, who act out their dreams. Needless to say, this is not a good thing for a sleeping organism to do.

On the second view, the dreaming mind is not just a noise-maker, and even if we talk and walk and act out dreams, we are still, although endangering ourselves, doing what dreams are designed to do. What, you ask, are dreams designed to do; what are dreams for? The answer given by the depth psychologists is that dreams are designed to express or reveal our deepest thoughts, feelings, desires, and needs. Dreaming is deep thought. Dreaming is a kind of thought designed to reveal what is deep and important, but concealed from the waking self, or at least that which is not typically entertained by or focused on by the waking self.

What the second view needs to add to have any plausibility is something like this idea: There is a gain, according to divine or natural design, that accrues from possessing mental capacities that allow us to express and/or reveal certain thoughts and feelings about ourselves and our relationships to ourselves that we are unable, for one reason or another, to entertain, express, or acknowledge while awake. This capacity is realized in dreams, and thus realizing this capacity is what dreams are for. To reap the profits of self-expression, or self-knowledge, or of knowledge of the plans or will of the gods for us is why we dream.

According to this view, which in one guise or another continues to be widely held, dreams are truthful, possibly the most truthful and valuable mentation that exists. This idea is familiar from ancient sources that saw dreams as containing messages from the gods, as well as more recently from Freud and Jung and their followers who, despite disagreements about the nature of the unconscious, would agree with Freud's famous motto that "dreams are the royal road to the unconscious."

The trouble is that judging that the function of dreams involves insights into one's complex psychological self or, alternatively, into the mind and will of the divine, says too little to yield a robust, determinate, and convincing answer to the question of the function of dreams, since there is an inconsistent class of views that shares the structure just described.

First, there is some question among the depth psychologists as to whether the function of dreams is satisfied simply by expressing or releasing certain deep thoughts or whether its function is served by expressing or releasing these deep thoughts and in addition coming to know, remember, or, in some other way, absorb what these deep thoughts mean—taking them, as it were, back into the world in the form of enhanced self-understanding.

Second, there is disagreement about the nature of the deep truths themselves. The purpose of dreams has been seen as providing a special way of expressing, releasing, or gaining knowledge about one's sexual and aggressive wishes (Freud), about one's deepest spiritual impulses (Jung), about the level of one's self-esteem (Adler), or about the moral quality of oneself. One could be ecumenical and say that the answer is "all of the above." There is, I think, *something* to the ecumenical view, since if it is genuinely inclusive it can be interpreted as saying that just about anything under the sun can be expressed in dreams—including nothing at all. And this is, I think, the truth. The fact remains that the depth psychological theories currently being considered tend not to be ecumenical in this way. They seek to identify *the* univocal message contained in dreams and see all dreams as meaningful.

In any case, it is not part of my current agenda to perform therapy on the various depth psychologies so that one or all of them can see their way clear to some more ecumenical view, and thus to some more credible view. But in reality, I cannot see how even an ecumenical view is credible so long as it holds on to the implausible tenet that all dreams express deep thoughts, even if these deep thoughts are multifarious in kind. Lots of dreaming is shallow thinking; some is meaningless nonsense.

Third, there is a problem bringing a depth psychological account into a comfortable relationship with evolutionary biology. Consider, for example, the view that dreams express or reveal deep truths about who one is and, in particular, that they yield knowledge about the moral quality of one's character and life. This sort of knowledge is something the gods might sensibly care about, but it is hard to imagine an evolutionary rationale for why such knowledge could matter. There is no known evidence, nor can I imagine that there is any unknown evidence, that humans committed to the Socratic maxims "know thyself" and "the unexamined life is not worth living" do any better when it comes to inclusive genetic fitness than those who have no interest in moral self-knowledge or moral self-examination. Furthermore, although the Socratic maxims call for relentless self-searching, Socrates does not, to the best of my knowledge, attribute any special value to dreams as a regular and reliable source of such knowledge.

Among depth psychological theories, the psychoanalytic view is the best candidate for a theory that like Socrates' emphasizes the importance of self-knowledge especially for the ill-of-heart, and at the same time works hard to make the theory of dreams consistent with late-nineteenth-century ideas from psychiatry, sexology, and evolutionary biology.

Freud's basic idea is that dreams are designed to release unconscious, repressed, and socially unacceptable wishes. These are part of our nature as *Homo sapiens* that need to be released somehow, lest we go mad. Better these wishes be released in hallucinations than in the world, and better that they come in the disguises of playful or seemingly nonsensical stories, so that normally they keep the dreamer from waking in horror, as she would were she to see clearly the sick and sinful desires she has, the naked truth about her sexual and aggressive self.

On the Freudian story, dreams provide release of things that need releasing so that while awake we can display standard Darwinian fitness, that is, so that we can work and interact cooperatively, civilly, possibly lovingly, with others.[5] Furthermore, thanks to a mind design that disguises from the dreamer the sordid nature of her wishes as expressed in her dreams, dreaming paradoxically protects sleep—allowing thereby, at one and the same time, the releasing of wishes the psyche needs to release and the conservation and restoration of the body for which sleep is also, possibly primarily, designed.

A system with the sort of sleep-dream design proposed by Freud is compatible with the plausible evolutionary idea that a well-designed awake mind is a well-honed epistemic-emotive engine, a detector of what is there and what is necessary for survival and reproduction, with the appropriate feelings and emotions (both naturally appropriate and socially acceptable) lined up with what is reliably detected so that fitness is maintained. A well-designed epistemic-emotive engine is a system in which knowing and feeling are in harmony—one sees and wants the succulent nourishing berries on the bush, fears and flees when the majestic but growling tiger approaches, detects that an appropriate mate is receptive and is experiencing and reciprocating lust, works the fields to harvest the crops with one's fellows, and cares (to a point) for how well one's relatives, especially one's offspring, are faring.

Freud did not call for relentless self-examination as a condition for making each and every life worth living, as did Socrates. However, Freud, unlike Socrates, provides dreams with a natural biological function—the wish-release function.[6] The theory also at the same time and for the same reasons suggests that dreams can be a valuable source of self-knowledge when such knowledge is needed to alleviate neurosis. Ludwig Wittgenstein, the great philosopher and fellow fin-de-siècle Austrian, thought Freud imputed far too much sexual meaning to dreams. It was not clear, Wittgenstein thought, that a Freudian had any room to interpret the dream thought of holding a branch as anything other than holding an erect penis. The fact that the theory commits one to interpreting all thoughts as deep, disguised, and sexual (or aggressive) makes psychoanalysis insufficiently open to the complex texture and uses of thought, and thus ironically to the difficulties of interpretation. In scattered remarks Wittgenstein indicates that he believed that some dreams have meaning and are not, in every case, either gobbledygook or disguised sexy (or aggressive) thoughts. Dreams are a kind of thinking, and we dream, just as we think, about rich and varied things, often in undisguised forms.

One problem for anyone who is attracted to the depth psychological approach is that there are incompatible depth psychological theories of dreams. Jungians and Adlerians also see dreams as self-revealing, and as subject to interpretation, to having their disguises removed. But each has a very different theory of the nature of the unconscious from Freud's and from the other's. For the Jungian, dreams upon examination reveal powerful spiritual impulses, whereas for the Adlerian they tell the tale of each individual's ongoing struggle with his birthright—his "inferiority complex." Furthermore, neither theory helpfully places itself within a Darwinian framework. It is hard to imagine any story that credibly links either the Jungian idea that in dreams we symbolically express the collective unconscious of the species or the Adlerian idea that dreaming functions to release or reveal our deep seated feelings of inferiority, inadequacy, and ineptitude with gains in reproductive success.

I conclude that of the depth psychological views I have mentioned, the only one that has any chance of credibly making a case for an evolutionary function for dreaming is Freud's. Even if Freud's theory of the nature and function of dreams is wrong—as it almost certainly is in some respects—it is worth taking seriously because Freud committed himself with the greatest intellectual passion to the project Patricia Kitcher appropriately dubs "Freud's Dream"—the dream for a complete interdisciplinary science of mind. It was this commitment that accounts for his concern to give an account of the psychological function of dreams that also met the demand of providing some sort of evolutionary rationale for dreaming. This, in itself, makes Freud's view the sole contender worth taking seriously among depth psychological views that attempt to answer the questions, "What are dreams for? What is it that dreams express or reveal?," since his theory but not Jung's or Adler's satisfies the demand that some work be done to fit the account of dreams into a theory that accepts some credible version of evolutionary theory as a background constraint. More about Freud later.

Dreams and "Theory of Mind"

There is a third view on the function of dreams that is a bit harder to describe and place than the nonfunctional dreams-are-noise view or the functional depth psychological views discussed so far. In part this is because this view, which among psychologists is called the "theory of mind" theory—"theory of mind" for short—is intended in the first instance as a theory of capacities that function while we are awake and that are utilized in assessing the mental states of ourselves and others and predicting behavior on the basis of these assessments. Indeed, there is, to the best of my knowledge, almost no discussion of dreams in the theory of mind literature, and thus no consensus among theory of mind theorists about whether dreams have *any* function whatsoever related to knowledge of one's own and other minds.

This means that I am open to the charge of making up a theory for theory of mind theorists that they themselves have not yet spoken on and may not like. So be it. I'll take my chances because I think there are fertile ideas worth developing in the theory of mind literature that pertain to our question: What, if anything, are dreams for? Here are some of the main tenets of the theory of mind theory:

- Humans are social animals who interact throughout life with conspecifics.
- Social interaction comes in many forms: competitive, cooperative, friendly, deceptive, informational, sexual, and so on.
- Animals that are both social and have the capacities to reveal and conceal information about their own mental states cause

what philosophers call the "problem of other minds." How can I tell what a conspecific—my mate, say—is feeling or thinking? Indeed, at the extreme, how can I know she is thinking and feeling anything at all, and is not simply a beautiful and beautifully behaved zombie—a creature with no inner life whatsoever?

- Nature has selected for capacities to read a handful of emotions off faces. But it is hard to read the thoughts, feelings, and mental representations of others.

- In order to assist us in the important task of reliably reading other minds, nature has done two things: first, she has designed us to develop a theory of our own mind, a theory that involves in the first instance developing the capacities to distinguish among our beliefs and our desires and our intentions; second, in addition to laying the groundwork for our reading of body language, especially the facial expressions of conspecifics, she has armed us with a default presumption that our conspecifics have minds like ours that can represent and misrepresent, that have beliefs, desires, and intentions on the basis of which behavioral predictions can be made.

Putting these points together, it follows that we are naturally designed to (develop to) be in touch with our own mental states as the states they are; that is, we don't normally confuse our beliefs, desires, and intentions with each other's. Furthermore, we are naturally designed to (develop to) be reliable detectors or inferrers of what is on the minds of others.

Of course, culture and learning are crucial components in the development of the skills of accurately assessing one's own and others' mental states. But the important point for present purposes is that (the theory of mind literature makes available the idea that) we are *naturally disposed* to develop the relevant mind-reading capacities in normal environments. In order for the idea to be interesting, I want to state it in a strong form. Think of the natural disposition to read other minds as akin to the disposition to develop language, what Steven Pinker calls "the language instinct." We are designed to read minds. We are "mental detectors," as my daughter Kate once put it when she was a little girl, amazed at her parents' ability to know what she was thinking.

At least one researcher in the field has stated the idea in this strong form. Sue Taylor Parker, a psychological anthropologist, argues that there were evolutionary selection pressures pulling for a powerful natural disposition to acquire a theory of mind. She writes:

> The general hypothesis is that self-knowledge serves as a standard for assessing the qualities of conspecifics compared to those of the self. Such assessment is crucial to deciding among alternative reproductive and subsistence strategies. The qualities that are assessed, which vary along taxa, range from the size and strength of the self to its mathematical or musical abilities. This so-called assessment model of self-knowledge is based on evolutionary biological models for social selection and the role of assessment in animal communication.

Suppose that theory of mind with this sort of evolutionist spin is true, and that it explains our fallible but reliable capacities to know our own minds and the minds of others. What does this have to do with dreams?

Here are two possibilities. The first is that the capacities of mind-reading, reading both one's own mind and other minds, is so valuable that nature has designed us to work on mind-reading while awake *and* asleep. We are thinking-feeling creatures, as are our conspecifics. It is a matter of such great importance to our inclusive genetic fitness that we get things about our own and other minds right that we are designed to work twenty-four hours a day on the project.

Sad to say, there is a big problem with this hypothesis. The motivating idea behind the evolutionist brand of theory of mind, which I have been advocating for the sake of discussion, is that the relevant mind-reading capacities were selected to give reliable information about our own and other minds. There is also the background assumption, as I read the literature, that despite the broad range and occasionally strange nature of ordinary awake human motives, intentions, beliefs, and desires, the right sort of theory of mind, the sort that will enhance fitness, is a relatively pedestrian folk psychology that attempts to detect or infer beliefs, desires, motives, and intentions that will yield reliable predictions—Johnny wants a cookie and believes that there are cookies in the cookie jar, so he goes to the kitchen, opens the cookie jar, reaches for a cookie, and eats it. For the most part, nothing like the wild and woolly motivational economies proposed by the depth psychologists need be assumed—

Johnny wants mommy and believes daddy to be a rival for her affection, so he wishes daddy ill, thus imagining daddy in a terrible accident, for example, being crushed to death by falling cookie jars.

The problem is that dreams seem especially ill suited to satisfy the aim of reliable interpersonal and intrapersonal understanding, explanation, and prediction, particularly given the assumption that this aim is best met with the apparatus of ordinary folk psychology. Unlike in my waking state, my mental states as represented in dreams often don't seem accurately to reflect me, who I am, and what I think, and even when they do reveal thoughts or wishes I can see— often embarrassingly—as mine, they do not do so in any sort of consistent way. Furthermore, what I dream about the feelings, beliefs, and behaviors of others seems at least as weird and unlikely—possibly more weird and unlikely—than dream thoughts I have about myself.[7]

The second, and more plausible idea, is one we have seen before in other guises as the reverberation, sensory residue, cognitive leftovers hypothesis. If mind-reading capacities have been selected for to function while awake, nature may well not also have worried about designing shutdown or damping devices for such mentation during sleep. To be sure, were we to believe our dreams we would often gain unreliable information about ourselves, our compatriots, the laws of nature, moral law, and so on, and were we to act on this information we would act foolishly and peculiarly. Fortunately, in addition to the fact that dreams don't normally wake us up, the contents of dreams insofar as they pertain to one's own and other minds (actually, insofar as they pertain to anything) are poorly remembered and thus may not be positioned in the mind in such a way that they are utilized in waking attempts to understand oneself or others, to predict behavior, or to act.

There is, of course, reason to worry about this last point, since there is a vast literature on the effects in waking life of things we cannot consciously remember or report—research, for example, on subliminal perception and implicit learning. This leaves open the possibility that dreams have effects, possibly even effects on identity, on the kind of person we are. This idea is available if one believes that one's self is to some significant degree a product of experience and allows in addition that the relevant experiences can be conscious or unconscious. Having alerted the reader to this possibility, I'll hold off on this important topic until later. The fact remains that the sort of account of dreaming I have suggested might be compatible with the theory of the mind approach does not provide dreaming with a fitness-enhancing function. Awake cognition was selected for and is maintained because it endows us with—among other things—reliable mind-reading capacities that produce gains in reproductive success. But dreaming insofar as it yields information about our own and other minds does so irregularly and unreliably. The awake capacity to read our own and other minds may be a biological adaptation, but serendipitously accurate dream thoughts about ourselves and others are at most a side or after effect or residue of this fitness-enhancing capacity. Gurgling sounds sometimes are produced in my stomach as I digest. Digestion is an adaptation, gurgling a mere side effect. And so it is with dreams on the theory of mind view.

There are aspects of the theory of mind view that I like and will utilize as I develop my thesis that dreaming as such was not selected for, but is still, to some degree, self-expressive, and that in addition to sometimes providing credible insights into one's own mind, into who one is and how one's life is going, dreams might also sometimes provide insight into the nature of others and into our relations with these others. Aristotle sensibly analyzed dreams that yield reliable predictions about friends as due to the fact that we know our friends well and thus are able to anticipate what they will likely do. Theories involving divine messages or precognition need not apply.

So theory of mind contains insights that will help us better understand the nature and function of dreams. That said, there are also aspects of the dreams are noise view and the depth psychological view that we will need to do some work in any credible theory.

A Brief Recapitulation

It is time to restate the three general views on the function of dreams that have been discussed since they will surface from time to time as we proceed.

The *dreams are noise* view is that dreams have no evolutionary proper function. The noise is created by the aftereffects when we sleep of some awake experiences and thoughts, as well as some of the stimuli in the surround while we sleep, interacting with a motley of memories and knowledge permanently or temporarily stored in areas activated by the haphazard firings originating in the brainstem. Happily, the noise is not so noisy that it interferes in any significant way with sleep, and assuming that sleep contributes to our inclusive genetic fitness, dreams don't interfere with sleep and whatever it does that is fitness enhancing.

The second view, *dreams as deep thoughts*, is the view that dreaming is functional in virtue of the fact that (according to its Freudian version) it serves as a time and arena in which real but socially unacceptable desires can be released. This release serves two functions: first, since the sordid wishes are disguised, sleeping is protected; second, the release of these wishes in sleep keeps them from ruining daytime interactions necessary for functioning well enough to achieve a modicum of maturity, which for Freud involved the abilities to love and work.

The third, the *theory of mind* view, comes in two forms. The first version says that in dreaming we continue to engage in the crucial labor of mind-reading which will help us to understand better ourselves and others and which will thereby aid us in the project of getting along with our compatriots while awake. The second, weaker and more plausible, version holds that our minds don't turn off completely from their day job of mind-reading during sleep. Thoughts about ourselves and others, personal and interpersonal worries and anxieties continue to reverberate. Electrical activity originating in the brainstem associated with REMing creates imagery, especially visual imagery, and the cortex takes the material provided, as noisy and poorly regulated as it is, and tries to make sense of things, to put the noise into semicoherent narrative structures, usually stories involving self and others. One might think of the mind as akin to old TV sets, which worked with numerous valve tubes rather than transistors. These TVs would hum for a while after the TV was turned off as the tubes crackled and cooled down. Sleep perhaps is like this. In one sense, sleep involves turning the system off, but some sort of humming—the hum of various kinds of dream mentation—persists through the night.

On both the dreams are noise view and the theory of mind view, dreams involve leftovers from the mind's day job—either leftover stimulation from the environment or leftover thoughts about one's own and other minds—which while asleep are poorly regulated or controlled.

I have not given a direct answer, nor a remotely complete answer, to the questions I posed: What are dreams for? What is the function of dreaming? I have tried, however, to provide an overview of several different credible answers—functional and nonfunctional—that have been given to the question. I hope also to have indicated that the question is both difficult and interesting.

My own view, as I indicated earlier, is that dreaming was not directly selected for. Sleep was. Certain aspects of dreams are due to noise left over from cognitive capacities that were selected for and that have a day job. Other aspects of dreams, especially the vivid imagery, are created in the first instance as side effects of different things the brain needs to do to accomplish its night job. Still, as we develop and acquire an identity—a vast store of memories, a certain temperamental style, characteristic emotions, and a set of personal concerns—a personality, a character emerges and takes on a complex structure. Our identity, now taken to include everything on the list, takes its place as a relatively complex dispositional structure in the brain. Furthermore, as creatures with distinctive identities engaged with the everyday world of work and play and relationships, our beliefs, emotions, and moods change, and as they do, so does who we are, how we feel, and so on.

The sleeping brain, with a sense of self both already in place and ever changing, is activated by both the residual activation of cognitive capacities that were at work before sleep and by the residue of things that were on our minds as we crawled under the covers. Also, the activities internal to the brain that are needed to occur for sleep to accomplish what sleep is for (I haven't told you yet what that is—that is the next chapter's business) create noise that activates the complex set of memories, emotions, and experiences that are held in the brain and that taken together make us who we are. But the sleeping brain is not designed, and therefore is not concerned one iota, to reveal who you are in a coherent way. Indeed, if I am right, the sleeping brain does not care whether you undergo any mentation at all during sleep. To put it slightly differently, despite the fact that typically sleep is responsible for dreaming mentation, the mentation is not necessary for sleeping to get its job done. This general thesis is supported by the existence of over one hundred patients with a variety of central nervous system problems who sleep but do not dream, and who, in virtue of sleeping normally, function satisfactorily when they are awake.

Consider this analogy: I once had a neighbor who liked to mow his lawn at just about the time we sat out on the deck to eat dinner. His sole aim was to mow his lawn, and I seriously doubt he was trying to create thoughts of murder in me. I did not murder him, nor did I ever (probably foolishly) complain about his mowing at dinner time, even though every time he mowed, feelings of anger, annoyance, and ill-will were aroused in me. My thoughts and feelings had no effect whatsoever on his accomplishment of his goal of cutting his grass, despite the fact that his mowing at dinner time invariably caused my thoughts and feelings.

One will sensibly wonder, if the analogy is apt, how is it that dreams sometimes make sense, assuming that they sometimes do. The quick answer is that the cortex, ever vigilant, takes whatever noise it is fed and tries its best to do its job. What job is that? There are several jobs the cerebral cortex has, but the one relevant for present purposes is to make sense of experience. The job is easiest when the flow of information is coming from a relatively well-behaved external world. But the cortex does its best, even when handed less-well-behaved information, to come up with some sort of coherent or semicoherent story. Since the noise created during sleep is not well-regulated or well behaved, the task is tough. Nonetheless, many, possibly most of the perceptions, thoughts, and feelings that are inadvertently activated by the sleeping brain are perceptions, thoughts, and feelings already on our mind (or recombinations thereof), which in addition are shaped by a more or less stable personality. This is the key to how dreams can be, sometimes are, self-expressive.

The upshot is this. All three answers discussed above to the questions "What are dreams for? What function does dreaming serve?" may, indeed will, if interpreted charitably, find some place in our analysis of the nature of dreams. But no one of these three theories by itself, nor any version melding all three, can provide a completely satisfactory theory of the nature of dreams. Most importantly, none of the three, except possibly Freud's brand of depth psychology (about which more later), provides any basis for thinking that dream consciousness might be a biological adaptation selected for because it enhances fitness.

What Are Dreams Like?

I have already mentioned that NREM dreams are typically dull in imagery, and although they can have a theme, it is often a perseverative rutlike theme. REM dreams, on the other hand, are rich in imagery and often have weird, bizarre, or disjointed plots.

I will use this pass at the question "What are dreams like?" to lay the ground for my claim that although dreams have no evolutionary proper function but are, as I have said, "spandrels of sleep," dreams are nonetheless, sometimes and to various degrees, self-expressive, identity constitutive, and cooptable for the project of self-under-standing.

Calling dreams "the spandrels of sleep" is good as an attention-getting device. It is also true. But it has potential for misleading if it is taken to imply that dreams and their contents are effects completely produced by causes intrinsic to the design of the sleep cycle. That is, that dreams are the result of what ultimately evolution designed sleep for and of what proximately the brain and body are trying to accomplish during sleep. The reason this isn't quite right is that the materials that go into the production of dreams crucially involve our individual histories—the experiences we have had; the memories we have stored; the beliefs, desires, motives, reasons, and values we have acquired; and the emotional states and moods we are in.

Dreams are, as it were, the complex result of cognitive and emotional capacities we possess, our individual histories, and the residue from recent waking life, possibly residue from the very day we fall asleep, as well as from noise created by and during sleep. The resonances created by thoughts and feelings and worries from the day together with the noise created internally by sleep and sleep-cycling all take place in a brain that houses one's self—or, as I am more inclined to say, that houses one's sense of self or one's self model—and whose cortex is designed to do the best it can to create coherent thoughts and stories out of the material with which it is provided, however ill suited the materials are to being made sense of. This much explains both why we dream and why dreams make sense—to the extent that they do make sense.

What I want to do now is say a bit more about the phenomenology of dreaming. I will not be providing anything like a complete answer to the question "What are dreams like?" In part this is because dreams come in too many varieties, too many shapes and forms, for me to provide a straightforward answer to this question.

My aim is limited to saying what dreams are like in two respects. First, I want to say a bit about what kind of mental phenomena dreams are. Are dreams like individual mental events, such as a per-ception of a yellow tennis ball in the car's trunk, or are they more akin to extended episodes of thinking, for example, planning the structure of one's day over breakfast? Or are they more extended still in the way telling someone whose father has died what her father was like as a colleague, about the joys and stories shared over the years as colleagues, about the fond way he spoke of his children, his grand-children, and so on?

The answer is that dreams come in all these forms. However, despite the fact that "all of the above" is the correct answer, there are simple interest-relative reasons to focus on dreams that extend beyond single thoughts, since the sort of meaning normally attrib-uted to dreams, and the sort of meaning I am wondering if dreams in fact have, is more extended usually than the meaning a single image or thought has.

Second, I want to play the devil's advocate and resist one common answer to the question "What are dreams like?," the answer that says, "Well, you know what awake thought and perception are like; dream-ing is not like that!" This is true, to a point. Dreaming and being awake are different. But there would not be a famous philosophical problem that turns on the difficulty of telling which is which, and that demands criteria to distinguish between dreaming and waking, if dreaming did not share certain properties with being awake.

It is a matter of unquestioned philosophical faith—thanks to a famous encyclical by the philosopher Thomas Nagel published in 1974—and thus something only a heretic would deny, that *there is something it is like to be* a conscious being. A corollary is that there is something that it is like to be in different kinds of mental states—tasting something, an apple, say, differs phenomenologically in how it seems from touching or holding that apple. There is, therefore, something it is like to dream, something it is like for the dreamer. Since we all dream, we may be able to say what dreams are like from something like an objective phenomenological point of view. The idea of objective phenomenology is not an oxymoron—although it might be better dubbed intersubjective phenomenology. It simply involves saying how things seem across some population, adolescent males and females, middle-class African Americans, cloistered monks or nuns, urban homosexuals, color-blind people, possibly just people, period.

Tactically, one can approach the phenomenology of dreams, the project of saying what dreams are like, from many different perspec-tives and with many different dimensions in mind. For example, there is the question of what sort of sensory experiences—visual versus auditory, tactile versus olfactory—are most typical in REM dreams. We address a different phenomenological question when we locate REM dreams versus NREM dreams along a bizarreness scale. There are questions about whether dreams are remembered or seem memorable, and if so which ones are memorable. There are questions about the content of dreams: Do many dreams have sexual or aggressive content, or are we more likely in dreams to be doing yard work, gassing up the car, or wondering where the mayonnaise is? And there are questions of metacognition: To what extent, and how often, are people aware that they are dreaming while they are dreaming?

A robust phenomenology of dreams will need to say how dreams seem across all these dimensions and others, where dreams fit on the spectrum that runs from a single individual thought or perception, say, a colored numeral flashed on a screen for less than fifty milliseconds at one end, to the type of mental state involved in sustained long term focus on a problem. This might be a problem of self or just a plain old problem—of the sort that might give rise to an autobiography or a proof of a difficult theorem such as "Fermat's last theorem," supposing, contrary to fact, that we were able to imagine the production of an autobiography or such a proof taking place while awake or asleep without interruption.

It is useful to distinguish between single mental events, such as seeing a red versus a green numeral flashed on the screen, and mental episodes such as wondering why one is in such a sorry mood, or trying to figure out what the boss really meant, or explaining to a student that the crucial premise in the cosmological argument for the existence of God is the one that says that the series of causes and effects cannot regress infinitely.

Whereas individual mental events do not have themes or, what may be different, do not have plots, mental episodes do. In trying to make sense of things, of what is happening outside us and inside us, we weave experiences, often experiences of series of events, into episodes. Episodes involve chunks long enough to have a theme, to constitute a scene—for example, the scene of a child eating a cookie—or chunks long enough to have a plot, to reveal a standardized script—for example, a little boy's display of the interpersonal savvy it takes to convince mom to let him have a cookie before dinner.

Individual perceptions, say, of a red numeral rather than green numeral, of a chocolate cookie rather than a piece of rubber, can come over time to fit into episodes, scripts, and scenes. So do episodes, scripts, and scenes come sometimes to fit into something larger—at a minimum, they fit into the set of episodes that constitute some temporally extended segment of one's stream of consciousness. We can tell stories about such segments. These are narratives. There is the narrative of what I have been thinking and doing over the course of the last two days, or over the past five years. Usually narratives are built around sets of thematically related episodes over an interval—there is the story of one's romantic life during one's adolescence, or of one's career or about how the kids are doing. As an ideal, but not in reality, we sometimes try—at least those who aspire to virtuosity in self-knowledge try—to reconstruct the complete story of our life. There is effort to construct the narrative of the things that have happened to me and that I have done over the course of my entire life, to tell the story about who I am, what I am like, what matters to me, and so on. Even in the grandiose case, relevant criteria related to judgments of what matters and what doesn't matter need to be made and applied, otherwise the narrative can neither be held in the head nor can it be told. "There is neither world enough nor time." And even if the whole story could be held in mind or told, no one should want to possess (or, even worse, listen to) the complete unabridged record of a life, since what one is *really* like, who one *really* is will be undetectable in the boring litany that fails to mark off matters of value and significance from the morass of meaningless details.

We can say a bit more about what dreams are like given the rough pragmatic distinction between mental events—for example, the perception of the oak, the thought that it is a beautiful day, mental episodes involving longer focus or rumination than mental events involve—for example, thinking through the process of replacing an out-of-reach light bulb; and still more extended narratives, the kind one might come to tell over years of psychotherapy about one's relation with one's parents or about one's love life, or about both, and how they fit together.

This much seems clear: many, probably most, dreams—both NREM and REM dreams—are more than single mental events. The reason one does not want to say that all dreams are more than single mental events is because certain hallucinations that occur as we doze off (hypnagogic hallucinations) or as we wake up (hypnopompic hallucinations) are exceedingly brief, fleeting images or auras. Many dreams, however, are episodes. Dreams have themes and plots, sometimes narrative structure. An episode typically does have narrative structure, but having narrative structure in the sense of displaying a theme or plot is not sufficient to make such an episode a narrative. Therefore, I have not yet claimed that some dreams are narratives. I will now do so. Some dreams are narratives. Which ones? Ones that string episodes together into some larger structure, that tell stories, possibly even dream series that occur over a period of nights, that link up over months, possibly years—the mental analog to a TV series—*Lassie, Leave It To Beaver, Bonanza, All in the Family, Kojak, The X-Files, Melrose Place, The Simpsons*, or, my favorite, *Sesame Street*.[8]

A skeptic of the line I am starting to flesh out might object this way: To say dreams are episodes with themes and plots, and especially with narrative structure, is really stretching it. Here you are falling into bed with the Freudians, Jungians, and other obscurantists who provide a theory that dreams have meaning and are not mere noise, but do so by maintaining certain incredible theses about the distinction between manifest and latent content (what you remember dreaming and what the dream was really about) as well as scientifically unsupportable theories about symbolism—ideas that can only be defended credibly within the framework of universally suspect Lamarckian views of evolution, the view that acquired characteristics can be passed on genetically over a single generation. Freud and Jung, after all, were both committed to the ideas that children pick up that stories about kings and queens, for example, may or do represent stories about their parents and then pass on the accrued set of symbols as a sort of prepackaged dream code to the next generation.[9]

The objection is a good one, one Freudians and Jungians and their ilk must face. But I can avoid making it stick to me. The idea that dreams sometimes, possibly often, have themes, plots, and narrative structure, and that they are typically to be classified on the side of the spectrum of mental state types that runs from episodes, extended episodes, to full-blown narratives, can be defended without falling in with the extremists among the depth psychologists. At this point, this is a promissory note. I'll be making good on it, to the extent that I can, by asking you to engage in phenomenological examination of your own dream life and, later, by looking at scientific research on the content and structure of dreams. But I want to be honest that I do need the premise that dreams—some of them, anyway—have themes, plots, and narrative structure, since such a claim is part of the overall view I am aiming to establish: that dreams are sometimes self-expressive and can yield knowledge, despite the fact that they do not have any proper evolutionary function.

Twisted Thinking

The final piece of business in this chapter involves trying to put you in a mood receptive to my overall argument by tinkering with your intuitions a bit, in particular, the intuitions that say that whatever else dreaming is like it is not like being awake. If awake mentation has a polar opposite, it is sleeping mentation. There is something right about this, but there is also something wrong about it.

To see this, consider these two true reports I shared with several neurobiology graduate students and post-docs whom I hardly know at all, and who knew virtually nothing about me, except that I was writing a book on dreams:

October 11th: *I am splitting firewood. Many of the insects living in the wood look like miniature dinosaurs. One creepy, crawly, creature bears an uncanny resemblance to a rhino. I wondered if I'd come upon a snake or a ferret in the wood pile. Then I thought that my daughter Kate should interview D. for her eighth grade term project on dreams, since D. is a psychiatrist.*

October 13th: *I saw the first bird of autumn appear on the new feeder. My mind turned from the fleeting sighting of the finch to a dim image of a Turkish city (I have never been to Turkey). I felt happy as I imagined having lunch later with G., and then pictured a scene in which a TV sports announcer urinated out the window of a nightclub onto two plainclothes officers staking the club out for drug traffickers. This seemed funny. But my mood shifted as I pictured Elton John and felt annoyed with him for changing the lyrics to his song about Marilyn Monroe for Princess Diana's funeral. I felt guilty and confused about feeling annoyed. Another bird perched on the feeder. I wished that a squirrel had tried for the seed instead, and imagined the squirrel being shocked—screeching and spinning end-over-end off the feeder never to return. I put my remaining raspberry yogurt on the dog's dry food, and drove off in a red Saab.*

The neurobiology graduates judged both dreams to be weird, in the way dreams are weird, and they offered various interpretations, noting especially certain obvious associations—insects are good candidates to morph into dinosaurs, imagining a bird in a dream might in the delirium of dreaming cause the mind to leap to the thought of a turkey (perhaps in deep unconscious) which might somehow take one to thoughts of the country Turkey, and so on.

Now I need to be honest. Neither the October 11th nor the October 13th reports were reports of dreams. (Nor did I tell you, the reader, or the budding neurobiologists, that they were dreams.) I am, of course, completely guilty of knowing that the reports would be understood to be dream reports, since I did everything to put that presumption in place and nothing at all to remove it. The fact is that both reports are reports of conscious awake stream segments, both of which I wrote down shortly after they occurred. I was wide awake when I thought those thoughts.

Setting aside without evidence or argument the possibility that I have an usually strange mind or that I am seriously disturbed, I want to suggest that many conscious stream segments of wide-awake persons are not dissimilar in apparent disjointedness, the occurrence of available but apparently undermotivated associations, and in seeming not to make sense especially as viewed from the third person point of view, especially if the third persons being called upon to do the interpreting lack information about the person having the thoughts, the context, and so on.

The demands of conversation or of public speaking help keep thought and talk on track, as do reading or writing an article or book, or watching a play or a film, or many other of life's tasks. But in my experience, much awake thinking while one is alone has thematically odd plot and narrative structure. However, such thinking episodes are not dreams nor are they daydreams.

My stream segments, and what makes sense of them, a sense I, at least, can explain, involves these facts. Take the October 11th wood-splitting segment. I did split wood, the insects looked like miniature dinosaurs, and one, at least, looked like a rhino to me—a very small rhino, to be sure, but a rhino nonetheless. I happen to like snakes and had been hoping to find some in the numerous stacks of unsplit wood piles created from downed trees left in the wake of Hurricane Fran the year before. Thinking about snakes led me to wonder about other animals—weasels and ferrets—that I might also come across. The neuroscientist next door works on the visual system of ferrets, so my mind was probably already primed to think of them. Thinking of ferrets caused this connection: My daughter Kate is in fact working on an eighth grade project on dreams. She is required to interview someone who knows about dreams, but parents are off limits. L., the next door expert on ferret brains, is married to D., a psychiatrist. Problem solved! Psychiatrists know something about dreams; therefore, Kate should interview D.

Regarding the October 13th stream segment, here are the facts. It was early morning, and I was drinking coffee, eating yogurt, and looking out onto the squirrel proof bird feeder purchased and mounted the day before over the deck in the back of the house. I saw a bird land on the feeder and then quickly fly away. Then I thought of my lunch date with my dear Turkish friend G., who had been having visa problems and had just returned to the States after five months back in Turkey. I glanced at the morning paper on the breakfast table and saw (I didn't really read it) that it contained the story about the sportscaster who peed on the cops (this struck me as hilarious) as well as the news that Elton John was in the area to give a concert, and my annoyance with him for messing with the lyrics of a great song resurfaced. Our dog, Bud, likes cottage cheese on his dry food, but we were out of cottage cheese so I gave yogurt a try. I brushed my teeth and drove off in my red Saab.

The first point I want to make is this. My mind while awake often travels to what might seem to be funny places, but are in fact places that matter to me and often are reasonable places to go to. Your mind behaves the same way. Waking thought—setting to one side daydreams and impossible awake fantasies—is not the neat and tidy, logically progressive, sequential world-negotiating, and problem solving process it is often cracked up to be. To be sure, some, probably much, awake thought and talk has such properties. But a lot of it doesn't.

The second point is that some dreams make sense, transparent sense, when we know more about the dreamer's life and state. Take my October 9th dream reported earlier. My old friend P.'s birthday is October 9th. Although we have only seen each other once or twice since 1976, P. often sends me e-mail greetings on my birthday in January, and it had been on my mind since the beginning of October to remember to do the same for her. My traveling partner G. in the dream is a philosopher friend who I had spoken with at length the day before the dream. I had last seen P. in 1995 at our college reunion, where I reacquainted myself also with A. (who P. morphed into). A. is an artist, but to the best of my knowledge, she does not smoke marijuana. Of course, in 1970, when we graduated from college, many people did. People also lived in communes in those days. Finally, the use of mind-altering substances was on my mind, since about a week before the dream my doctor had told me that alcohol would mix badly with medication he judged I needed to take. Thus, the October 9th dream.

Regarding the sportsjacket dream: I am unusually fond of my dark brown washed silk jacket. I purchased it for a dear friend's wedding in August 1997 at the sort of men's clothing store I would not normally frequent. They specialize in fashion. I have received many compliments about the jacket, including one a couple of days before the dream from a man who is known around Duke for his attention to his wardrobe. He wears blue suede shoes.

Perhaps this much explains why I had the perseverative NREM dream about where the coat was hung. The background makes sense of my dream without making my dream reasonable and without providing it with any psychological function. It helps explain how this particular perseverative thought rut was available to me.

Please Remember This

There are two take-home points from this chapter. First, dreams sometimes, possibly often, possess meaningful, interpretable structure. What structures dreams possess is often, related to what I know, remember, or what is otherwise on my mind. Therefore, dreams can be, and often are, self-expressive. Second, despite the fact that dreams are a nonstandard kind of consciousness, the sane standard of waking thought to which dreams are contrasted when we say that dreams are nonstandard is not all that easy to specify. Some, possibly much, waking thought isn't as nondreamlike—is not as "normal"—as initial intuitions might make us think.

The reader might be confused, and rightly so. I announced at the start that I reject certain functional views of dreams, but I have been lately defending the idea that dreams sometimes function self-expressively and thus can be utilized in the project of gaining self-knowledge. I have also made it clear that I aim to provide a strategy for getting around Descartes' dream problem, the skeptical worry that at the limit there is no way of being sure when one is awake if, that is, one is ever awake and not on every occasion wrapped in a dream. It might seem that I have not lately been helping myself set the ground for the solution or dissolution of Descartes' problem, since I have just been stressing how, from a phenomenological point of view, some, possibly much, awake consciousness is weird, disjointed, and freely associative in the way we often think is uniquely characteristic of dreams. Thus I have muddled the picture of what makes dream consciousness distinct and distinguishable from awake consciousness.

I never promised that my analysis of the nature of dreams would be simple. Furthermore, it is best to let various subtleties, complexities, and obstacles surface if one aims to build a robust and credible theory. It sometimes makes sense in theory construction in mind science to study a phenomenon abstracted from its normal ecological niche or niches and to bracket questions about its evolutionary origins. Indeed, this is often the best strategy in the earliest stages of theory construction. We would not understand as well as we now do how the eye works had it not been for simplifying experiments on cats in the 60s and 70s by Torsten Hubel and David Wiesel on differential cell activation in visual cortex (area V1) to differently oriented lines. Thanks to seminal work such as this, the visual system is now the most well understood sensory system by far.

Dream research is very young. Eugene Aserinsky and Nathaniel Kleitman reported the discovery of REM sleep in the journal *Science* in 1953, the same year James Watson and Francis Crick discovered the double-helix structure of DNA. I was four years old when the discovery was made. REM was discovered long after the laws of mechanics, thermodynamics, gravity, and the atomic structure of matter. Even general and special relativity predate the discovery of REM sleep by almost half a century.

The fact is that it was only after 1953 and thanks almost completely to Aserinsky's and Kleitman's discovery that the era of night-long recordings of brains in sleep labs (the brains were actually in people in sleep labs) began in earnest. Tremendous progress has been made in our understanding of sleep and dreams thanks to the path broken by this pioneering work. Indeed, thanks to personal computers hooked up to nonintrusive "night-caps," dream research can take place now in the comfort of one's home. It would be deeply disrespectful to the phenomena of sleep and dreams and to the many researchers who have dramatically advanced our understanding of sleep and dreams over the last four decades to oversimplify things. So onward. What is it we now know about sleep? What are the connections between sleeping and dreaming?

Notes

1. A vast literature exists on the rationality of deception for resources, food, territory, and mates. The possibility that it may be better to seem good than to be good is the topic of a famous debate between Socrates and Thrasymachus in Plato's *Republic*. David Hume's "sensible knave" is rational but not good in exactly the sense that he watches for chances for knavery with high payoffs and low probability of detection.

2. It is important to stress that on the evolutionary story, it is inclusive genetic fitness that matters, not individual reproductive success. An ant or an aunt who fails itself or herself to reproduce but who assists close relations in the project of reproduction, say by killing termite enemies or nurturing nieces and nephews, contributes to the spread of its or her genes inclusively, in virtue of the reproductive success of close genetic relations, without reproducing itself or herself.

3. We will, of course, on any view, want there to be some mental capacities that are vigilant, so that if a predator comes on the scene, or the winds of a tornado start to surface, or the baby cries, we will wake up. It would seem from an engineering perspective that the system could be in some sort of default mode such that it is designed to wake up just in case the baby cries. However, it is not clear what good NREM perseveration about the possibility of the baby's crying could do except to make for a disquieting sleep.

4. This may or may not be sound psychonutritional advice. I do recall that I had very bad dreams once after a Greek meal that included retsina wine. The next day did not go very well either.

5. This reading of Freud is very charitable since he was by no means a genuine Darwinian. The great historian and philosopher of science Frank Sulloway makes clear that Freud's ideas about evolution were more Lamarckian (see n. 8) than Darwinian.

6. In the "Crito," Socrates reports a premonitory dream that convinces him that his hemlock cocktail party will be delayed a day. This dream works as a literary device for Plato, one familiar to his audience. Socrates in the early *Dialogues*, the texts thought to best represent his views, develops no general theory on the source or function of dreams. In the "Republic," however, Plato does suggest that humans sometimes express their seamy sides in dreams.

7. Although I will not develop the idea here, one might imagine a response along these lines that would blend a Freudian sort of view with

a theory of mind view. What you dream about your own mind and the minds of others is in fact reliable. It is just that the thoughts you have about yourself and others in dreams can seem to contradict the thoughts you have about yourself and others while awake. The key is to remember that we are creatures with contradictory beliefs, desires, and impulses. Taken together, the mind-reading we do while awake and that which we do while dreaming provide a more complete and accurate picture of our own and other minds than would either by itself.

8. I emphasize that I only mean to leave open the *possibility* that there might be dream series in the way that there are TV series. In fact, for reasons that will become clearer as we proceed, I doubt that there actually are such dream series. On a related point: many people claim to have repetitive dreams—exactly the same dream over months, years, even a lifetime. The data gathered by dream researchers, although not conclusive, provide no evidence that there are such repetitive dreams.

9. Lamarckianism is the view that (in the present case) thoughts, beliefs, or symbols that are learned at a particular historical time can be biologically encoded, make their way into genes, and be thereby passed on genetically. In this way the second generation is spared having to learn what the first generation had to learn. Genes provide the relevant thought for free. Suppose for example that in some ancient culture a story was invented and told that taught the youth that fathers were (like) kings and mothers were (like) queens. This generation acquires the symbol. The next and all subsequent generations are born knowing that parents are royalty. Jung's idea of the collective unconscious is the idea that a certain set of symbols were utilized by our distant ancestors and are passed on genetically. Freud is less explicit that the symbols we use are acquired in such a Lamarckian way. But he can certainly be read that way. Indeed, Freud displays his Lamarckianism in the "Three Essays on Sexuality" of 1905, when while wondering about how penis envy could occur in a young girl who for whatever reason doesn't see a penis at the right developmental time, responds that the girl will remember unconsciously what a penis is, and is like, due to the enormous significance of the penis to the species.

3

Sleepy Heads

There she met sleep, the brother of death.

—*Homer*, The Iliad

Sleep and Death

When I was a little boy the first prayer I learned was this:

Now I lay me down to sleep.
I pray the Lord my soul to keep.
If I should die before I wake,
I pray the Lord my soul to take.

There are many things I like about this prayer. It is short. It assumes and thereby teaches what is true, that we humans can do things to ourselves—"I lay me down to sleep." Furthermore, a child is taught the prayer not just so that he or she can express some egoistical desire about himself or herself. The prayer is taught because in learning to say it, one also learns that others love and care. The prayer expresses a communal wish that if one is to leave this earth alone, as each of us surely will, be it while sleeping or while wide awake, that others hope that we fare well. "Fare thee well" is used to express wishes for a good and safe journey. "Farewell" is used to say good-bye, often, at least in dramatic contexts, good-bye for good.

But the prayer is puzzling in one respect. One learns this prayer only when one has language, can remember complex sayings, and has the rudimentary capacities required for engaging in rituals—bedtime prayers at least. This means that one learns the prayer at an age when the dangers of dying during the night are low relative to being taken while awake. However, no morning prayers I learned as a child reflected this fact. They had to do with praising God and the Blessed Virgin, asking that God's will, as incomprehensible as it might seem at times, be done, affirming one's faith, and so on.

Why were there no morning prayers that said things like this?

> Now I rise from this sweet bed,
> to face the world with much to dread.
> If I should die before nightfall,
> I pray the Lord my soul to call.

My experiences, my exposure to certain ideas linking sleep and death, I have learned, were not unique, not simply based on some idiosyncratic 1950s New York Roman Catholic views on sleep and death. In Greek mythology, for example, Nyx, the goddess of night, is a descendant of the god of the infinite, Chaos. Nyx had many children, including the goddesses of Destiny (Moros) and Fate (Ker), and the gods of sleep (Hypnos) and death (Thanatos). Furthermore, Hypnos and Thanatos were twins. Sleep and death—twins born of the same mother, Dark Night.

One reason for connecting sleep and death is that despite what I have said about the safety of sleeping—especially in the locked suburban house of my youth, relative to being up and about in a world of rushing streams begging to be traversed, as well as huge and irresistible climbing trees, not to mention cars and trains, drunks, child molesters, and murderers—most people die while asleep. They don't die because of sleep, of course. Accidental death, the kind most likely to befall the young nowadays, is often preceded by a period, however brief, of what we call "unconsciousness." The terminally ill, both old and young, typically enter some such state before nodding off for good. The person about to die can look remarkably like a person sound asleep. Conversely, sleeping people can appear as if dead. Dead people are rarely up and about; they are usually horizontal and still. So it is behaviorally with sleeping souls.

It is also likely that the link between sleep and death is based on an alleged phenomenological similarity between the two. This is a paradoxical way to put it, since phenomenology has to do with how some state *seems*, and the view I am now entertaining conceives of the similarity as involving being in a state, to invert Thomas Nagel's idea, for which there is *nothing* it is like to be in that state. The view has been considered by many wise persons. Aristotle and John Locke, living two thousand years apart but each possessing the best medical knowledge of his times, believed that some of the night is dreamless for each of us and that some people may never dream. If one thinks of death as "eternal rest," as a state of not-being, where nothing happens in or to the mind, then the mind at sleep may mimic that state—insofar as a state of not-being can be mimicked—at certain times for each of us, and for some people all the time.

Sleeping and Dreaming

Sleep and death are not the same thing, despite having certain features (for example, immobility) in common. Sleep and dreams, or sleeping and dreaming, are also different from each other and require different analyses. The Greeks understood that sleep and dreams were different, despite being intimately related. Morpheus, the god of dreams, is the son of Hypnos, the god of sleep. One argument for distinguishing sleep from dreams and for analyzing them separately is based on the premise that although dreams occur in sleep, some sleep is dreamless. Consider this analogy. Every day— indeed, every minute of every day, there is weather in San Diego and Seattle. In San Diego it rains only a little, in Seattle it rains a lot. But most of the time it rains in neither place. Knowledge of the nature and cause(s) of precipitation is important, but it is only one of the many things a good meteorologist needs to know. Precipitation is only one sort of weather, only one way weather can be.

Perhaps this is how it is with sleep and dreams. We sleep for six to eight hours. Some of us, the San Diego types, dream only a little during that time, while others, the Seattle types, dream a lot during that time. But no one dreams all the time he or she sleeps. Therefore, dreaming and sleeping are not the same. The idea is represented on the right, moonlit side of Figure 3.1, where episodes of dreaming are shown as occurring during only some of the time we sleep. Representing the contrast between different types of dreamers would require simply increasing or decreasing the number and the duration of dreaming episodes for particular individuals.

There is also the view that there are daydreams that are just like the dreams that take place in sleep except that we are awake during them. This idea is represented on the left, sunlit side of Figure 3.1. Since daydreams occur while we are awake and not asleep, dreaming and sleeping are not the same. Ergo, another proof for the same point.

I want to reject the assumption that these otherwise different models share, namely, that dreaming occurs during only some of the time we are asleep. This is the "common sense" view, and it is widely held by many, if not most, sleep scientists. The view I am going to assume is that we are always, while alive, conscious. If it is true that while alive we are always conscious to some degree, and if it is true that we are always alive and not dead when we are asleep, then it is true that we are always conscious while asleep. We are always dreaming while we are asleep. Figure 3.2 represents this idea.[1]

I don't know that it is true that we are always dreaming while asleep. Francis Crick has tried to convince me that during certain portions of deep sleep the mind is totally blank, thoughtless, and senseless. And Alan Hobson, on whose research I depend heavily for

Figure 3.1 Represents the view that dreaming is the mentation that occurs during REM sleep and during daydreams. On this view we dream only during some of the time we are asleep.

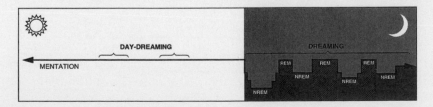

Figure 3.2 Represents the view that we are always dreaming when we are asleep.

my insistence that we dream in NREM sleep, believes that the case for dreams in deepest sleep, delta dreams, is hard, although not impossible, to make. The fact that two great philosophers, René Descartes and Gottfried Wilhelm Leibniz, living in the seventeenth and eighteenth centuries respectively, also believed that we are always conscious whether we are asleep or awake is only mildly consoling, since their reasons for thinking this were conceptual, not empirical—a thinking being is, by definition, a being that is always in some conscious mental state or other.

For reasons that will become clearer as the argument proceeds, I am not prepared to abandon the hypothesis that all sleep is dreamy. But even if Crick and Hobson are right that some sleeping is dreamless, it will not harm my overall argument that dreams are the spandrels of sleep.

One reason I want to assume, at least for the sake of argument, a very strong link between sleep and dreams is to meet a certain type of savvy critic who might object that my target thesis that sleeping was selected for and dreaming came along as a free rider is a total nonstarter, not even worth entertaining, on grounds that sleep and dreams are too tightly wound up with each other for this to be true. If sleep has a proper biological function, then dreams do, too, and that function is one and the same.

The best strategy for me to meet this objection is to allow the critic to assume as intimate a connection between sleep and dreams as he wants. I claim that there is no credible thesis about the intimacy of the connection between sleep and dreams that has any prospect of undermining the claims that they are different phenomena, subject to different analyses, and, despite initial appearances, actually able to be disentangled.

An especially strong, but ultimately highly implausible claim that might come from the lips of someone who expects the story of sleep and dreams to be unitary and unified would involve arguing that decoupling the nature and function of sleep from the nature and function of dreams is like decoupling the nature and function of water from that of H_2O, or the nature and function of salt from NaCl, or the morning star from the evening star and both from Venus. Identical things require identical analyses. Sleep and dreams are identical, therefore the strategy of providing them with different analyses is misguided and will prove futile.

The analogy upon which this argument rests is not credible. It is necessarily true that water is H_2O. But it is not necessarily true that sleep and dreams are identical. The widely held view discussed above that maintains we dream only some of the time we sleep is motivated by the claim that sleep and dreams are not only not necessarily identical, they are not identical at all. It may be false that there is dreamless sleep, as I think it is. But there is nothing incoherent about saying that there could be sleep without dreams, whereas there is something incoherent about saying that there could be water that is not H_2O.

A different, and superficially more credible, objection is this: Even if the attempt to distinguish the nature of dreams from the nature of sleep does not depend on the futile strategy of decoupling something from itself; even if it does not involve an attempt to provide different analyses for things that are, strictly speaking, identical, it makes an equally deadly mistake. The strategy I favor of distinguishing sleep and dreams and analyzing them separately—even granting that they are not identical—runs the risk of missing an important systematic unity that sleeping and dreaming possess. Claiming that sleep and dreams can be understood separately is akin to claiming that the nature and function of the human heart can be understood separately from the nature and function of arteries, veins, capillaries, blood type, blood pressure, red and white blood cell ratio, and so on. Despite being true to a certain extent, this claim misses the point that these things taken together are part of one unified system—the circulatory system. The story of the nature and function of the circulatory system will interweave truths about all the parts that make it up.[2] And so it is with sleep and dreams.

The guiding impulse behind all the criticisms mentioned is that the phenomena of sleep and dreams, as well as their natural history, are so tightly bound together that they are either one complex phenomenon—call it "the sleep-dream complex"—or, more likely, they are part of one larger phenomenon deserving a unified explanation akin to the way the story of the heart is part of the larger story of circulation.

There is something right about the picture of sleep and dreams as integral and connected parts of some larger story, the story of what it is to be our kind of animal (and many other kinds as well). Sleeping and dreaming are without question important aspects of human life. *Homo sapiens* are creatures that sleep and dream. It is part of the essence of being a human animal to sleep and to dream. Despite these facts, there are empirical as well as conceptual reasons for providing different analyses of sleep and dreams.

Imagine that there is no such thing as sleepless dreaming—that daydreams are not real dreams or, to put it differently, that there is no such thing as dreaming when one is not asleep. Imagine, further, that sleeping and dreaming invariably co-occur. That is, imagine that the relation between sleeping and dreaming is not one of strict identity like that between water and H_2O, but instead like the relation of the temperature of a metal and its volume. If the volume of a metal changes, so does its temperature. Mercury in a thermometer visibly represents this scientific truth in everyday life. Furthermore, it may be that the relation is bidirectional. Not only is it the case that if the volume of a metal changes then so does its temperature, but also that if the temperature of a metal changes, then so does its volume. Even if this were so, it would not follow that understanding the nature of metal would yield a full understanding of temperature. One reason is that temperature works differently in plasma from the way it works in metals.

Or consider more relevantly the relations among being alive, circulation, respiration, and digestion (or metabolism). In the normal human case, these four things co-occur. But they are not identical. To be sure, these phenomena interact in important, and not always symmetrical, ways, so that circulation is necessary for respiration and digestion. But the key point is that these things despite always co-occurring are not the same.

Suppose analogously that alive persons are always mentating. They also, if alive, had better be breathing and digesting. These phenomena co-occur. But they are not the same thing. An answer to a question on a biology exam about the nature of digestion that spent too much time talking about thinking, breathing, and circulation will be graded *F*.

The implications for the case of sleep and dreams is straightforward. One can believe that humans while alive are always in some conscious state or other and thus by implication that sleeping and dreaming always co-occur and still believe that sleeping and dreaming are different phenomena.[3] Let the picture be as represented in Figure 3.3, and there is still no obstacle to providing different analyses for sleep and dreams.

We should not expect in the case of sleep and dreams that there will be a unified evolutionary story of the selection pressures that

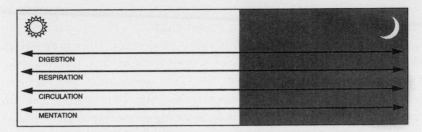

Figure 3.3 Represents the view that thinking (mentation) is just like digestion,
respiration, and circulation. It occurs at all times in living human beings, but
differs qualitatively during sleep.

drew them into being. Nor, and for many of the same reasons, will
there be a unified story of the functions of sleep and dreams.

Some of nature's wonders that universally co-occur turn out upon
study to be identical, to be one and the same thing. Salt and sodium
chloride (NaCl), water and H_2O, gold and the substance with atomic
number 79, and the planet Venus and the morning star and the
evening star are all like this. But not all things that co-occur, not all
things that are constantly conjoined are one and the same thing. It is
(almost) true that where there is smoke there is fire. Despite this, fire
and smoke are different things, subject to overlapping but ultimately
different analyses. Metallic volume change and temperature change,
as well as respiration, digestion, and circulation, are similar kinds of
examples. And so it is with sleep and dreams, even if it is true that
wherever and whenever there is sleeping there is dreaming.

What Sleep Is

My overall argument will gain credibility if I can say some enlighten-
ing things about sleep, independently of speaking of dreams. Even
if, like living and breathing, sleep and dreams always co-occur, it
will be good to know what sleep is independent of its ever-present
companion.

The question "What is sleep?" seems unlike most interesting scientific and philosophical questions, such as "What is the speed of
light?"; "What is the relation between mental events and brain
events?"; "Does God exist?"; "What is the nature of time?"; "Why is
there something rather than nothing?"; "Why is there anything at
all?" The difference can be put crudely this way. Anyone knows what
sleep is firsthand. Sleeping is what we are doing when we are not

awake. That is all there is to say on the matter. If you know what being awake is, then you know what sleep is. No further inquiry or investigation is required. Question answered. Move on to something worth an inquiring mind's time.

This naive response is, of course, just that. Firsthand experience reveals virtually nothing about what sleep is, other than a certain vague phenomenology about what sleep seems like—which ranges from the idea that sleep seems like being dead, to the idea that it seems like tripping on LSD, or a bit of each.

It takes science to tell us what sleep is. It is important to know what it is, not just how it seems, if we are to make progress on the questions of whether sleep is a single kind of bodily state or several related states; or what happens to the mind-brain and to the rest of the body during sleep; or what, if anything, sleep is for. The first step, then, is to try to discover the hidden structure of sleep. Neither the nature nor the function of sleep is revealed at the phenomenal surface, from the first person point of view, from the introspective pose.

One tactic for revealing the hidden structure of sleep and answering questions such as those just posed is to study some animals, for example, humans, some who are awake and some who are asleep according to our usual behavioral criteria for determining waking and sleeping. Next, measure brain waves and see if there are differences between those individuals who are awake and those who are asleep. And indeed there are.

Brains wave. Brain waves can be measured and characterized in terms of the rate at which the waving occurs and the relative distance the waves move from some point determined to be the point of rest or the meridian. When we are awake, brain waves occur very frequently, in quick succession, in rapid-fire form. Measures of the rapidity of neuronal firing are measures of frequency.

Awake brains are characterized by high frequency waves—by as many as fifteen waves per second. Despite the fact that the brain is rapid firing while we are awake, its electrical activity is low voltage. This is slightly counterintuitive, since if we picture a person frantically waving good-bye compared to one waving her arm slowly but higher and lower than the first, we think of the first as waving more energetically. And indeed, in the literal sense, she is. But it is a general truth about wave phenomena such as pendula, light, sound, and brain waves that the farther they move side to side or up and down from some resting place or set meridian, the greater the amplitude and the more energy emitted. In the case of brain waves, amplitude is a reliable measure of voltage. The greater the distance between the top and the bottom of a wave, that is, the greater the amplitude of a wave, the higher the voltage. Awake brain waves are rapid firing, but their peaks and valleys don't go very high or very low. Brain waves slow down as our heads hit the pillow, and within an hour or an hour and one-half of going to sleep the brain has descended stepwise to slower and slower waves with much higher peaks and far deeper valleys than the awake waves display.

EEG—electroencephalographic—representations of an awake mind look like traces of the journey of an extremely fast creature—a cheetah, jaguar, or road runner—running full tilt up and down a series of steep, small hills of similar height. By comparison, the EEG of a person in deep sleep looks more like a map plotting the path of an adventurer who climbs Squaw Mountain in the Sierra Nevada range and then redescends into Squaw Valley, followed perhaps by an ascent of Pike's Peak, after which the Grand Canyon attracts his interest. This journey has long time periods between blips (low frequency). But since it goes to both higher and lower places than the brain goes while awake it has high amplitude, that is, high voltage.

So far the story of the sleep cycle is relatively neat and tidy. This is true despite the fact that the neuroscientists who were in charge of naming the different kinds of brain waves used to differentiate the different stages of sleep seem to have known some Greek letters. But out of ignorance or orneriness they refused to follow the order of the letters as they appear in the Greek alphabet when naming the sleep stages. To make matters maximally confusing, the waves that characterize wakefulness are called beta waves, after the second letter in the Greek alphabet. As we dose off, beta waves are replaced by alpha waves (alpha is the first letter of the alphabet). Alpha waves quickly give way to even lower frequency theta waves (stage 1)—theta is the eighth letter. Eventually, the peaceful, melodic string music characterizing alpha and theta wave orchestration is joined, in the wonderful metaphor of Peretz Lavie, by occasional drumbeats and trumpet sounds. Although these orchestral novelties (they are the blips of K-complexes and sleep spindles) look disruptive from the outside, their occurrence is the sign that the individual is at a point in the cycle when she can no longer be easily awakened, quickly clear her mind, and return to beta waving. This is stage 2 NREM sleep. About ten to fifteen minutes after the drums and trumpet join the strings in stage 2 NREM sleep, delta (delta is the fourth Greek letter) waves, the ones that climb Pike's Peak and descend into the Grand Canyon begin to appear. A saxophone riffs. Then the sax leaves stage and a droning trombone joins the orchestra. This is stage 3 NREM. Eventually the droning trombone gets the other players to exit the stage and we are in deep, delta sleep, stage 4 NREM sleep. The droning of stages 3 and 4 NREM can last for as long as thirty or forty minutes.

Then comes the big surprise. REM sleep. The mind-brain's move to REM sleep, the type of sleep identified with bizarre mentation, delirium, and psychosis, begins with a rapid trip upwards towards wakefulness through stages 4, 3, and 2 and then into REM sleep. Allan Hobson's view is that REM dreams are not simply like psychoses, they *are* psychotic episodes—but they are neither unhealthy nor abnormal given why they occur and the context in which they occur. On an EEG, REM looks very much like being awake. It is characterized by rapid-firing (high frequency) and short-distance blips (low amplitude).

The total sleep cycle, comprising the descent through the four stages of NREM sleep, the rapid ascent to REM sleep, and a period of REMing lasting twenty to thirty minutes, takes in total about ninety to one hundred minutes. An eight-hour sleep will typically divide into six hours of repeated descent into NREM, in which a total of one to two hours will be spent in deep (delta) sleep and approximately one and one-half to two hours in REM sleep.

The data I have cited so far based solely on EEG recordings might give rise to this thought. REM sleep, insofar as its EEG profile is virtually the same as one sees in an awake person (see Fig. 3.4), is not a stage of sleep at all, but a stage of being awake. The idea is not crazy. But to keep it from getting too much of a grip we need to define sleep and distinguish it from wakefulness by using more than only EEG criteria. EEGs are a crude measure of total brain activity, especially neurochemical activity, and it is neurochemistry that largely, but not exclusively, differentiates REM thinking from awake thinking.

People studied by sleep researchers are hooked up to an EEG which yields the information about cortical activity, as well as to an electrooculogram (EOG) that records the frequency, direction, and speed of eye movements, and to an electromyogram (EMG) that records muscle tone and bodily movement. The ever expanding tool kit of the cognitive neuroscientist also sometimes involves magnetoencephalography (MEG) in studying sleep oscillations, and imag-

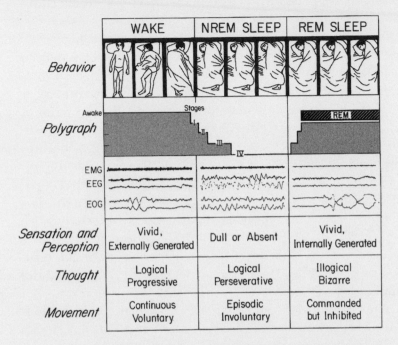

	WAKE	NREM SLEEP	REM SLEEP
Behavior			
Polygraph			
	EMG EEG EOG		
Sensation and Perception	Vivid, Externally Generated	Dull or Absent	Vivid, Internally Generated
Thought	Logical Progressive	Logical Perseverative	Illogical Bizarre
Movement	Continuous Voluntary	Episodic Involuntary	Commanded but Inhibited

Figure 3.4   Sleep stages. From Hobson and Stickgold, "Dreaming: A Neurocognitive Approach." © Academic Press 1994. Used by permission.

ing techniques such as fMRI (functional magnetic resonance imaging) and PET (positron emission tomography) to see more precisely areas of activation during sleep and wakefulness.

The data compiled EEG, EOG, and EMG are together sufficient to warrant classifying REMing with sleep. The EOG shows that the eyes are moving wildly beneath closed lids in REM, but not during NREM, when they are relatively stationary, nor during wakefulness, when our eyelids are open, saccading from place to place as we take the external world's measure. More importantly, whereas EMG recordings reveal that NREM sleep is characterized by lots of shifting movement as well as intact reflexes, during REM periods muscle tone is lost, and the capacity to move—twitching and movements of the facial muscles aside—is eliminated, as are the normal reflexes of wakefulness. During REM periods, the mentation results largely from internal processes, whereas while we are awake much of our thinking is under the control of external stimuli. Furthermore, PET shows that limbic activity is high and forebrain activity is low in both REM and NREM sleep relative to wakefulness. In phenomenological terms, feelings are more active during dreaming than is executive control, and this is reversed to some degree during wakefulness.

The point is that REM sleep, EEG patterns aside, is a stage of sleep and not of wakefulness. The reason REM is a stage of sleep is that we are asleep during REM. This is neither a tautology nor based on a pronouncement from this philosopher's armchair. Like most cognitive phenomena, sleep is characterized by a set of criteria not all of which can mutually coexist. A person cannot be in stage 2 theta wave sleep and stage 4 delta wave sleep at the same time. But a person is asleep at either stage. One is sleeping, just as one is depressed, or suffering from bipolar disorder, or an insomniac, or awake, if one satisfies some sufficient set or number of conditions for being judged to be in the relevant state or condition. It is rare to require that all the relevant conditions need to be satisfied.

Advice and health columns in the newspaper often contain little quizzes that might help you decide if you are diabetic, or alcoholic, or depressed. A perfect score warrants immediate action. But normally a score of around 70 percent, that is, having 70 percent of the symptoms listed is deemed sufficient reason for seeking professional advice or a checkup to see if one really has the problem in question. Psychiatrists use the profile or symptom lists in the approved diagnostic and statistical manual, *DSM IV*, their bible, in just this way in making their diagnoses. If every criterion for some psychiatric disorder was required for diagnosis of that disorder, almost no one would be diagnosed with psychiatric disorders.

Using a similar methodology, an essentially identical form of inference, it follows that during REM periods we are asleep. That is, despite the awake-like brain waves—which help explain the rich and robust phenomenology of REM sleep—we are asleep because our eyes are closed, because mentation is under the control of firings originating in the brain stem and not from stimuli in the external world, because our bodies are in an essentially paralyzed state, because oxygen usage is higher than in NREM but lower than when we are awake, because the profile of neurotransmitters is totally out of whack with the profile of an awake brain, and because phenomenologically we are "out of this world." REM sleep is truly a stage of sleep. That is that.

So far, as planned, I have been staying as close as I reasonably can to the topic of sleep, sidestepping until the physiological profile of the sleep stages is in place the question of the type or types of consciousness that occur in sleep. It is time to begin to speak more directly to this topic.

REM: A Long, Strange Trip

Here is a REM dream I had last night. How do I know it is REM? Theory tells me so. First, I'll tell you about the dream. Then I'll tell you what my brain was doing besides thinking these odd thoughts. How do I know what my brain was doing? Again, theory tells me so.

> October 26th: *I was in North Carolina with a group of teenage boys and girls. The boys were planning to raid an all-girls post-graduation party. The girls approved, especially one named L., who was physically identical to A., an undergraduate student of mine. So, we guys arrived at the party. I felt awkward hanging out with these young men, especially when I met the parents who were hosting the party and who were roughly my age. My wife, J., was there in the body of a colleague's wife. J. said to the parental hosts of the party: "Owen has lost weight, he looks good, doesn't he?" This annoyed and embarrassed me. The guys stayed downstairs during the party. The girls, we were told, were upstairs watching a basketball game, and would be down soon. Limousines appeared at the same time the girls did. The guys, myself included, were disappointed as all the girls were chauffeured home. J.'s best friend, C., arrived from Massachusetts and took me off to two homes in Vermont where several old relatives, including a great-aunt* [who died in the late 1960s] *were vacationing. Their car batteries were dead and I was trying to get them jump-started in the snow and cold. My success was mixed.*

The plot or my memory or both trail off at this point. In any case, here are some other things I know about what I was doing during this dream in addition to having this dream. First, as I have said, I was in REM sleep and not in NREM sleep during this dream. Second, I used less oxygen while having this dream that I would have used had I been up and about actually doing what the dream had me doing. Third, the imagery used in constructing this dream was due to the activation of cortical regions by waves originating in my brainstem, which also got my eyes darting around. Fourth, regarding neurochemistry, amounts of aminergic neurotransmitters such as serontonin and norepinephrine were very low during the dream, whereas my brain was awash with acetylcholine.

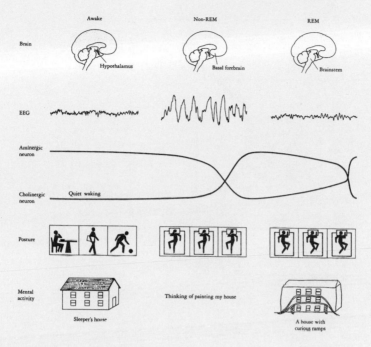

Figure 3.5 Sleep cycle. The hypothalamus, the basal forebrain, and pontine brainstem are believed to control states of waking, REM sleep, and non-REM sleep. As we go from one state to another, a series of coordinated changes occur in EEG signals, neurotransmitter level of activity, posture, and mental activity. Posture shifts during the transitions to and from REM sleep. The vivid perceptions of reality in waking shift to thoughtlike, nonvisual cognition in non-REM sleep and then to the bizarre visual imagery of dreams. From Hobson, *Sleep.* © J. Allan Hobson 1989:24. Used by permission.

The AIM Model

Here is the model, the theory I depend on to say much of what I just said (represented in Fig. 3.6). It is what Alan Hobson, its creator, calls AIM, for the three features of the mind-brain used to explain dreams, indeed, consciousness, generally. According to AIM, A is *activation level* and can be thought of as referring to the frequency of waves measured by an EEG. I refers to *input source,* for example, whether, visual thoughts are caused by things in the external world or by internal activation of brain areas that produce visual imagery. M refers to *mode* or *modulation level* as determined by the kinds and ratios of various neurotransmitters active in the brain, for example, serotonin and norepinephrine, two important amines, and acetyl-choline, a well-studied choline.

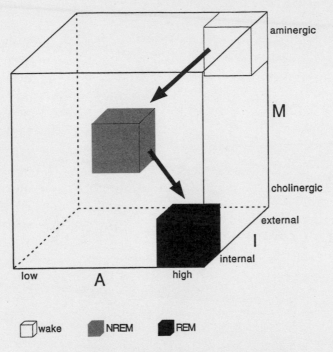

Figure 3.6   The sleep cycle portrayed in the AIM model. Adapted from J. Allan Hobson, *Sleep*. © J. Allan Hobson 1989:141. Used by permission.

Figure 3.6 visually displays the model and locates waking, and both NREM and REM sleep in the state space. AIM is designed to depict the underlying neurobiological and neurochemical features of sleep and dreams, indeed of the mind-brain generally. Waking is a state of high activation—the brain waves with the highest frequency, beta waves, are dominant. External stimuli are the main input source, and amines such as serontonin and norepinephrine have relative domination over acetylcholine in modulating such capacities as attention, learning, memory, and reasoning. So the representation for the awake state is at the back top right of the cube.

On the other hand, the input source for both NREM sleep and REM sleep is represented as internal, not external. But NREM, comprising stages of increasing slow waves, is to the low activation side and at a middle *mode*, since both the aminergic and cholinergic systems retain a balance in NREM even as these neurotransmitters decrease in overall quantities relative to wakefulness. Because REM has waves of virtually the same frequency as wakefulness, it sits with wakefulness on the scale of activation. But because cholinergic neurotransmitters take over in REM, the REM representation sits at the nadir of the mode, at the aminergic bottom.

The AIM model is an excellent but not perfect way of representing differences among wakefulness, REM, and NREM. The A(ctivation) axis is good at representing EEG activation; it is less clear that it can also at the same time represent oscillation patterns as detected by MEG. Also the I(nput) axis is good at distinguishing whether input is received from the external world as in wakefulness or from the brain itself, but it is not good at distinguishing among proximate input areas activated in the different states. For example, recent PET studies indicate that limbic areas responsible for emotions may be more active during REM than during wakefulness, and prefrontal cortical areas responsible for attention, planning, and control are less active in REM than when we are awake. These points are not objections to what the AIM model represents or to how it represents what it represents. The points simply suggest the not-surprising fact that even a three-dimensional cube may not be able to represent all the relevant differences among wakefulness, REM, and NREM.

Going to Bed and Staying There

We are now in possession of a fair amount of information about the hidden structure of sleep. Many important questions remain. First, why (and how) despite involving vivid experiences do dreams involve shutdowns of the logical, motor, and memory systems and (relative) insensitivity to disturbance by external stimuli? Second, why does the phenomenology of NREM and REM mentation differ in the ways it does? Third, what function(s) does sleep serve and how does the clocklike cycling of NREM and REM sleep contribute to these functions?

The short answers to the first two questions are these: Sleeping in general is controlled by a clock in the suprachiasmatic nucleus of the hypothalamus. The hypothalamus is an area importantly implicated in the manufacture of hormones and in thermoregulation. This clock gets us into NREM sleep, a hypometabolic form of sleep, and moves us through its four stages. There is a second clock in the pons (the pontine brainstem) that sets off REM sleep and its accompanying mentation.

In REM sleep, pulsing signals originate in the pontine brainstem (P, for short) and reach the lateral geniculate body of the thalamus.

When we are awake this area (G, for short) is a relay between the retina—on certain views part of the brain itself—and visual processing areas. Other pulses go to the occipital cortex (O, for short)—the main visual processing area of the brain. The general picture then is this: the pons (P) initiates waves that go to the lateral geniculate body of the thalamus (G) and to the occipital lobes (O). PGO waves are the prime movers of REMing.

This much accounts for the saliency of visual imagery in the dreams of sighted people. But the PGO noise is going to lots of different places and reverberating every which way. This is why people who work at remembering dreams report auditory, olfactory, tactile kinesthetic, and motor imagery as well as visual imagery. There is nice convergence of neuroscientific and phenomenological data here. Recent studies out of Rodolfo Llinás's lab at New York University using PET, fMRI, and MEG show that the parts of the brain that reveal robust activity during different types of awake perception are also active during episodes of related dream imagery. This strongly suggests that dream imagery operates on the same anatomical areas as does awake perception. This helps explain why prosopagnosiacs— braindamaged persons who don't see faces as faces—don't report dreaming of faces and why people with right parietal lobe lesions who can't see the left side of the visual field report related deficits in their dream imagery. But the main point is that PGO waves are dominant during REM sleep and quiescent during NREM sleep, and this explains by inference to the best available explanation a good deal

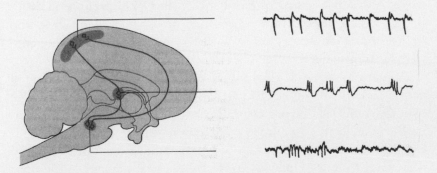

Figure 3.7   The visual brain stimulates itself in REM sleep via a mechanism reflected in
EEG recordings as PGO waves. Originating in the pons (P) from neurons
that move the eyes, these signals are conducted both to the lateral geniculate
(G) body in the thalamus and to the occipital cortex (O). Adapted from J.
Allan Hobson, *Sleep*. © J. Allan Hobson 1989:82. Used by permission.

about why the mentation of REM sleep involves vivid, bizarre, and multimodal imagery.

One hypothesis I have for why many researchers underestimate NREM dreaming, even to the point of thinking it is not dreaming, has to do with overrating the importance of robust sensory imagery, especially visual imagery, in dreams. Once sensory imagery is taken as definitive of dreaming, then dreaming is equated with mentation occurring during REM sleep, and the sensorially dull, but thought-like, mentation of NREM sleep is ignored. This then leads to the mistaken conclusion that NREM sleep, especially stages 3 and 4 NREM sleep, is a period of unconsciousness.

Blind Dreams

The issue of REM dreaming among the blind invariably comes up, usually at this point, when the dominance of visual imagery in REM dreams is reported. The facts are these. Blind people dream. People blind from birth have both ordinary sensorially dull NREM dreams, as well as the wild and crazy dreams characteristic of REM sleep, but with no visual imagery. People born sighted but who lose sight due to damage at the sensory periphery (but not due to serious damage to visual cortex) before age three or so have impoverished visual imagery in their dreams, sometimes no visual imagery at all. If blindness occurs after seven or eight years of age, visual imagery is much richer. The longer any person is blind, the less rapid eye movement occurs during REM. But other markers of REM sleep remain without much REMing, as it were. For such persons, identifying the stage of REM sleep relies primarily on EEG (looking for the return of beta waves) and EMG (watching for muscular-skeletal paralysis).

The answer to another piece of the puzzle, namely, why don't we in fact get up and do or try to do the things we dream about doing, has to do with the fact that the stages of NREM sleep involve muscular-skeletal relaxation. During REM sleep, the area in the brainstem containing the bulbar reticular formation neurons sends hyperpolarizing signals to the spinal cord, blocking external sensory input and motor output. In REM sleep we are essentially paralyzed.

From a motivational point of view, NREM dreaming—worrying and perseverating about next week's meeting with the boss, semicoherently reliving one's afternoon swim, wondering anxiously how algebra is going for one's son, and so on—does not typically involve the sorts of thoughts that one would normally, especially if the urge to sleep has taken hold, want to get up and do anything about. The fact is that we can still get up during NREM sleep. Our body allows it. This is why sleepwalking, sleep-talking, tooth-grinding, and night terrors—these are different from nightmares, which occur during REM sleep—occur, if and when they do occur, during NREM sleep.

People in REM sleep have, it would seem, much more motivation to act out the elaborate stories their brains construct. REM mentation presents lots of interesting action to get involved in or get away from. Fortunately, it seems to the dreamer as if she is acting out the drama she dreams, so the bodily paralysis characteristic of REM does not produce frustration. Still, there are individuals with brainstem lesions that eliminate the normal REM paralysis and who do get up in the middle of the night and do dangerous, wild, and crazy things: dancing with Fred Astaire, trying to thwart the mugger with a karate kick to the face of one's sleeping (now very surprised) husband, trying to tackle the floor lamp imagined to be the opposing quarterback ready to launch a touchdown pass. It is good not to have these lesions, and it is good not to share a bed with people who have them.

Sleeping Beasts

I need to address directly the question "What is sleep for?" This question takes us to, or close to, the heart of the matter. However, in trying to say some illuminating things about the function of human sleep and sleep-cycling, it will be helpful to say a bit about how sleep and sleep cycling work in nonhuman animals.

Opinions vary a bit on this question. Some say that fish and amphibians rest but do not sleep. Most researchers think that ancient reptiles have only low-grade NREM sleep, while more recent reptiles and birds have robust NREM sleep and some REM sleep. Until recently it was thought that all mammals save one, the egg-laying marsupial echidna, or spiny anteater of Australia, have REM sleep (many suspected that the duck-billed platypus, the other nonextinct species of monotreme, was also REM-less). Now there is some evidence that even the echidna and the duck-billed platypus partake of REM a bit, possibly as much as male rabbits who, unlike their female counterparts, REM very little. Furthermore, very intelligent social mammals such as dolphins and some species of seal may not REM at all.

How does one establish that some type of creature rests but does not sleep? Fish and amphibians certainly satisfy behavioral criteria of sleep. EEG patterns do not cooperate, however, which leads many to conclude that what appears to be sleep is just rest. But here one might worry that our criteria for sleep are anthropocentric or mammalocentric. Consider this analogy: Breathing involves, indeed it is for the sake of, oxygenating blood. Do fish breathe? Well, not if we think of breathing as taking in oxygen through lungs in a nonaqueous environment. But if we think of breathing as encompassing various ways of oxygenating blood, for example through a gill-filtering system, then fish, like humans, breathe. Or if this way of putting things bothers you, both fish and humans stay alive by utilizing blood-oxygenating systems. The question of which animals breathe or respirate is transformed into a question of whether a certain goal is accomplished, regardless of the precise mechanisms that do it. So too it may be with the distinction drawn between sleep and rest. Marking different ways in which different kinds of creatures renew themselves is important, but it is equally important to mark the fact that whether one calls it sleeping or resting, the creature in question is accomplishing the tasks of renewal, restoration, and rejuvenation that its body requires.

Not surprisingly, sleep and sleep-cycling—considered now as one complex phenomenon—has certain characteristics one would expect if it is an evolutionary adaptation. Animals such as bears and elephants who are not preyed upon sleep uninterrupted for long periods of time. The elephant, interestingly, sleeps standing up during NREM periods and then lies down for REM sleep.[4]

Antelope not only run fast, they do everything fast. They mate in a matter of seconds while on the run, birth takes place rapidly, and the newborn is immediately up and about, alertly scanning the environment as if it knows that dangers lurk. Eating and drinking occur in frequent but very brief episodes. Likewise, antelope sleep comes in brief spurts, never lasting for more than a few minutes at a time. Giraffes and rabbits sleep this way, too, as do most birds; in fact, some birds sleep during the allotted short spurts with one eye open.

Research on Atlantic bottle-nosed dolphins done in Moscow by Lev Mukhametov and his colleagues in the late 1970s presents a very interesting case. First, these dolphins never display brain waves characteristic of REM sleep. Since they don't REM it is plausible to think that they don't have REM dreams. But most dolphins—witness Flipper—are smart, friendly, and psychologically well adjusted. Second, dolphins do sleep. But they sleep one hemisphere at a time—while the left hemisphere sleeps the right remains totally alert, and this pattern alternates every one to three hours during sleep between the two hemispheres. When dolphins are given sleeping pills, both hemispheres go to sleep, and the creatures almost drown. This has led to the hypothesis that in dolphins all respiration is under voluntary control, which can only be exercised while at least one hemisphere is awake.

Humans have both a voluntary and involuntary way to control breathing. Normally, we breathe effortlessly and involuntarily. But when speaking or swimming, one has to make voluntary adjustments to the involuntary respiratory pattern. The dolphin research on the connection between respiration and sleep may be relevant to the important ongoing research on people with sleep apnea, a relatively common, but potentially dangerous, breathing disorder.

In creatures that REM, REMing is universally more frequent at the earliest stages of development and is perfectly correlated with relative immaturity of the animal at birth. In the first week or so of a kitten's life, it is REMing 90 percent of the time, whereas guinea pigs, which are born relatively mature, REM the same amount as newborns as they do when they age. For humans, newborns are REMing during half the sleep cycle. This drops to 33 percent at three months, and at puberty REM sleep comprises about 25 percent of all sleep. REM sleep decreases in relative amount as we age, as do stages 3 and 4 NREM sleep.

One important question raised by the discussion of REM sleep in beasts and human infants is this: Supposing REM sleep gives rise to REM mentation, what is REM mentation like in a deer or an elephant or a human infant? Do human infants have dreams that are about anything? Aristotle thought not, and his reason was a good one: To have thoughts about anything, one needs to have spent time communing with the world, catching on to the self-world distinction, forming mental representations, and learning to think and feel in terms of these representations. A December 16, 1997, headline in the *New York Times* Science Section asks the right question in a memorable way: "What Would It Mean If a Duck-Billed Platypus Had a Dream?" The answer, I am pretty sure is "nothing." The duck-billed platypus might have a multitude of images during REM, a platypus dream, if you like, but for reasons Aristotle gave, it is unlikely that these would add up to anything that really meant anything.

What Sleep Is For

Studies of the sleep patterns and habits of hundreds of species make it fairly clear that NREM sleep is older than REM sleep. The fact that NREM is the oldest form of sleep and is hypometabolic suggests the following hypothesis: NREM sleep was selected to serve restorative functions or energy conservation or body-building functions, or some combination of these. Some people find this hypothesis empty—akin to saying sleep is for rest which, although true, is thought to be uninformative. But things are not so gloomy if we can specify some of the actual restorative and conservatory processes and some of the building mechanisms in detail. And we can.

Pituitary growth hormone levels peak during NREM sleep in both children and adults. For children, growth hormone helps the child to grow. In both children and fully grown adults it also promotes protein synthesis throughout the body and thus aids in the process of new cell growth, which helps with tissue repair. For example, cell repair of the skin is well studied and known to occur with greater frequency during sleep than during wakefulness. Protein synthesis in the cerebral cortex and the retina follow the same pattern of occurring at a higher rate in NREM sleep. And, of course, the amount of food needed for survival is lowered when the metabolic rate is. REM sleep is also hypometabolic compared to being awake. Remember that the muscular-skeletal system is pretty much nonfunctional during REM.

One might think of the work the brain-body does on the night shift as a sort of detail work best left to quiet time. Imagine the construction of a beautiful chapel. During the day, there are many strong construction workers on the job, carrying and cutting wood, hammering and framing the structure, mixing and pouring mortar. Incredible amounts of energy are expended, and it shows as the structure rises quickly from the ground and reaches completion. Come late afternoon and early evening, and once the hectic dusty site clears, the finish carpenter works on some cornices and moldings. The artist hired to paint frescoes in the spandrels created by the arch and column design gently smooths the plaster in the curved spaces where he will eventually do his art. The craftsman in charge of the stained-glass design appears to observe the evening light as he did the dawn's light before the day crew arrived at the construction site.

All this work occurs during quiet time, after hours. Furthermore, less energy is expended than during the day shift, but what is getting done is vital to whether and to the way the whole chapel comes together. In certain respects the after-hours work requires a kind of delicacy, meticulous attention to detail, and types of patience not always displayed by the day crew.

And so it is with sleep. The endocrine system readjusts all its levels during sleep. During wakefulness, the adrenal glands release cortisol, which, when plentiful, helps maintain and regulate the rate of metabolism required by the day's activities. Extra doses of cortisol are released in stressful situations, especially when life and limb are endangered. Cortisol is depleted by bedtime. But starting about halfway through the night, the adrenal glands begin refilling the tank, over several intermittent shifts, so that the cortisol tank is full at awakening.

Another example is the gonadotrophic hormones secreted by the pituitary. These hormones are responsible for the secretion of sex hormones by the testes and ovaries, which during puberty are causally implicated in the growth of the sex organs as well as in the development of secondary sex characteristics. During puberty the gonadotrophic hormones work the night shift almost exclusively. This is less pronounced after puberty. But the fact remains that testosterone in grown males levels are depleted while they are awake, regardless of whether any sexual or aggressive behavior has occurred, and are restored during sleep. Indeed, levels peak at dawn.

Melatonin is a hormone secreted by the pineal gland—the place where Descartes believed the incorporeal mind meets the brain. Melatonin serves several functions related to sex, skin pigmentation, and the maintenance of our biological clock. Hefty amounts of melatonin are produced in darkness among sighted people, and this has an effect on the sleep-wakefulness cycle. To put it simply, melatonin makes one drowsy. This has led to widespread use of melatonin pills by people traveling across time zones in the attempt to adjust their sleep-wakefulness cycles. Sleep disorders are more frequent among the blind. This may well have to do with the fact that the pineal gland does not get the right kind of information about the light in the world that tells it when it is melatonin release time.

The Functions in Sum

To be sure, much more needs to be said and can be found in medical textbooks about the restorative/conservatory/building processes that are fitness enhancing and associated with sleep, especially NREM sleep.

Regarding REM sleep, two functions suggest themselves. First, the much larger percentage of REMing in development across mammals suggests that it is important in helping to build and strengthen brain connections, particularly ones in the visual system, that are not finished being built in utero. On the other side, the prominence of significantly greater time spent in REM sleep as an infant, when one doesn't know or care about right and wrong, than as an adolescent bubbling over with vivid and new socially unacceptable wishes, should go the other way if anything like the orthodox Freudian view of dream function were true. What instinctual impulses, what sexual and aggressive fantasies are being released by a newborn or, even less credibly, by thirty-week-old fetuses, which, according to some experts, go through phases of REMing twenty-four hours a day? Similar problems for the Freudian present themselves in the case of the social, sexy, promiscuous dolphins that don't REM at all and that, therefore, may not have opportunities to get rid of their "dirty thoughts." Perhaps they don't even have such thoughts.

The biggest difference between waking and NREM sleep and REM sleep has to do with the ratios of different types of neurochemicals, modulators, and transmitters in the soup. In particular, the ratios of aminergic and cholinergic neurochemicals flip-flop. Neurons known to release serotonin and norepinephrine (noradrenalin) shut off in the brainstem during REM and neurons secreting acetylcholine are on.

What good could this do? One credible hypothesis is that norepinephrine is crucial in getting the frontal and posterior cortical subsystems to do a good job of attending. Indeed, there is good evidence that both norepinephrine and serotonin are implicated in learning, memory, and attention (as well as in thermoregulation); and dopamine has been shown to play an essential role in learning, at least in sea slugs.

In waking, serontonin is working hard, as is norepinephrine. The aminergic neurons that release these neurochemicals quiet down in NREM sleep and turn off during REM sleep. This helps explain why memory for dreams is degraded. Meanwhile, neurons releasing acetylcholine turn on. Here is a credible hypothesis for why this might be: By a massive reduction in firing during REM sleep, the neurons releasing the neurochemicals most directly involved in attention, short term memory, and learning get a rest. While resting, they synthesize new neurotransmitters. The evidence points to a major function of REM sleep as involving stockpiling the neurotransmitters that the brain will need in the morning for the day's work.

Another hypothesized function of sleep and of REM sleep in particular implicates the acetylcholine bath that occurs during REMing in something like disk maintenance, compression, trash disposal, and long term memory consolidation. The guiding idea is that for memories to be retained they must be converted from storage in the halfway house of distributed electrical patterns into stable protein structures within neurons, in particular at the synapses. To get a feeling for the need here, imagine your computer crashing and the difference *save* makes. The idea is that memory reactivation involves the reactivation of the neural networks whose synaptic strengths have been altered. What happens during REM sleep is that the cholinergic neurons that are on and releasing acetylcholine interact with the temporary but connected electrical synaptic hot spots constituting a memory from that day or from previous days, and change those hot spots to a more stable form—to some sort of protein structure.

Another and importantly related idea championed by Francis Crick and Graeme Michison is this. Information taken in during the day is temporarily stored in the brain in a manner that is both *distributed* over many synapses, and *superimposed*; that is, a single synapse is involved in storing several different pieces of information. Superimposition allows a single synapse to play a role in remembering how to say "hello" in French, what happened on a first date, and what a peach smells like. A system that uses distributed and superimposed representations is efficient so long as it has a way of pruning excessively overlapping memories so that confusion resulting from remembering too many things at once does not occur too often. Pruning, or what has been called "brain-washing," is accomplished, according to Crick and Michison, by a process of "reverse learning," a process consisting of weakening the strengths of the associations among the already less firmly associated distributed and superimposed memories held in the system. The weak branches are pruned so that the strong may grow.

If the first process, memory fixation thanks to acetylcholine baths, is like performing *save* on your computer, the second process, weakening unwanted associations through reverse learning, is akin to putting things in the *trash* or, less drastically, of neatening file divisions.

Much more needs to be said about established and hypothesized functions of sleep and sleep-cycling for the story to be remotely complete. However, I trust that enough has been said to indicate that there is a credible basis for thinking that sleep serves a proper biological function. But what about the mentation that occurs during sleep? What about dreams? Even supposing dreams occur as a result of the good and important work that the sleeping brain is doing, do the dreams themselves have any proper biological function? When framing the chapel, imagined above, it was necessary to pound hundreds and hundreds of nails into wood. The chapel would not stand if framing did not occur. Wood and nails needed to be joined. Their joining serves an essential function in the creation of the chapel. But what about all the noise created by the nailing? This was caused by the process of framing, to be sure. But did it serve any function itself? Suppose that non-noise-producing hammers and nail devices were created, would anything be lost if we used them, anything important, anything other than the noise? This is the sort of question I want to address next.

Notes

1. I believe we are having experiences even when we are knocked unconscious. One piece of evidence comes from a military researcher who once questioned me about the "dreamlets" (his word) reported by fighter pilots who quickly lose blood to their brains and go unconscious during certain high speed defensive maneuvers. These pilots had brains pretty much voided of blood but still claimed to have had thoughts— quick shots of naked women, for example. There is also some tantalizing evidence mentioned earlier that even general anesthesia does not produce complete unconsciousness.

2. Although I won't fuss over it, the fact that the circulatory system is, in a sense, a unified system cuts not at all against my argument that sleep and dreams are to be analyzed separately. Different components of the circulatory system serve different functions and, in all probability, have different natural histories. This is one reason a physician concerned about your persisting fever will want to check your white cell count,

whereas the physician concerned about your dizzy spells will be concerned with aortic valves and arterial build-up of fatty deposits. The circulatory system is unified, but it is hardly a unitary phenomenon. Furthermore, the different components comprising the system and the coordination among them were most certainly subject to distinctive selective pressures over the course of evolution.

3. Since it will not make any difference to my argument, I will follow my intuitions and deny that daydreams are *real* dreams despite the fact that the word "dream" occurs in depicting them. In *The Chemistry of Conscious States,* Allan Hobson provides evidence that there are interesting phenomenological differences between the most bizarre daydreams and dreams—dreams are two and one-half times as crowded with characters and scenes and settings as daydreams, and laws governing space and time are more regularly violated. Hallucinations caused by LSD or mescaline are not dreams either. It seems a credible enough idea to think that a mental episode is a *real* dream if and only if it occurs when we are asleep. Hypnagogic hallucinations—rapidly changing, jumbled images and thoughts often related to what was last seen, heard, or thought of before nodding off—as well as the hypnopompic hallucinations that sometimes occur as we wake up are probably best classed as in-between states.

4. I like to think of us humans as very safe. The trouble is, as many great thinkers have emphasized, for example, Thomas Hobbes in *Leviathan* and William Shakespeare in *Hamlet,* we are especially prone to being killed while asleep by our fellows during times of war and when we are targets of revenge. William C. Dement takes the title of his great 1972 book on sleep and dreams, *Some Must Watch While Some Must Sleep,* from *Hamlet* (Act III, Scene ii), where all sorts of murder and mayhem, real and imagined, are being carried out on sleeping souls.

4

Dreams: The Spandrels of Sleep

Things cannot be other than they are. . . .
Everything is made for the best purpose. Our
noses were made to carry spectacles, so we have
spectacles. Legs were made for breeches,
and we wear them.

—*Dr. Pangloss in Voltaire's* Candide

An adaptationist program has dominated
evolutionary thought in England and the United
States during the past forty years. It is based on
faith in the power of natural selection as an
optimizing agent.

—*Stephen Jay Gould and Richard C. Lewontin, 1978*

Function and Design Among the Artifacts

It has proven to be a good research strategy in biology, cognitive psychology, and cognitive neuroscience to ask of any trait or capacity: What function does it serve? What was it designed for? How does it work?

Strictly speaking, these questions do not ask exactly the same thing. Things serve functions for which they were not designed—a paper bag can serve as an umbrella. And learning how some device works can leave one clueless about its function. Imagine an expert explaining to me the intricacies of his latest invention without ever explaining what it is for, or, alternatively, explaining what it is for without my being able to comprehend what he is talking about. Suppose, for example, that understanding the device requires knowledge of quantum physics. If so, I won't understand how the device works, although I might well understand what it does. In any case, these questions about function, design, and how something works form a family. Typically, asking and answering one involves asking and answering the others, at least partially.

Explaining how something works often answers all interesting questions about function. This is because describing how something works normally involves specifying the end aimed at or achieved. If I provide a detailed explanation of how my bird feeder works and why, in particular it succeeds at attracting such large numbers of diverse species of birds, I will need to explain several things: how its design allows plentiful perches; the different kinds of seed used; and how it successfully keeps squirrels away (it contains a nine-volt battery that provides an electric shock to any creature large enough to stand on the metal base and complete the electrical circuit by touching its mouth to the metal that surrounds the openings the birds eat from).

Artifacts are designed to serve some end, some purpose. Washers, dryers, drills, lawn mowers, sewing machines, needles and thread, combs, soap, bicycles, cars, and art are designed to serve certain functions—in the case of art, to produce an aesthetic effect. Artifacts work if they achieve the function for which they were designed. The function for which an artifact was initially designed is its *primary* function. A primary function has to do with original intentions.

A car that no longer works as a car can acquire a *secondary* function. It can serve as a used parts shop, as a place to store moonshine, as a shelter for field mice, as a rust-producing factory, and as many other things besides.

Sometimes nonworking cars are simply left on the back-forty (or the front lawn) to decompose. They are not intended to function as art; indeed, they are not intended to function as anything at all. Supposing we do not store the moonshine in them and that no vermin move in, we are inclined to say that they do nothing, they serve no purpose, indeed, that they are a blight on the landscape.

Even the car that is just decomposing in the yard is doing something. For example, it is releasing oxygen and nitrogen as it rots away. This affects the surrounding soil and air, and the shadows it casts change the way grass grows near it and beneath it.

We can say of cars, and of most any artifact that one can purchase new or that some artisan takes the time to design, that they have a primary function. When artifacts stop performing their primary function, they can perform a secondary function, such as serving as a moonshine storage facility. A car that has ceased to serve its primary function and has not been adapted to serve any secondary function may come to serve no function at all. However, it will, even in virtue of just rusting away, still have effects.

I have been giving examples of how an artifact might come to lose its primary or original function but still be put to some other, secondary use. But it is important to emphasize that an artifact can work just fine to perform its primary function and also be used to serve some additional function or functions. Thus a car that runs well can also serve as a moonshine storage and delivery device. That is, a car can serve a primary and a set of secondary functions at one and the same time.

Furthermore, brand new artifacts that could serve their primary function perfectly well can be coopted for secondary functions. I purchased a one hundred-foot-long dog lead to hang between two trees above the deck to hold bird feeders. The lead would work just fine to keep the dog in the yard, for which purpose it was designed. I just use it for a purpose different from the one for which it was designed or intended. In a sense, I endow the dog lead with a new primary function.

To keep things straight, think of artifacts that do the job for which they were initially designed as artifacts that serve their primary function. Some, possibly many, artifacts serve their primary function, as well some set of secondary functions—the car's glove compartment, the trunk in which we keep sports equipment, the ski rack mounted on the roof have primary functions, all of which are secondary functions relative to the primary function of a car. Broken artifacts, we have seen, can be adapted to serve new secondary functions. Broken artifacts differ from the new dog lead used to hang bird feeders between trees in that they could not, without being fixed, perform their primary function. Finally, artifacts like the decomposing car, that serve neither their primary function nor any secondary function, still in virtue of decomposing and casting shadows have *serendipitous* effects. Often we say, and say rightly of artifacts that have only serendipitous effects, that they are utterly useless.

In sum, for human-made artifacts there are primary functions, secondary functions, and serendipitous effects. One and the same artifact can have primary and secondary functions, as well as serendipitous effects, at one and the same time. An artifact can also lose its primary function and come to be of use only for some secondary function. Or it can retain in principle its primary function, as does my dog lead, which I have reassigned to be a bird-feeder hanging device. No matter how primary and secondary functions are gained, lost, and combined, serendipitous effects are always present, even if barely noticed.

Biological Design

How do function and design work for biological characteristics, traits, and capacities? There is, on the one hand, a powerful tendency to think that Mother Nature works hard to design all the things in her dominion as human designers do, that is to do some job and to do it well. The world is filled with living things that fit their environmental niches beautifully, and the world abounds with artifacts that do what we need done. Despite the extraordinary number of well-adapted, well-designed, and well-functioning living and nonliving items that populate the natural and human-made worlds, it is important to remember that both Mother Nature and the R&D divisions of small and large firms have tested, and continue to test, many pathetic designs. Such designs don't work well, or at all, which explains why we rarely see them. Mother Nature and human manufacturers produce and reproduce on the assembly lines the designs that pass muster, that do the job, and they do all this relative to cost-benefit analysis. In particular, a complete redesign of a satisfactory design is usually too expensive to get by the accountants in the R&D division.

There is a very large number of ways to build bridges that do not work. These tried, tested, and failed designs—mostly imagined—are extinct. At least no reputable bridge builder still keeps on the books designs known to result in bridges that collapse. Still, there are many ways to build beautiful bridges that do the job. So it is with respect to biological phenomena. Mother Nature tries various designs. Only the designs that work survive over long periods of time, and they survive precisely because they work.

The fact is, however, that in both the design of artifacts by humans and in the work of biological design by Mother Nature some design features appear—over time—as design improvements. A rearview mirror is a good design feature on a car. Using the terminology introduced above, a rearview mirror has as its primary function the sighting of vehicles approaching a car from the rear. Rearview mirrors do not, strictly speaking, contribute to the primary function of a car. Until recently it was a side effect of having a rearview mirror that glare was created when a car approached from the rear at night (new model mirrors can be flipped upward to prevent glare). Suppose, probably contrary to the facts, that a certain amount of glare and the required visual readjustment to light were the only side effects of standard rearview mirrors. No one designed rearview mirrors to produce the glare; it just came, we'll suppose for argument's sake, as a neutral, serendipitous side effect of what a rearview mirror is designed to do.

Car manufacturers also, of course, build cars with features designed to catch the buyer's eye and thus the buyer's dollar. Jazzy dashboards, flashy wheel covers and grilles, and hood insignias contribute not one iota to what a car's primary function is, although they may serve secondary functions such as making the driver feel good about himself. [1] And of course when a particular design feature catches the eyes of buyers, cars with those features rise in sales relative to the competition.

Especially rich manes on male lions, especially long and colorful tail feathers on certain birds, may contribute similarly to mating chances, reproduction, and thereby to an increase in the genes relevant to producing similar traits in the next generation relative to the competition.

Is the male lion's majestic mane, or the peacock's possession of spectacular tail feathers adaptive or an adaptation? What about human capacities to walk, talk, see, hear, introspect, and dream? Are these adaptive or adaptations? The issues are fairly complicated, so it will be wise to revisit briefly some important recent work in the philosophy of mind and biology to understand what it means for a trait to be adaptive, or, what is different, an adaptation.

Adaptedness and Adaptation

One might think we can make quick work of the main problem—Is dreaming an adaptation or not? Does it serve any function?—so long as we can show that across most any meaning of adaptive or functional that consciousness is adaptive and that dreaming is a type of consciousness.

What, however, does it mean to say of some trait or capacity that it is adaptive or an adaptation? This is a topic of considerable discussion. One sense of "adapted" means, roughly, well suited or a good fit. Some trait is well suited or a good fit relative to some task or end. So we might say of some trait that having it contributes to the organism's well-being, to the quality of its life. A well-adapted heart is neither too small nor too large to efficiently pump blood. Well-adapted eyes (especially prior to the invention of lens crafting in the seventeenth century) are eyes that can see in the 20/20 range. We might also say of some person that she is gifted mathematically, that her mind-brain is unusually well adapted to doing mathematics. One even hears the word "adapted" used to describe personality traits: He is so well adjusted, he has such a positive outlook on life, that he can adapt to whatever comes his way.

We also say of mechanical devices, intentional human acts or act-types, and cultural institutions that they are adaptive or functional. Here we mean that the device, act, act-type, institution does what it is designed to do.

One further distinction within the nest of meanings of the terms "function" and "functional" will be helpful to have in view: this between a causal contribution sense of function, and a functional versus dysfunctional sense. To use Philip Kitcher's example, mutant DNA causing tumor growth is functioning as it is supposed to from the point of view of the relevant cell lineages; it is making the causal contribution we expect, but it is dysfunctional—bad biologically and psychologically for the organism in which the tumor is growing.

Evolutionary biologists normally use the term adaptation in a way that is more restricted in meaning than the terms adapted or adaptive or functional. The preferred sense of adaptation is a historical one. A trait is an adaptation if, and only if, the trait arose due to selection pressures for it. The guiding idea is to tie the concept of an adaptation to selection pressures operating when the trait appeared. To say that a trait is an adaptation is to say something about the causal history of the trait. The abilities to walk and run are likely adaptations. Being able to walk and run enable us to be able to waltz, and tango, and tap dance, and pole vault. But Mother Nature did not give a hoot about these add-ons. So the ability to tango is not an adaptation. Presumably, Mother Nature selects for traits that contribute to reproductive success, to inclusive genetic fitness. A trait which is an adaptation in this historical sense might no longer be fitness enhancing in the present. For example, sexy tail feathers that attract mates have gotten so long and weighty in some birds that the birds can no longer fly, thus subjecting them to greater chances of being preyed upon.

Conversely, suppose a trait such as horns in a certain species of beetle originally arose for fighting. The horns could be and were used incidentally for digging, but they were selected for to do battle. The horns were so successful in the business of waging war, let us suppose, that all enemies have long since departed. The beetles now use the horns only to dig for food. The horns were well adapted for digging from the start. But suppose that digging for food was not necessary in the original selective environment, that all necessary nutrients were above ground. In the original selective environment, the horns were exclusively an adaptation for fighting. That was their primary or original function. And they could still do that job if it were ever required. Suppose that in recent times, say over the last twenty thousand years, even as enemies have disappeared, food sources have gone underground, so the beetles dig. If we assume that digging and finding food is fitness enhancing, then there is reason to believe that the current selective environment works to maintain the horns and possibly even to modify them to be better digging devices. We have a secondary function (or a new primary function, if you like) emerging out of or coopted from a primary function with different selective pressures involved in the origination and the current maintenance and modification of the trait. Thinking of adaptations historically involves both the ancient and modern history of the trait.

It is no objection to the historical criterion of an adaptation that some trait might no longer serve the function for which it was selected. Suppose there is another Great Flood, but this time no Noah and no ark. Then all the creatures saved on the original ark, including *Homo sapiens*, are done for. Aquatic beasts meanwhile do just fine. Despite the fact that all land dwellers are now extinct, the fact remains that the respiratory system of land dwelling animals are adaptations—notice that there is a pull that must be resisted to use the past tense and say "were" adaptations. It is just that due to an environmental catastrophe, the relevant adaptations can no longer serve the function for which they were designed. If you take in oxygen through a lung system but cannot keep your head above water for forty days and forty nights (dolphins, porpoises, and whales, if it comforts you, will survive even this flood), then your adaptation fails you because it is not adapted to your current environment. But it does not fail you because it is not an adaptation.

Having a grip on the different meanings of adaptive, adapted, and adaptation helps us understand why someone might say that aggression is an adaptation but not adaptive, or, conversely, that being able to read and write is adaptive but not an adaptation.

For example, Stephen Jay Gould argues that the abilities to read and write "are now highly adaptive for humans." But the abilities to read and write were not selected for during the Pleistocene age, when we evolved. These abilities may have emerged during the Pleistocene era, but not because they themselves played any fitness enhancing role as the ice melted.

These abilities—to read and to write—came as free riders on brains selected to do other things, to hunt, forage, mate, and communicate with conspecifics. Thus the capacities to read and write are not adaptations. Even if literate people were once more reproductively successful than nonliterate people, this would not show that then or now there are any differential selection pressures pulling for brains that can learn to read and write. There is no strong reason to believe that human brains have undergone any significant evolutionary changes over the last ten thousand years. Brain-damaged persons aside, all human beings can become literate. When and where one is born determines whether literacy is acquired. The smarts are invariably there—as they were even for our Pleistocene ancestors living at the end of the last Ice Age. Literacy will occur if it has been invented in one's locale and if the proper social, nutritional, and educational resources are in place. Except for malformed individuals, all humans since *Homo sapiens* evolved on the African savannah have possessed the neural equipment to become literate. Natural selection requires variation. And with respect to the capacities required for literacy, there is no reason to think that sufficient variation exists within the species to undergo differential selection. To make matters worse for anyone who wishes to claim that there is genetic variation among literate and illiterate types, say between people from Belgium and Bangladesh, and that literacy is fitness enhancing, the fact is birth rates among literate people are at all time lows.

Even if literacy is not an adaptation in the sense that it evolved because it contributed to our reproductive success during the Pleistocene age, we still might be inclined to say that literacy "is highly adaptive." But here we would mean things like literacy contributes to human flourishing, to happiness and well-being.

Epiphenomenalism About Dreams

If being an adaptation involves a trait's being selected for because it is fitness enhancing, then we may call the denial that some trait is an adaptation "evolutionary epiphenomenalism," or, as I will sometimes call it for brevity's sake, "epiphenomenalism." According to the view being broached here, dreams are evolutionary epiphenomena. Evolutionary epiphenomenalism about dreams is an empirical claim, and a strong one at that. It says that the presence of dream consciousness has no adaptation explanation—there is no fitness-enhancing effect for which dream consciousness was selected and maintained when it first came on the scene, nor is there any fitness-enhancing effect for which dreaming was coopted, as was the case with the beetle horns discussed above. One can be an evolutionary epiphenomenalist about a specific type of consciousness, for example, dream consciousness, or one might be an evolutionary epiphenomenalist about consciousness generally.

It is no accident that the status of the conscious mind was considered a problem by early evolutionists, since it was considered a problem for everyone. Traditional puzzles about human uniqueness, about the physicality of mind, about the nature of mind's interaction with the brain and the body were still on center stage in the nineteenth century when news of the blind watchmaker hit the stands—as they are still, in many respects, on center stage even today.

Thomas Henry Huxley, "Darwin's bulldog," so named for his relish in debating the merits of evolutionary theory, relative to the Master's reticence, stated the view that consciousness was epiphenomenal—something the Master himself almost certainly did not believe—in the clearest possible terms:

> The consciousness of brutes would appear to be related to the mechanism of their body simply as a collateral product of its working, and to be completely without any power of modifying that working, as the steam-whistle which accompanies the work of a locomotive engine is without influence on its machinery. Their volition, if they have any, is an emotion *indicative* of physical changes, not a *cause* of such changes. . . . The soul stands to the body as the bell of a clock to the works, and consciousness answers to the sound which the bell gives out when struck . . . to the best of my judgement, the argumentation which applies to brutes holds equally good of men. . . . We are conscious automata.

Huxley was almost certainly an evolutionary epiphenomenalist about consciousness, as indicated by the claim that consciousness is "a collateral product" of the workings of the body. However, the view expressed in this passage is stronger than an evolutionary epiphenomenalist need maintain. Huxley's claim is that consciousness is a side effect of the body (itself a complex adaptation or set of adaptations) that itself has no further effects. Consciousness is "completely without any power" to affect the body. The fact that some trait is not itself an adaptation, but is an effect of an adaptation does not in any way imply that it does not or cannot have effects. Suppose, as I think is the case, that literacy is made possible by cultural selection for previously untapped potential of brains selected for because they were good at hunting, gathering, foraging, communicating, and mating. Assuming that literacy is acquired by and realized in the brain and that it results in such practices as reading and writing, then despite not being a biological adaptation, it has all sorts of effects on our bodily behavior—for example, it leads us to buy and read newspapers and to write and respond to letters. Notice that Huxley speaks explicitly of consciousness as a side effect. Consciousness is "a collateral product" of the body's working and "is completely without any power of modifying that working."

Needless to say, if epiphenomenalism were true of the conscious mind generally in the excessively strong form stated by Huxley, then it would follow as a trivial consequence that dream consciousness is epiphenomenal. But evolutionary epiphenomenalism is false, or at least highly implausible, as a general thesis—and, as I have just argued, Huxley's sort of epiphenomenalism is even stronger than anyone who believes that some mental traits are evolutionary epiphenomena need maintain. It is not completely uncontroversial, but it is pretty close to being uncontroversial that sensory consciousness is an adaptation and that awareness of our sensory states is used in guiding action.

The fact remains that even if the conscious mind, as a whole, is not epiphenomenal, some types of consciousness might be epiphenomenal. And so it is, I think, with dreams. Still, the thesis is subject to misunderstanding since, as we have just seen, epiphenomenalism comes in various forms. We need to proceed carefully.

To say that dreams are evolutionary epiphenomena is to say that there is no fitness-enhancing effect of dreams for which they have been selected, maintained, or coopted. But evolutionary epiphenomenalism about dreams does not draw into question the existence of dreams, nor need it draw into question the causal role of dreams in, say, affecting the day's mood or in being utilized in the project of self-knowledge. Evolutionary epiphenomenalism just says that, as a matter of (ancient and recent) historical fact, having dreams is not a trait that was selected for by natural selection. Culture may come to select for having or remembering dreams of a certain sort, as well as for certain techniques of dream interpretation. It could do this, as it has for playing bocci ball or bridge, without the activity affecting's biological fitness one way or another. Furthermore, my own view is that it is unlikely that *what sleep is for* is enhanced by dreaming things that can be interpreted as having a certain significance, or even by an entire population becoming virtuoso dreamers, dream reporters, or dream interpreters.

Geometry, calculus, and physics are important. We cannot, in a sense, do without them. But being able to do these things is an evolutionary epiphenomenon of selection for big brains designed originally to gather, hunt, communicate, and mate.

I hope this much makes clear that to say of some characteristic, trait, or capacity that it is epiphenomenal is not to disparage it. Epiphenomenal just means "secondary appearance" or "side effect." Usually, the intention to disparage a side effect involves saying something like, "It is *just* a side effect"; "it is a *mere* side effect"; or, as Huxley maintained, that it itself is caused but does not, indeed, cannot produce any effects. That which is epiphenomenal despite being a secondary appearance or side effect might be just as important from any number of perspectives as the adaptation that allows it, that produces it, or that contributes to its realization. This will become clearer if we enlarge the picture of how evolution works.

Spandrels and Exaptations

Evolution simply means unfolding or unrolling. Everyone who does not believe that the world stands still—thus, everyone—believes in evolution—even creationists.

The theory of evolution by natural selection says more than that the world unfolds over time. It says that evolution is largely or primarily guided by the process of natural selection, the process of modification of heritable traits over generations thanks to the differential reproductive success of organisms that possess the traits.

All Darwinians believe in evolution by natural selection. Stephen Jay Gould writes that "natural selection [is] a paramount principle (truly primus inter pares)." But he goes on to insist that neo-Darwinian pluralists, like himself, believe that "a set of additional laws, as well as a large role for history's unpredictable contingencies, must also be invoked to explain the basic patterns and regularities of the evolutionary pathways of life." What Gould calls "ultra-Darwinian fundamentalism," adopting a phrase of his colleague Niles Eldridge, privileges the principle of natural selection in the way Skinnerians once privileged the principles of operant conditioning in explaining all learning. According to ultra-Darwinian fundamentalists (if there are any), *all* evolution is evolution by natural selection; all persisting traits are adaptations (although they needn't now be adaptive). Pluralists admit the importance, possibly the primary importance, of natural selection, but insist that there are other principles and processes that can give rise to the traits, characteristics, and capacities of living things.

Darwin himself was a pluralist. In the first edition of *The Origin of the Species,* published in 1859, he wrote these words at the close of the Introduction: "I am convinced that natural selection has been the main but not the exclusive means of modification." Darwin repeated these words in the last (1872) edition, expressing the hope that this self-quotation might serve to defeat the powerful forces of "steady misrepresentation."

Darwin was right: not all traits are due to natural selection. Since natural selection works only to produce adaptations, this claim amounts to insisting that not all form, function, and behavior of nature's bounty consists of adaptations.

According to terminology introduced by Gould and Lewontin and Gould and Vrba, we can divide biological traits into three non-mutually exclusive types. These are adaptations, spandrels, and exaptations.

Spandrel, as discussed earlier, is an architectural term that refers to the triangular space left over when arches are placed next to each other at right angles, so as to begin mounting a dome, as in many great churches, or in a straight line, as in the magnificent Roman aqueducts. Spandrels are inevitable by-products of arch and column designs.

In Roman aqueducts, spandrels are unambiguous architectural by-products of a design aimed at carrying water, possibly people and farm animals. In aqueducts, normally, spandrels are not decorated. Perhaps paganism and the weather explain this. The spandrels exist because a decision was made to line up arches and not to put up a wall across the river. The desire not to make a dam explains this.

Spandrels are, of course, decorated in churches. It would be silly

Figure 4.1   Arches provide a solution to the problems of large-scale stone architecture, such as the Pont du Gard in France. Often the spandrels (see Fig. 1.3 and Fig. 1.4)—as well as the area inside the arch from the line of its "springing" to the bottom of the keystone, called the tympaneum—are decorated (see Fig. 4.2). But spandrels and tympaneum need not be decorated. Adam, *Classical Architecture*, © 1991. Used by permission.

Figure 4.2   Some variations in decorative spandrels. Adam, *Classical Architecture*, © 1991. Used by permission.

not to use these spaces for religious art—for representations of angels and saints, Mary, God the Father, the Holy Spirit, and the rest of the heavenly host. Roman Catholicism explains why. It is, after all, a form of monotheism with a panoply of important accompanists of the One True God—accompanists ideal for representation in statuary, frescoes, paintings, mosaics, and stained-glass windows.

What Gould sometimes calls the "principle of spandrels" is targeted to deflate "panadaptationism," the view that everything is an adaptation. Biological spandrels exist and are nonadaptations, therefore, panadaptationism is false.

The color of blood is an example of a biological spandrel. Mother Nature cared a lot about the details of the circulatory system and the many features of blood, including the ratio of what we call red and white blood cells. But the features of these cells that worried Mother Nature did not involve any direct or indirect concern with coloration. Notice, this is not because Mother Nature never cares about color; she sometimes does, as the ostentatious sexually attractive feathers of many birds and the surreptitious camouflages of many animals clearly attest. It is just that she never cared, even for a second, about the color of blood. Red (actually purple) blood is good to have if you are human. If you have green blood you have a problem and should see a doctor. But this is not because red blood is an adaptation. Red blood comes as an inevitable side effect of all the important features of blood that were on Nature's mind as she worked out this complex system designed for oxygenation and for various immune functions. The color of blood is a biological spandrel; it is a by-product of the primary design intentions for blood. As I have said, if your blood is not red, you have a problem. But again, blood's turning out to be red rather than green was not because Mother Nature was trying to help doctors detect rare diseases. It is just that once blood turned out to be red it was rightly taken to be an abnormality to have it any other way.

The sound of a human heartbeat, as I explained in the first chapter, is diagnostic and in that sense useful to humans. However, it is utterly implausible to think that the noise hearts make played any role whatsoever in the evolution of the heart by natural selection.

Examples such as these form part of the evidence for the philosopher of biology Robert Brandon's argument that "not all traits are adaptations." Brandon gives two examples (one involves gene linkage, the other pleiotropic connections) of what he calls "epiphenomenal traits."

> When a not particularly deleterious gene is closely linked on a chromosome to a gene being strongly selected for, it can hitchhike its way to prominence. Pleiotropic connections are similar but more permanent. . . . For example, a gene may code for an enzyme that helps detoxify a poisonous substance common in its environment. It does so by converting the poison to an insol-

uble pigment. Two new traits become common in the population over generational time. One, the ability to handle the toxic
substance, is an adaptation. The other, the resultant color of
the organisms having the first property, is not an adaptation. Its
presence is not explained by what it does but rather by its
pleiotropic connection to an adaptation.

In both the example of the neutral hitchhiking gene—imagine that a
dimple gene free rides on some percentage of chromosomes that code
for taste buds—and the example of the creatures who become darkly
pigmented as a side-effect of selection for the detoxification trait, we
can imagine that neither the hitchhiking gene's effects nor the effects
of the creatures' coloration have any effect on fitness. These traits are
nonadaptations that do no good, nor do they do any harm.

Exaptations, on the other hand, enter the world either as neutral
traits, as nonadaptations that serve no purpose, or as adaptations for
one purpose that are then coopted to serve some other purpose. The
wing buds of insects and the feathers of birds are believed to have
been initially selected for to serve some thermoregulatory function.
Proto-birds, especially ones with larger-than-average wing buds, running from predators and flapping these feathered appendages got
away from these predators better than their less-well-equipped compatriots, and thus wings that eventually gave rise to flight emerged.
So now we have birds that can stay warm *and* that can fly. [2]

Exaptation, the concept of a trait that is not originally designed
for a certain end—for example, flight—but gets pulled out to perform that function, provides a way around the dangerous idea of
"preadaptationism"—the idea that, for example in the case of
winged-flight, Mother Nature produces 5 percent of a wing many
centuries before wings emerge because she sees in advance that
wings can be a very good thing to have. Exaptations can provide grist
for the mill of natural selection without endowing Mother Nature
with prescience, with powers of precognition. Although every adaptation, in virtue of having a natural history, has its origins in an exaptation, the concept is useful precisely because it helps mark the
process—the process of exaptation—by which natural selection
works to modify the raw materials at its disposal.

Exaptations differ from spandrels in that although both can arise
as nonadaptations (the first feather we assume neither enhanced
nor detracted from the fitness of proto-birds), exaptations are coopt-

ed by natural selection to serve the function they eventually serve. An exaptation becomes an adaptation relative to that new function. Spandrels are not coopted by natural selection for any fitness enhancing function (if they are, then the seeming spandrel is in fact an exaptation). So long as a spandrel does not come to detract from fitness, it can sit there forever as a side effect or free rider without acquiring any use whatsoever.

Sometimes spandrels are utilized for biological purposes, but not because they are, as it were, useful to the internal biological economy of organisms that possess the spandrel. Again, both the color of blood and the sound of a beating heart are biological spandrels because they are not adaptations to begin with and they were never coopted by subsequent selection pressures to become adaptations. But the fact that neither the color of blood nor heart sounds are adaptations or exaptations, but rather spandrels, does not detract from the usefulness of deviance from the norm in medical diagnosis. Medical diagnostics is a cultural invention maintained by forces of cultural selection. Our biology obviously allows for medical practices to develop, but there is no interesting sense in which we could credibly call such practices biological adaptations.

On the other hand, wings were exapted from proto-wings by natural selection to subserve flight. Wing buds first arose as random mutations or as side effects of other structural features of nonflying insects and proto-birds. They happened to enhance fitness thanks to their thermoregulatory effects. Soon all the creatures in certain species were sprouting wing buds. Then the next miracle occurred. Some members of the species had larger than average wing buds. Like Orville and Wilbur Wright, they could stay briefly aloft. And this was fitness enhancing. Soon full-fledged wings were abundant, and flying insects and birds were everywhere. The Wright brothers flew a couple of hundred feet. Now, less than one hundred years after they took off, many thousands of aircraft flights take place each day over very long distances. Biological evolution did not work as fast on winged flight as the aeronautical industry did on plane and jet design, but selection operated in both cases—natural selection in the first case, cultural selection in the second.

Relatedly, we can imagine how it could go with the creatures Brandon imagines who got dark color as a side effect of their capacity for detoxification. Suppose that a predator is introduced who sees these creatures less well the darker they are. And suppose that there is some variation in how dark members of the species are. The lighter creatures get eaten and the number of darker ones increase in virtue of being better able to withstand the predation pressures. In this case, the dark color which was originally a nonadaptation comes to serve as an exaptation, a trait that is now, in the new environment, actively worked on by Mother Nature to produce an adaptation—coloration that is a couple of shades darker than the coloration of the ancestral population.

Surely, Consciousness Is an Adaptation

So what about mind, and, in particular, the conscious mind? Is consciousness an adaptation? If we can explain how and why we came to be conscious, and in particular if we can show that consciousness has been selected for because it is fitness enhancing, then we may rest assured that it at least once served a function. Since dreaming is a type of consciousness, its place among the functional traits and capacities of *Homo sapiens* will be made more secure if the case for the functionality of consciousness, more generally, can be made. Or, so it seems.

So how is it for consciousness? Darwin called the eyes "organs of extreme perfection." There is little doubt that visual consciousness is an adaptation. Just as certainly, pain states are adaptive. You place your hand in a fire. The fire is hot. Your hand hurts. The pain causes you to remove your hand from the fire. Pain has certain effects relative to human bodies that figure in explanations of our overall capacity to avoid serious injury. Pain in humans is an adaptation for, among other things, causing us to remove our hands from fire and other sources of injury.

Generalizing from cases like vision and pain, the standard view is that consciousness evolved because it conferred on its bearers an adaptive advantage. Since dreams are a kind of consciousness, we can generalize further and secure for them functional status. Here is the argument:

1. Consciousness is an adaptation.
2. Dreaming is a type of consciousness.
3. Therefore, dreaming is an adaptation.

This sort of argument is common in my experience. But it is a terrible argument.

First, it implicitly assumes that consciousness is a single kind of trait, characteristic, or capacity and that every instance or subspecies of the trait is an adaptation. This is unlikely. Indeed, it is almost certainly false, since there are counterexamples. Schizoid thinking is a kind of consciousness, but it is not adaptive nor is it an adaptation by any reasonable standard. Second, the argument says absolutely nothing about what the function of dream consciousness is. At least in the case of visual consciousness and pain consciousness there is a plausible story waiting in the wings about what good each does. There is no similarly plausible story, so I claim, for dream consciousness.

Considered at the coarsest grain, conscious states share the property of being experienced. Conscious mental states seem a certain way; nonconscious states don't seem any way at all. Without consciousness there is no subjective, phenomenological point of view. Conscious mental states share the property that "there is something that it is like" to be in such a state.

Beyond the common feature of there being "something that it is like" to have or be in a conscious mental state—beyond the common feature of having phenomenal properties—conscious mental states vary greatly in *how* they seem. There are at least five kinds of consciousness in the sensory modalities. Within a sense modality, experiences differ in how they seem. Experiences of red differ from experiences of green; the taste of black tea differs from that of green tea; the smell of an apple orchard in autumn differs from that of a rose garden in summer; the sound of a piano differs from that of a violin; and so on almost to infinity. Besides the senses, there are emotions, moods, dreams, and conscious thoughts about states of affairs; there are various kinds of neuroses and psychoses. There are somatosensory states such as sexual arousal, hunger, and thirst, and much more besides. All of these are kinds of conscious states. Figure 4.3 provides a partial picture of the heterogeneity of conscious mental states, as conceived from the phenomenological point of view, from the perspective of the ways things seem.

An important task for a complete theory of the conscious mind is to provide a way of mapping the phenomenology onto neuroscience, of mapping types of states that seem certain ways onto types of brain states. We want to know how the varieties of consciousness are realized in the brain. There may be some neural property, say, a certain oscillation frequency that is necessary for a conscious experience to occur.

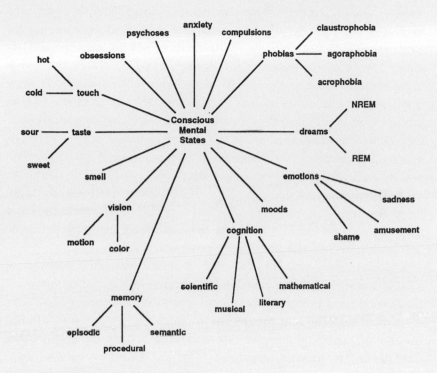

Figure 4.3 Heterogeneity of conscious states.

But even if there is some necessary marker of all conscious mental states, this marker is certainly not going to be sufficient for distinguishing among types of conscious mental states. Thanks to advances in brain imaging techniques we now know that when a visual perception, a visual image, or a visual hallucination occurs, it is the visual cortex that is active. Likewise, when the experience is auditory, or tactile, or involves language, different areas of the brain light up. Possibly the lit-up areas all share some single feature in common, for example, a distinctive oscillatory pattern. But even if some such marker of the occurrence of conscious mental states were discovered, and even if it could be used to distinguish reliably conscious states from nonconscious ones, it would not help us distinguish among different kinds of conscious mental states. The reason is simple. The marker would be identical across all conscious states and thus could not by itself signal any differences among them.

Thus, even supposing that some reliable marker for distinguishing conscious from nonconscious states will be discovered, we will still need to know what marks the differences among kinds of conscious mental states. We will still need to ask such questions as, What makes a conscious experience a visual one rather than olfactory one? The answer, an important part of the answer, at least, is that the exact brain areas and the specific input and output pathways that are activated make a conscious mental state a state of a certain sort—in the present case, a visual perception rather than an olfactory experience. Of course, the story is more complicated than the story told by brain images. Brain-imaging techniques pretty much detect only electrical activity, neuron-firing rates, oxygen use, and blood flow. But we also know, thanks to work on neurotransmitters, many of which are yet to be discovered, that neurochemicals are crucial to determining what mental states we are in, which emotions and moods we experience, and whether an experience can be remembered later.

The main problem with the argument is this: Even if consciousness, generally speaking, or waking consciousness, in particular, is an adaptation, it does not follow that all manifestations or types of consciousness—paranoia or dreams, for example—are themselves things Mother Nature aimed to be experienced *because* they were fitness enhancing. In the case of dreams, Mother Nature did, I am sure, *cause* us to dream, but not *because* it was fitness enhancing. Mother Nature caused us to dream because dreaming is what you get as a nonadaptive side effect of putting in place certain adaptations, especially ones involving selection for sleep and sleep-cycling, and ones designed to produce efficient awake minds and bodies.

No one thinks that Mother Nature cared as she built our brains or cares now about the powers realized by the great minds in the history of astronomy, quantum physics, special or general relativity, mathematical logic, string theory, or, for that matter, evolutionary biology. To be sure these monumental theoretical productions of great minds are good, important, and wonderful to have around. But this is a long way from saying that the capacities that produced them are functional in any interesting biological sense. The capacities to generate such theories are neither adaptations in the historical sense of having been selected for originally because of their fitness enhancing properties, nor are they adaptive in the narrow biological sense of serving some function related to biological well-being, the way, say, two working kidneys or two decent eyes are. The reason we can confidently assert that the capacities to do science, higher mathematics, philosophy, and cognitive neuroscience are not adaptations is the same reason that we can say that the capacities to read and write are not adaptations, not selected effects of natural selection, but rather are some kind of evolutionary epiphenomena. The reason is that the brain has not, as best we can tell, changed since *Homo sapiens* became a distinctive species tens of thousands of years ago. But all the afore-mentioned capacities are very recent developments, and Mother Nature does not do several hundred century look-aheads when engaged in design by natural selection. It is as simple as that.

Sleep, Dreams, and Ideal Adaptation Explanations

I return now directly to sleep and dreams. My thesis now put in the terms of the current discussion is that sleep and sleep-cycling in humans have proper evolutionary functions and thus are adapta-tions. But dreams do not have proper evolutionary functions, and thus are not adaptations.

The complaint voiced earlier that sleep and dreams always co-occur might make my argument look impossible. How can one sub-ject things that always co-occur, items that are, quite possibly, simply proper parts of one and the same phenomenon, to different analy-ses? Well, the first point is that although sleep and dreams may always co-occur for us, they did not always co-occur over the phyloge-netic long haul. Many creatures that sleep are not thought even now to be consciously mentating—lizards and fish, for example. Second, there are cases of humans who sleep normally but do not dream, and thus the claim that sleep and dreams invariably co-occur in the human case is false. All normal humans dream and in that sense dreaming is universal. But there is a small and telling number of exceptions.

I can make my argument that sleeping is an adaptation, but dreaming is not, from a slightly different angle than I have attempted so far by using some of the lessons gained in our discussion of adap-tations and nonadaptations. According to Robert Brandon, there are five elements of an ideally complete adaptation explanation:

(1) Evidence that selection has occurred, that is, that some types are better adapted than others in the relevant selective environment (and this has resulted in differential reproduc-tion); (2) an ecological explanation of why some types are bet-ter adapted than others; (3) evidence that the traits in question

are heritable; (4) information about the population structure from both a genetic and a selective point of view, that is, information about patterns of gene flow and patterns of selective environments; and (5) phylogenetic information concerning what has evolved from what, that is, which traits are primitive and which derived.

It should be clear that few, if any, ideal adaptation explanations can be given for any trait. But explanatory ideals are important in matters of evolution precisely because aspiring to them helps reign in flip "just-so" storytelling of the sort that Dr. Pangloss engages in when he explains in Voltaire's *Candide* that the bridge of the nose was designed to hold spectacles (imagine how bad off, not to mention ugly, we would be if our nostrils were mounted right against our faces), or that Rudyard Kipling engages in when he constructs fantasies for children about how the camel got his hump or the leopard got his spots.

I cannot provide an ideal adaptation explanation for sleep (no one can). But I want to give a sense, repeating several things I have said in earlier chapters, that will indicate why it is plausible to think that sleep is an adaptation. There is more than a "just so" story to be told about the fitness-enhancing function(s) of sleep.

In order to provide a story about why sleep was favored by natural selection that aspires to, but does not reach, the status of an ideal adaptation explanation, one first needs some evidence that selection for sleep has occurred. The phylogenetic record just mentioned reveals this much. There are some amphibians, bullfrogs and tree frogs, for example, that rest and thereby conserve energy but do not show typical physiological signs of sleep. However, most creatures do sleep, and as is the case with vision, sleep appears to be a solution to certain design problems nature has faced in different contexts, along different evolutionary pathways. It has recently been suggested that one function of REMing is to keep the eyes healthy by oxygenating them. Thus the lineages leading to birds led to birds that sleep, and the separate lineages leading from certain reptiles to mammals to humans led to mammals that sleep. Sleep conserves energy, allows for refilling various depleted endocrinological and neurochemical tanks, and occurs at times, places, and in a manner in which an animal is at its least vulnerable.

The demand for a plausible ecological explanation of selection for sleep can also be met. Look at the sleep patterns of different animals. Predators sleep longer than prey. When there are exceptions, such as in the case of bats, certain squirrels, and hamsters, all of whom sleep a lot, there are also ecological variables that help explain the exceptions. For example, such animals retire to the safety of caves or deep burrows with escape routes.

Furthermore, there is evidence of heritability with regard to sleep. There are distinctive species-specific modes of sleep and sleep-cycling. Humans, dolphins, birds, giraffes, lions, falcons, chickens, cats, and mice all sleep, but they do so in different species-specific ways. Sleep habits, especially among humans, are subject, of course, to social learning, to the amount of daylight at different latitudes at different times of the year, to job demands, and so on. But the reliability of certain patterns within a species across environments is striking evidence for powerful genetic pressures to sleep and to sleep in a certain species-specific way. Certain congenital sleep disorders, including fatal familial insomnia, also suggest the heritability of sleep-related traits.[3]

I hope this much gives a sense of how the argument for providing an ideal adaptation explanation for sleep would proceed, given that many pieces of the puzzle, even by Brandon's exacting standards, are already in place.

Dreams: Adaptations, Exaptations, or Spandrels?

Enough theory and data are now on the table, I hope, to see why I think sleep is an adaptation but dreaming is a nonadaptation. The hypothesis can be formulated somewhat more precisely given what has been said so far. It is that sleep and the phases of the sleep cycle—NREM and REM sleep—were selected for *and* are maintained by selective pressures. They are adaptations in the biological sense. However, the dreams that occur during NREM sleep and REM sleep are likely epiphenomena in the sense that they are serendipitous accompaniments of what sleep is for. Whereas an ideal adaptation explanation can be sketched for sleep, it is exceedingly hard to imagine even the beginnings of such a sketch for dreams.

Some things that were originally selected for to serve a certain function end up being able—with some engineering modifications—to serve another function. Selection pressures work to modify and eventually to maintain the adaptation because it serves both purposes, or to put it another way, both the original trait and the extended or secondary one serve to increase fitness. As I have said, feathered buds (when they constituted only 5 percent of a wing) were probably selected for thermoregulation, but now selective pressures work to maintain feathered wings because they enable flight as well serving to regulate body temperature. Insect wings are the preferred example here, since it is known for certain that it was aerodynamically impossible for the first wings to serve to get insects aloft. Initial selection was definitely not for flight.

It is standard in evolutionary biology to say of some characteristic that it is a nonadaptation only if it is a concomitant of a trait that was selected for and if in addition no concurrent positive selection or independent modification operate on the trait. So the capacity to fly was a sequela of selection pressures for efficient thermoregulation, but feathered wings that enable flight are an adaptation because despite being a sequela (literally, a follow-up), they were (and are) subject to positive selection and independent modification pressures. On the other hand, the color of blood and bones, the sound of a beating heart, and the human chin are examples of sequelae that are true nonadaptations. They are spandrels, and it is pretty clear, even if they have been put to various uses—chins for sporting goatees, and the color of blood and bones and the sound of the heart for medical diagnoses—that these uses have not called any selection pressures into play.

My diagnosis for why it is so hard to imagine a plausible sketch of an ideal adaptation explanation for dreams is that there simply are no plausible theories about how it is that dreaming is, or even might be, fitness enhancing. Recall, an ideal evolutionary explanation is launched when we explain (1) how the trait in question is or at least was fitness enhancing, and (2) how it is that the particular ecological niche that creatures with the trait occupy, or occupied when the trait evolved, makes sense of why it is that the trait is, or was, fitness enhancing. We launch a plausible proof of sleep's being an adaptation when we satisfy these two demands. The problem is that there simply are no plausible accounts or theories of dreams that satisfy the first two requirements for an ideal adaptation explanation. On the other hand, there are plausible reasons for thinking that dreaming is a concomitant of sleeping that has not undergone positive selection or independent modification. We can, as it were, start to sketch an ideal nonadaptation explanation for dreams, whereas we cannot start to sketch an ideal adaptation explanation. I have stressed that the biological notion of an adaptation and of a non-adaptation need to be marked off from such notions as adaptive, functional, dysfunctional, and neutral. As I have just been emphasizing again, the biological notion of an adaptation is tied to selection pressures that contribute to reproductive success in a particular environment or set of environments.

My thesis is this: Sleep and sleep-cycling is an adaptation for the multitude of reasons given—it restores, conserves, and builds; and we can specify some of the specific things it does and the mechanisms these are done by. But there is good reason to be positively dubious about the adaptive significance of the phenomenal experiences that supervene on REM and NREM sleep. Dreaming, broadly construed, is pleiotropic, an automatic sequela, a spandrel. It is doubtful that dream consciousness once in play as a sequela of causal processes originating in the brain stem that tickle the visual areas producing REMing was subjected to positive selection pressures and modification. That is, it is doubtful that dreaming is an exaptation.

So dreaming is not an adaptation, and it is not an exaptation. What then is it? There is only one possibility. Dreaming is a spandrel. Dreams are the spandrels of sleep.

Perhaps I can put the point in a kinder, gentler way. The brainstem is designed to activate the visual system to finish building it during the first year of life. All the evidence from animals like humans that REM a disproportionately large amount of time as newborns points to some sort of developmental function: dedication to the project of completing the visual system. However, once the system is built, the continuation of the activation of the visual system serves no obvious further developmental function. Furthermore, whereas the PGO waves of REM sleep are implicated in the processes of stockpiling neurochemicals for the next day's work, for making what is learned more stable so that it can be remembered, and possibly for trash disposal, there is no reason to believe that these jobs require mentation of any sort.[4]

Two Neurobiological Hypotheses About the Function of Dreams

I can make this point in the most provocative and thus, I hope, memorable way by contrasting my view with those of Allan Hobson and Francis Crick and Graeme Michison. We all agree that a brain-based explanation of sleep and dreams is necessary, and that such a theory will have little in common with traditional depth psychological views. The difference is this: Hobson and Crick and Michison remain in different ways functionalists about dreams. All, I think, believe that dreaming is an adaptation (which leaves open the possibility that dreaming was once an exaptation), whereas I think dreams are spandrels. In particular, Hobson and Crick and Michison think that dreams serve important cognitive functions such as firmly fixing, filing, and consolidating memories worth keeping or forgetting things worth forgetting. My view is that these cognitive functions are served by sleeping, but not by dreaming. Let me explain why this is a difference that makes a difference.

Hobson indicates in his three books on sleep and dreams that he is attracted to views that posit memory-stabilization as one function of REM dreams. One such theory that we have discussed is that high levels of the neurotransmitter acetylcholine fix memories during REM sleep. Even if this is true, there is no phenomenological evidence that as electrical patterns are transformed into protein structures the associated mentation involves the activation of the thoughts worth remembering. People remember nonsense syllables better after sleep than if tested right after learning but before sleep. But to the best of my knowledge, people never report dreaming about nonsense syllables. Nor do students of mathematics work through the proofs of the previous day in dreams. It may well be that the proof of the Pythagorean theorem would go in one ear and out the other if we didn't sleep in between. But I would place large bets that one will have trouble getting any phenomenological reports of sophomore geometry students' dreaming through the steps of the theorem in REM sleep (although they may well worry about the imminent exam during NREM sleep). The point is that PGO waves are causally implicated in the neurochemical stockpiling of amines (serotonin, norepinephrine, etc.) and in setting acetylcholine to the task of bringing stability to what has been learned. But there is no reason, so far as I can see, to think that the content of the mentation initiated by the PGO waves is causally relevant to these processes. The right circuits need to be worked on, but no mentation about the information that those circuits contain is needed; and typically such mentation does not occur. The visual, auditory, propositional, and sensory-motor mentation that occurs is mostly noise—at least as measured against what one is trying to learn and remember. One might be drawn to a different conclusion if the mentation were about exactly those things one needs to stabilize for memory storage, but phenomenologically that seems not to be the case.[5] It can't be the actual thoughts that occur during the bizarre mentation associated with REM sleep that the system is trying to stabilize, remember, or store—most of that is weird. Of course, some is not weird, but even the nonweird stuff isn't the sort of stuff you should be thinking about if you are a student who wants to pass tomorrow's test.[6]

The problem with Hobson's functional theory about dreams arises from the fact that the content of dreams and the content of memories worth securing don't seem to match. Hobson toys with epiphenomenalism about dreams towards the end of his 1994 book, *The Chemistry of Conscious States,* but overall he seems wedded to the memory-fixation, or to the related, but somewhat different view that dreams involve some sort of cognitive rehearsal or imaginary practice of things we need to rehearse or practice. Again, I don't think the phenomenology of dreams—most of the dream narrative data I depend on was gathered by Hobson's group—provides much support for this idea, since what is rehearsed or imagined in dreams isn't very often the sort of thing I need to practice, let alone do, in the light of day.

Hobson offers two different responses to my sort of view. One floated in conversation and correspondence is to suggest that since most of what we dream is not remembered, we may still in fact think or rehearse and thus fix useful thoughts, say, about how a new acquaintance tends to behave—but not remember them upon waking. This is possible. But it seems that there should be more data supporting the idea that such rehearsal occurs in the dream reports of good dream rememberers. But there aren't such data.

The second response involves a more firm admission of the genuine prospect that the epiphenomenalism floated in the 1994 book might after all be the truth. This idea appears in preprints—some now published—of work by Hobson's group that he and his dream team have generously shared with me. Here the suggestion is one that I am happy with, namely, that "it is REM sleep itself, and not the subjective experience of dreaming, which has functional significance for cognition that cannot easily be deduced from dream content."

Supposing Hobson and his colleagues have now seen the light, what prevented them from seeing it clearly and defending it resolutely over the past twenty years? Here I admit to amateur speculation on the cause of one glitch in an otherwise brilliant theory. My suspicion is that Hobson has followed too closely Michel Jouvet's brilliant work, from the early 1960s, on reenactment by cats of instinctual behaviors, for example, apparently stalking a mouse during REM sleep. Jouvet got cats to do this by preventing motor paralysis associated with REM by lesioning the pontine brainstem. There are three problems with extrapolating to the human case from these results. First, it is unclear why a cat should need to practice in dreams behavior that is hard wired or instinctual. Second, and relatedly, even if some practice is required for the instinct to emerge (and there may be, since orphaned animals often don't show the same natural savvy they would show if raised by their own kind), it is not clear that any images or thoughts need to be imputed to animals imitating or practicing instinctual behaviors. Third, as I have insisted, according to Hobson's own data, as well as data from other sleep researchers, humans don't report much rehearsal of what it is they are trying to learn or might reasonably be expected to want to practice.

My skepticism on this point also affects Francis Crick and Graeme Michison's idea that dreaming is important for memory because it is important for trash disposal. Recall that Crick and Michison's hypothesis is that a parallel distributed processing system such as the brain will be in danger of overload, of making too many associations, of not being able to keep sorted out the salient facts from the multitude of irrelevancies. The alleged danger follows pretty straightforwardly from working out some of the mathematics of distributed and superimposed representations. The wide distribution across synapses of memories and the fact that certain synapses will be implicated in remembering several different facts can, if everything takes firm hold in memory, lead to hyperassociation, a sort of Proustian state where everything is reminiscent of everything else. This would not be a good state of mind to find oneself in on a permanent basis. Fortunately, the danger can be prevented if the system has capacities of reverse learning, of eliminating or at least weakening the strength of things not worth remembering and of minimizing, as necessary, synaptic overload. And indeed, according to the hypothesis being proposed, the system has what it takes—a brain-maintanence system that cleans out what is not worth knowing or remembering, and that prunes and reconfigures overloaded circuits.

In both their 1983 and 1995 renditions of the view, Crick and Michison claim indirect support for their hypothesis by pointing to the muddled phenomenology of dreams. Reverse learning occurs when proto-memories that are not worthy of entering the hallowed halls of true memory are weakened or washed out. This is revealed by the odd things we think during REM dreams. Surely, these are exactly the sort of strange facts and associations that one should not want to remember.

There are three problems with this view, at least insofar as the phenomenology of dreams is brought in as support. First, on most views, the fact that some thought makes an appearance in consciousness, especially a second appearance, is widely believed to aid in remembering that thought. So the idea that in dreams we are conjuring up the stable of thoughts worth forgetting is paradoxical to say the least, since conjuring up thoughts—re-experiencing them—is widely believed to contribute to remembering them and to making it harder to forget them. Second, and relatedly, the functional view of Hobson, and Jouvet before him, is based at least in part on the claim that we dream about things worth remembering. Crick and Michison's claim, on the other hand, is that we dream about things that are worth forgetting. The two positions on the function of the phenomenological content of dreams are at odds.[7] On one view, our dreams have the content they have in virtue of that content being of the sort worth remembering. On the other view, our dreams have the content they have in virtue of that content being the sort of thing worth forgetting. Third, the phenomenological data fail to support the claim that the content of dreams involves conjuring up things worth forgetting just as much as they fail to support the view that we dream about things worth remembering. It is hard to see how many of the nonsensical thoughts I have in dreams are things that I need actively work to forget since I was never really entertaining them in the first place. I have dreamed about having fun at amusement parks on the rings of Saturn. I didn't in fact do so, and I have never entertained, by the light of day, that I have visited Saturn. It is not something I needed to remember in order to forget. But, suppose my thoughts about Saturn were side effects of my mind-brain working to forget what I had for breakfast each day of the week before the dream. A good brain with finite storage capacities should do this sort of thing. An efficient mind-brain should not want to keep a reliable log of all one's breakfasts. But again, on this scenario, the scenario in which the Saturn dream is a consequence of the system working to dump the breakfast files, it seems that the phenomenology, the content of the dream—it is about Saturn—is utterly irrelevant to the process of forgetting that I had Special K for breakfast last Thursday. To forget about the Special K, the brain just needs to do whatever it needs to do to erase (or neglect to secure) memories of experiences that are not worth retaining. But if that is right, then the bizarre phenomenology of dreams is neither relevant to what the mind-brain is trying to forget, nor evidence one way or the other for the trash-disposal hypothesis.

I need to emphasize, so as not to be misunderstood, that I think that the most promising hypotheses about the cognitive functions of sleep, especially but not exclusively REM sleep, involve memory consolidation functions, save and trash. My point is simply that there is no evidence that what we dream about is relevant to what the mind-brain should be trying to remember, or trying to forget, for efficient cognitive functioning by daylight.

My recommendation for Hobson and Crick and Michison is to abandon altogether their different functional views of REM dreaming. REM sleep is functional. REM dreaming is not. Neither, for that matter, is NREM dreaming. But they are not dysfunctional either.

Raining on the Parade

Dreams are a special but by no means unique case in which the epiphenomenalist suspicion has a basis. Dreaming is to be contrasted with cases in which phenomenal awareness was almost certainly selected for. Take normal vision, for example. It is, I am convinced, a biological adaptation. Blindsighted persons who have damage to area V1 in the visual cortex get visual information but report no phenomenal awareness of what is in the blindfield. However, they perform well above chance if asked to guess what is there, or reach for it, which is why we say they are getting some information. The evidence suggests that the damage to V1, which is essentially implicated in phenomenal visual awareness, explains both why blindsighters claim to see nothing and why the performance is degraded. And this suggests that the phenomenal side of vision is to be given an adaptationist account along with, and as part of, an adaptationist account of visual processing generally. This is not so with dreaming.

The phenomenal aspects associated with sleeping are nonadaptations in the biological sense. The question remains, does dreaming serve a function? If it does, it is a derivative psychological function

constructed by way of mechanisms of cultural imagination and utilization of the fact that despite not serving a direct biological or psychological function, the content of dreams are not totally meaningless. Thus dreams can be used to shed light on mental life, on
well-being, and on identity. What I mean by the last remark is that the
cortex's job is to make sense out of experience, and it doesn't turn off
during sleep. The logically perseverative thoughts that occur during
NREM sleep are easy for the cortex to handle since they involve real,
but possibly "unrealistic" ideation about hopes, worries, and so on.
Indeed, from both a phenomenological and neuroscientific perspective, awake mentation and NREM sleep mentation differ more
in degree than in kind.

REM mentation is a different story. It differs in kind. Phenomenologically and brainwise it is a radically different state, closer to psychosis than to any other mental state types.[8] Still, the cortex takes
what it gets during REM sleep and tries to fit it into the narrative,
scriptlike structures it has in place about how one's life goes and how
situations—for example, restaurant scenes, visits to amusement
parks, to the beach, and so on—go.

Suppose one dreams, especially that one dreams persistently
about one's current partner and one's old boyfriend. Mentation
about one's current true love and one's old true love might be informative about what's on your mind, or it might be uninformative, just
the best story line the cortex can bring to the materials offered up.
But this could be true and such a dream could still be a good place to
start from in conversation with a psychiatrist or friend if your love life
is going badly, or if you are suffering from any psychosocial malady.
Other dreams might be memorable but pretty much unrevealing
about oneself or have nothing like the meaning we are inclined to
assign but nonetheless be a good conversation starter for someone
trying to figure out the shape of his life. Obviously, from what I have
said, the cortex is expressing what's on your mind, how you see
things. Your dreams are expressions of the way you uniquely cast
noise that someone else would cast differently. This view leaves plen-
ty of room for dream interpretation. During REM sleep, the cortex
must, insofar as it can, work up a story that builds largely on the contents activated by the PGO waves. Often these contents are not the
building blocks a teller of literal tales would start with. These contents will enter into the dream narrative, but it will be up to the cortex to determine where the image of, for example, the Museum of

Modern Art can be fit, and this will be determined and will be interpretable (if it is interpretable) by seeing how this image is situated within the larger narrative structure of which it is a part.

So things remain the same; dreams make a difference to your life. They may get you thinking in a certain way upon waking. You may find yourself in a hard-to-shrug-off mood despite learning that the imagined losses of loved ones causing that mood were dreamed and didn't really happen. You may be inspired to write a poem or a mystical text, or you may work at the project of interpretation. This is not silly. What you think while awake or while asleep is identity expressive. The project of self-knowledge is important enough to us that we have learned to use the serendipitous mentation produced by a cortex working with the noise the system produces to further the project of self-knowledge and identity location. This is resourceful of us. [9]

Spandrels can, but need not, serve functions even though they are sequelae of the design the architect is focused on putting in place. Being a spandrel doesn't make something nonfunctional. Spandrels are beautiful accompaniments of dome and arch designs. They are probably nice enough to look at as a matter of structural geometry if left plain, but painting them and putting mosaics on them makes the world more beautiful. So it is with dreams. They are mental spandrels, but we can work them into all sorts of useful, creative, and fun things we have learned to do in our lives. If we choose to do so, if we choose to work and play with dreams, it is due to human inventiveness and ingenuity, and it is testimony to our creative capacities to make something out of things which are, from a purely biological point of view, epiphenomenal, that are nonadaptations.

This all needs more explaining. I feel as if I may have rained on your parade, that I may have popped your favorite balloon. If I have done this, I apologize. I now want to inflate a new balloon, one I hope you will like even more that your old one. Trust me, the old balloon has been on the verge of popping for a long time.

So how is it that dreams can be spandrels, nonadaptations, and epiphenomena—matters of such insignificance from an evolutionary point of view—and, at the same time, self-expressive, possibly identity-constituting, sources of self-knowledge, things of great and central importance to a good life, to living well? Explaining this is the job of the next chapter.

Notes

1. Much depends on the eye of the beholder. If a car's primary function to a buyer is transportation, then appealing hubcaps are not part of the primary function. If a car's primary function from the buyer's perspective is to be a "transportation device with sex appeal," then the hubcaps contribute to and are partly constitutive of the primary function of a car. Sales, rather than transportation, are of course the primary function of the cars on the lot from the dealer's point of view.

2. Kingsolver and Koehl tested insect fossil models, comparing aerodynamic and thermoregulatory hypotheses offered by other scientists, and discovered that the thermoregulatory hypotheses was much more plausible than the aerodynamical hypotheses for wing buds, and that, furthermore, for any size insect there is a point of wing enlargement at which no additional thermoregulatory advantage accrues whereas aerodynamical advantages do.

3. Patients with fatal inherited insomnia have a strong genetic tendency to suffer severe degeneration to the anterior thalamus, which is well known to be involved in sleep regulation and in the origination of sleep spindles during theta sleep, the first stage, one might say, at which one is really getting some rest.

4. One big puzzle has to do with people who don't REM but don't seem to suffer learning, attention, or memory problems. REM suppression helps many depressed patients, and Peretz Lavie reports a patient, Y. H., who has a lesion in the pontine brainstem and never REMs, apparently without ill effect. Mark Solms has collected data from 112 patients with global cessation of dreaming and finds that brainstem lesions are relatively rare in this population, while frontal and medial occipital lesions are far more common. But there is no one place that is always knocked out in such patients. Furthermore, Solms insists that many of these patients who do not dream still REM. Solms is the only sleep-dream researcher I have read who insists as strongly as I do that although REM sleep and dreaming almost invariably co-occur, they are different phenomena. Although all of the 112 patients suffering from global cessation of dreaming have neurological problems, many of them remain cognitively adept with good memories, and so on, despite not dreaming. More research is needed on such patients to really get at the behavioral and psychological effects of dreamless sleep. The main feature Solms notices, and I don't know what to make of it, is that these patients don't sleep very well. This leads him to suggest that Freud was right that the function of dreams is to protect sleep. But he shares none of Freud's premises for this conclusion and in fact has no evidence for it other than the bare-boned fact that these neurologically messed up patients who don't dream don't sleep as well as the average person with a healthy brain.

5. Of course the so-called day's residue makes occasional appearances in dreams. It would be surprising if it didn't. It's on your mind. The incorporation of external stimuli is also easily explained—the system is designed to be relatively insensitive to outside noise, but it would be a pathetic survival design if it was completely oblivious to outside noise. So dripping faucets, cars passing on the street outside, are being noticed but in a degraded way. They won't wake you, but a growling predator at your campsite will.

6. According to important work by Wilson and McNaughton, rats that have learned certain spatial tasks have the relevant neural circuits worked on during sleep. Why the rat would need to be thinking the "right" spatial thoughts in addition to having the "right" circuits worked on is utterly obscure—especially given that the content of dream reports of humans are not normally about what they need to remember and indeed typically do remember after a good night's sleep—a tempting inference, but totally unwarranted as best I can tell.

7. One could claim that both functions—remembering and dismantling memories—are accomplished by different types of dreams. I look forward to hearing someone work out the details of such a view. In the meantime, I'll remain skeptical.

8. Things are a bit more complicated than this simple way of putting things suggests. Neurotransmitter levels in NREM are more like they are while awake than they are in REM, whereas REM waves are very close to awake waves and both are dissimilar from NREM waves.

9. Inventing a new function for a biological characteristic might or might not change the characteristic. Using the sound of heartbeats has not, I assume, changed the nature of heart-beating. The case may be somewhat different with dreams. Using dreams for gaining self-knowledge, for creative projects, and the like, may have affected the content of dreams as well as the abilities of individuals to remember or even to control dream plot and content. The literature on lucid dreams (dreams that involve awareness that one is dreaming) contain some evidence that individuals can learn to control dream plot and content. It wouldn't be as if natural selection was working on dreams or dreamers, but rather that certain social practices were discovered that lead via some sort of feedback to micro-adjustments in the brains of certain dreamers that enhance real-time awareness and control of dreams. One would predict that lucid dreamers have more frontal cortical activity during dreams than nonlucid dreamers, and that there are some changes in the neurochemicals that subserve memory in people with good dream recall and those with poor recall. Both hypotheses are testable, although I don't know that they have been tested yet.

5

Self-Expression in Dreams

Every dream reveals itself as a psychical structure which has a meaning and which can be inserted at an assignable point in the mental activities of waking life.

—*Sigmund Freud*, The Interpretation of Dreams, *1899/1900*

On the rare occasions when our dreams succeed and achieve perfection—most dreams are bungled—they are symbolic chains of scene and images in place of a narrative poetic language; they circumscribe our experiences or expectations or situations with such poetic boldness and decisiveness that in the morning we are always amazed when we remember our dreams.

—*Friedrich Nietzsche*, Mixed Opinions and Maxims, *1879*

The Twist

Freud was wrong about the meaningfulness of every dream. Not all dreams are meaningful. Many, possibly most, aren't. Nietzsche was wrong, too. There is no poetically bold or talented homunculus inside you trying to get out the right poem while you sleep—sonnet, haiku, even free verse. But Nietzsche was right to notice that even if you assume an inner poet, most dreams are bungled. The inner poet is a bad poet or it is not alert.

Forget the views that all dreams are meaningful or the work of a bad poet inside you. Here is a better view: Dreams are produced by activity originating in the brainstem that awakens stored or semi-stored thoughts and memories that are then put into some sort of narrative structure by higher brain sectors that are designed to make sense of experience by light of day, but continue to work, less efficiently, when the lights go out.

Now comes the pivotal claim, the twist in my argument. Even though dreaming is a type of consciousness that is not an adaptation nor even especially adaptive, some dreams, possible many, are self-expressive.

So far I've argued that dreaming is not an adaptation with a primary biological function, nor is dreaming an exaptation with a secondary biological function. Dreams are mental spandrels, side effects of adaptations and exaptations, that serve no fitness-enhancing function whatsoever. It is this thesis that makes my view more deflationary than either Allan Hobson's or Francis Crick and Graeme Michison's views, which assign a fitness-enhancing function to dreaming. I deny that dreams have such a fitness-enhancing function. Sleeping does, but that is a different matter. It is this deflationary thesis that made me feel as if I was popping, or gradually letting the air out of, your balloon—that I was raining on your parade.

I don't in fact consider what I've said bad news. But I know from experience that many react to the suggestion that dreaming is not fitness enhancing as if I have just told them they have one month to live. This is a crazy reaction. Many of the best things in life—literature, musical composition and performance, sports, science, mathematics, philosophy, law, libraries, government, and education—are not adaptations. Does this make you sad? No? Good, nor should it. Showing that some capacity, practice, or institution is not explicable in terms of natural selection deflates the pretension—if anyone has it—that evolutionary biology can explain just about anything. But claiming that dreaming, or any other phenomenon, is not an adaptation does not have any implications for the existence or the importance of dreaming, or the other phenomena.

Most people think that arguing that dreams are the spandrels of sleep pretty much implies that dreams are garbage. This is a mistake. Spandrels are side effects of dome and arch designs or of arches lined up in a row. Are they garbage? Of course not. And so it is with dreams. Dreams are mental spandrels. But they are just like architectural spandrels in being interesting, often eye-catching, and worth embellishing (even by free association) effects of the primary design intentions of the relevant architect—nature or persons.

Have I given you some new balloons? Have I stopped raining on your parade? You are not sure? Fair enough. I need to say more. But trust me: I come to celebrate dreaming, to convince you that your dreams, despite serving no biological function, matter to your life, to who you are. Let me spell out the argument. But first we will need to spend some time talking about what a person or a self is before we can say whether and how it is that dreams might contribute to identity and be self-expressive.

Personal Terminology

It will be useful to set out some terminology that I'll be using in discussing the question of self-expression. The following concepts are distinct but mutually helpful in addressing the issues of whether dreams are meaningful, whether they can contribute to who you are, and whether they are worth attending to or analyzing.

- *Personal identity* refers to what it is, if anything, that makes an individual the same person over time, what makes an individual the unique person she is. What, if anything, makes me the same person over time?
- *Identity-constituting* or *identity constitution* are terms refering to whatever goes into making a person who or what she is. How and why do my friendships matter more to who I am than my breakfasts?
- *Self-expression* or *self-expressive* refer to bodily behavior or mental acts (including speech) that *reveal* or *release* information about one's identity, about who one is. When I choose what to speak about and thereby reveal what interests me, reveal what I care about, what about myself, or what aspect of my self, am I expressing?
- *Self-knowing, self-knowledge,* or *soul-searching* refer to the activities or the state of coming to possess justified true beliefs about one's nature, about who one is, about what has made one who one is, and about how one expresses or reveals who one is. Who am I? What is the best story about who I am?

What a Person Is

In order to understand the nature, value, and meaning of dreams, and in particular to understand what, if anything, dreams contribute to personal identity, we will need to have some feel for what it means to be a person, some sense of what a person is.

There is a philosophical consensus about what are the wrong answers to the question of what makes an individual person who she is. One wrong answer posits an immutable "I," a transcendental ego, a soul that stands behind or inside each individual and makes that individual the same person over time. Another wrong answer grounds identity in the continuity of a living body. On the first view, I am identical with my immutable soul; on the second view, I am wherever my embodiment takes me.

The mistake of the first view is twofold: It posits the existence of a mysterious, nonnatural entity, a soul or transcendental ego, and it assumes incorrectly that personal identity involves or requires that identity be, and be grounded in, something unchanging. But our criteria of personal sameness are grounded in something much weaker than strict identity and immutability. Some strong degree of continuity and connectedness will do.

This is easy to see. It was Paul (then Saul), the person Paul, who underwent a conversion experience on the road to Damascus that resulted in his becoming St. Paul, one of Christ's apostles and a grandly successful missionary for Christianity. Likewise, St. Augustine's transformation from the ultimate party animal to the devout theologian, intellectual, and Bishop of Hippo involved one and the same person, Augustine. We want rightly in both cases to say that the person changed. They did not change so much that we have an altogether new person on our hands. But they changed enough that they are very different later than they were earlier. If this way of thinking is right, then it cannot be something unchanging, such as a soul, that accounts for personhood. Saying that Paul or Augustine were the same persons before and after their conversion experiences involves thinking that there was some strong degree of continuity and memory connectedness between each individual's self, pre-transformation and post-transformation.

Whereas the first mistaken view—that an immutable soul makes us who we are—is too strong, the second view is too weak because it underestimates the prospect that our bodies can change radically, yet we can still remain the same. Witness Christopher Reeve, aka Superman. It is too weak also because a continuous living body in deep coma may be John's, but John may no longer be "home." Emily may be physically continuous with Emily, but becoming schizophrenic in her early twenties has made Emily an entirely different person than she used to be. Similarly, David's Granny in the nursing home with late stage Alzheimer's is physically continuous with a certain baby girl born in 1915 who later became mother to David's mother and was his attentive, fun-loving grandmother when he was boy, a young man, and into his own early middle age. But she is no longer the same person, she is no longer David's Granny in some significant sense, despite being physically continuous with that baby girl born in 1915.

The ills of both the soul-based view and the bodily-continuity view can be cured with the same prescription. It is neither a soul nor a merely continuous living body that makes for identity. Personal identity requires a properly functioning mind-brain in a continuous living body. A well-functioning mind can do the job of maintaining the sort of continuity and connectedness, the memory connections, the sense of personal sameness, and so on, required for being a person. A degraded mind-brain, one destroyed by Alzheimer's or alcoholism or trauma can, at a certain point, lose the capacity to house a person, to sustain a self. This much—living a life with a properly functioning mind—is a necessary condition for having an identity, for being a person. But surely not everything we do, not every memory we have, is equally important for making us who we are. Nor does every fact about us go into the narratives we use to understand ourselves and describe ourselves to others.

Identity Constitution

Everyone thinks that what one experiences and does during the day matters to who one is, although, of course, not every experience or action matters equally. Gustatory experiences over breakfast, for example, normally matter less to who one is than do sexual experiences before or after breakfast. What about experiences that occur while one is asleep? Do dreams contribute to one's identity? Do they express who one is? If so, doesn't it follow that there is something to be gained from trying to remember and make sense of one's dreams? If not, why not?

If thought while asleep is discounted when it comes to determining who one is, how is the discount rate determined? It would be good to know the argument behind whatever discount rate applies to dreams. It might be that dream experiences count less than waking ones because they are poorly remembered, and identity is tied to memory. Or, it might be that we have reason to think that the signal-to-noise ratio is exceedingly high on the noise side when we are dreaming. Or, it might be that common sense reveals that the really important identity-constituting events, such as school, college, marriage, raising children, one's career, take place during wakefulness, not during sleep.

Indeed, there is almost certainly something to each of these rationales for applying a discount rate to dreams. Still, it is important to remember that many waking experiences—such as what one had for lunch last Thursday—matter not one bit to who one is, and also that some waking hours are wasted—for example, aimlessly channel surfing for a couple of hours—and for that reason also matter little to one's identity.

Harry Frankfurt, a philosopher at Princeton, has provided a compelling argument according to which the importance of an experience or event is tied subjectively to how much the individual involved cares about the experience or event. Frankfurt, however, rightly shies away from trying to provide a calculus for determining the relative importance of important events. I too doubt that we could come up with a satisfactory measure of the value or, what is different, the contribution to identity of different experiences. But if we try to construct an informal metric, consensus about two things will emerge. First, people will differ in what they consider valuable or wasted experiences. Second, despite the fact that sleep and dreams will appear repeatedly on lists of less, rather than more, valuable time and experiences when it comes to identity-constitution, this establishes nothing about the actual causal contribution of experiences one has while asleep to who one is, to one's identity.

The point is this. Most everyone thinks that experiences significantly determine who we are. But we don't think that all experiences matter equally to identity. We think that time I spend aimlessly surfing among football games matters less to who I am now, as well as to my future self, than would spending the same amount of time doing something more important, such as comforting a friend who has suffered a great loss or attending the performance of a great play.

Both the ideas that not all experiences contribute equally to who we are and that not all experiences are equally valuable seem obvious. But we need to beware the slide from thinking that because one thing is more valuable than another, it has greater influence on identity. Surely, however, that I choose to spend those two hours on Sunday afternoon in front of the TV is self-expressive. Why do we think that a wasteful choice I make, or a wasted experience I have, affects less powerfully who I am than a less wasteful one, given that we don't think it is necessarily any less self-expressive?

We assume that it is reasonable to apply a discount rate to wasted experiences when assessing the relative importance of different kinds of experiences to the process of identity formation and constitution. I even think there is something to the intuitions behind this practice.

But I don't see that anyone has provided a well-articulated rationale for hugely discounting some experiences and not others. The fact that we do so falls in the domain of taken-for-granted practices, rather than in the domain of practices that have a mother lode of evidence and argument behind them.

The reason this issue matters in the present case has to do with the fact that it is commonplace to apply a steep discount rate to dream experiences. Two quick reasons for so doing might be that dreams are poorly remembered and largely meaningless. The former is true, the latter less obviously true. But let us grant both for the time being. There is still a big problem: We know from good experimental work on implicit learning and subliminal perception, that relatively meaningless events an individual cannot consciously remember having occurred are in fact often remembered and affect subsequent performance. For example, there are words such as "bank," that without being placed in context are ambiguous (the shore of a river or the place where you go to get money). If we flash the word "dollar" so quickly that a subject has no idea what, if anything, she saw, she will nonetheless show priming for interpreting the word "bank" as money bank over river bank.

The upshot is that whether dreams are mostly noise or not, the issue of their causal impact on one's identity remains very much a live issue. But at present we lack any good theory about what, if any, causal contribution dreams make to one's character, one's personality, or one's identity, and if they do not make any significant contribution, no one has explained why they don't. In fact, the issue is rarely addressed among dream researchers. A complete theory of the nature and function of dreams will need to speak to this issue.

Self-Representations

One might doubt that dreams are identity constitutive but still think they are self-expressive. Consider this analogy with sports rooting. I express my desire for the Duke basketball team to win by cheering for them whenever they play. But my expressing my desire that the Duke basketball team reign victorious is not, in any deep sense, part of who I am. It is for some of my friends and colleagues, but not for me. If I worked at the University of North Carolina, I'd root for the Tar Heels and not the Blue Devils. My love for my children, to draw the contrastive space, is identity constitutive. There is virtually no imaginable scenario under which I'd shift my love, affection, loyalty, and income from Ben and Kate.

While awake I express some preferences and desires that are not in any deep sense identity constitutive. Dreams seem an even more likely arena than wakefulness for frivolous self-expression. And thus it is perfectly plausible that I might dream about flying to the moon without that desire's being a strong, central, or standing desire of mine—perhaps without its being a desire I possess at all, just mere noise.

That said, while awake we represent ourselves to answer certain questions of identity. Given that I am a person, what kind of person am I? Getting at identity in this sense requires more than being a good detector of the fact that one is the locus of a certain kind of psychological connectedness or is housed in an enduring body. It requires in addition that one have representational resources and cognitive abilities to access and issue reports about the various states, traits, dispositions, and behavioral patterns that make one the person one is.

When we represent ourselves for the sake of gaining self-knowledge, we aim to detect and express truths about the dynamic integrated system of past and present identifications, desires, commitments, aspirations, beliefs, dispositions, temperamental traits, roles, acts, and actional patterns that constitute who we really are. We aim to get at what really makes us tick.

It will be useful to distinguish two different aims of self-representation, which in the end are deeply intertwined. First, there is self-representing for the sake of self-understanding. This is the story we tell to ourselves to understand ourselves for who we are. The ideal here is convergence between self-representation and a true but abridged version of the story of who we are. Second, there is self-representing for public dissemination, whose aim is underwriting successful social interaction. I have been focusing so far on the first function of self-representation. But the two are closely connected. Indeed, the strategic requirements of the sort of self-representing needed for social interaction, together with our tendencies to seek congruence, explain how self-representation intended in the first instance for "one's eyes only," and thus which one might think more likely to be true, could start to conform to a false projected social image of the self, to a deeply fictional and farfetched account of the self.

Self-represented identity, when it gets things right, has one's true identity (or some aspect of it) as its cognitive object. Because representing one's self is an activity internal to a complex but single system, it does not leave things unchanged. The activity of self-representation is partly constitutive of identity, as is the activity of self-expression or of seeking self-knowledge. This is true in two senses. First, even considered as a purely cognitive activity, representing one's self involves the activation of certain mental representations and cognitive structures. Once representing one's self becomes an ongoing activity, it realigns and recasts the representations and structures already in place. Second, the self as represented has motivational bearing and behavioral effects. Often this motivational bearing is congruent with motivational tendencies that the entire system already has. In such cases, the function of placing one's self-conception in the motivational circuits involves certain gains in ongoing conscious control and in the fine-tuning of action. Sometimes, especially in cases of severe self-deception, the self projected for both public and first-person consumption may be strangely and transparently out of kilter with what the agent is like. In such cases, the self as represented is linked with the activity of self-representation but with little else in the person's psychological or behavioral economy. Nonetheless, such misguided self-representation helps constitute, for reasons I have suggested, the misguided person's identity. It affects who she is.

So for whom does my narrative, self-represented self play? The answer should be pretty clear and painless by now. It plays for third parties, and it plays for one's self. The "I" or self for which my narrative self plays is me, the whole information-processing system, from which the narrative self emerges and for which it plays a crucial role. Often I express and grasp snatches of my narrative self and utilize these representations in monitoring and guiding my life. This way of thinking about our reflexive powers makes matters fairly unmysterious. I am a system constituted in part by a certain narrative conception of self. Sometimes I hold that conception in view as I think about things. I, being more than my narrative self, can comprehend it, utilize it, and, in concert with outside forces, adjust it.

The philosopher Daniel Dennett insists that the self that is the center of narrative gravity is a fiction—a useful fiction, but a fiction nonetheless. "Centres of gravity" are "fictional objects . . . [that] have only the properties that the theory that constitutes them endowed them with." What might this mean? If our highest-order self, our dominant model of the self, the model in whose embrace we find identity and meaning, is a fiction, then the epiphenomenalist suspicion seems secure, at least as regards the self. This inference, however, would be a mistake. The idea that the self is in some sense a fiction is compatible with its being real and its playing a functional role in an individual's psychological economy and social life.

The idea that the self is a fiction is in part a way of expressing the fact that it is, for the reasons given, a construction. Mother Nature does not start us off with a full-blooded self. She starts us off caring about homeostasis, and she equips us with the equipment to distinguish "me" from "not me." She does not wire in a personality or an identity. Identity is the joint production of many sources, including one's own developing self and the ever-evolving story one uses to locate who one is to oneself and to others. So the self is a fiction because it is constructed and because the narrative in terms of which we construct and express it is open-ended, subject to further developments. The idea that the self is a fiction also captures a second feature of identity. The self I am is subject to constant revision. This is true in two ways. Not only do new things I do change the ongoing story, the past is also sometimes reconstructed or filled out from the point of view of hindsight. Sometimes these reconstructions are self-serving ("I never really loved her anyway"). Other times they involve rendering various indeterminacies determinate, revising certain hypotheses about what we are like in light of new evidence, and answering questions that arise now, but didn't arise before. For example, one wonders in one's thirties why one cares so deeply about a certain worthless thing, and one reconstructs some story of one's distant past to explain to oneself, and possibly to others, why things are as they are. Most such reconstructions are uncorroborated; some are uncorroboratable.

The self is fictional because it is a construction and because it involves all manner of revisitation to past indeterminacies and reconstruction after the fact. Dennett has us imagine John Updike making the Rabbit trilogy into a quartet not by writing about a still older Rabbit Angstrom (this, in fact, Updike has now done) but by creating the story of a very young Rabbit Angstrom (similar to what George Lucas has just done with *Star Wars*—creating a series of "prequels" to the original). The extant trilogy constrains what Updike can say about the Rabbit who existed before the Rabbit of *Rabbit Run*. But the indeterminacy of Rabbit's former life is vast, and thus there are numerous credible ways in which the story of the earlier years could be told. For

certain parts of our lives we have similar degrees of freedom in how
we tell the story of our selves.

There is a third way in which the picture of the self as a fiction is
appropriate. A piece of fiction starts off from some narrative hook or
set of hooks, and pins a character and his story on those hooks. In
the case of pure fiction, the author has complete freedom in choosing what hooks to pin a character on. But if she wants to sell copies,
she had better make sure that there is something compelling about
her characters and their stories. The same principles apply in the
first-person case. A life is satisfying from the inside and respected
from the outside when its central themes are built around worthy
aims and values. But what aims and values are compelling to one's lis-
teners and worth respecting vary temporally, culturally, and subcul-
turally. Different kinds of narratives work at different times and in
different places. The book-buying and interpersonal markets create
selection pressures favoring certain kinds of narratives and disfavor-
ing others. We see these pressures at work in everyday life when one
presents oneself primarily as a concerned parent in one context and
as a professional philosopher in another. The features of one's identity that are dominant in one form of presentation recede in the
other—as they should. Presenting the wrong self or the wrong
aspects of oneself given a certain context is rightly perceived to be
odd or neurotic. The parent who responds to a teacher's concern
about his child's behavior with "Well, I just got a big promotion at
work!" displays an odd side of himself. If he displays himself this way
consistently his child has better than average chances of being malformed as well.

This brings me to a fourth way in which the self trades in fiction
rather than fact. The self that is the center of narrative gravity is constructed not only out of real-life materials, out of things that really
have happened to me; it is also constructed so that it holds, abides,
and strives to maintain certain ideals not yet realized. The narrative
is in many cases organized around a set of aims, ideals, and aspirations of the self. But since these have not yet been realized, they are
fictions, albeit useful and necessary ones.

To conceive of the self as a fiction seems right for these four
reasons:

- It is an open-ended construction.
- It is filled with vast indeterminate spaces and a host of tentative hypotheses about what I am like that can be filled out and revised post facto.
- It is pinned on culturally relative narrative hooks.
- It expresses ideals of what one wishes to be but is not yet.

But there are two important respects in which the analogy of the self with a piece of fiction can be misleading. First, there is the issue of constraints. The author of a genuine piece of fiction has many more degrees of freedom in creating her characters than we have in spinning the tale of our selves. Despite the indeterminacies operative in construction of the self and despite the fact that different narrative emphases will be reinforced in different communities, there are firmer and more visible epistemic constraints in the case of self-construction than in the case of ordinary fictional construction. There are, after all, the things we have done, what we have been through as embodied beings, and the characteristic dispositions we reveal in social life. Third parties will catch us if we take our stories too far afield. We may also catch ourselves. There are social selection pressures to keep the story that one reveals to one's self and to others in some sort of harmony with the way one is living one's life.

Some people are, of course, massively self-deceived. Self-deception makes sense only if selves are not totally fictive, that is, only if there are some facts constraining what is permitted to go into our self narrative. Self-deceived individuals sequester certain facts from view, possibly unconsciously. In this way they keep these facts from entering the narrative. Some alcoholics know they have a problem but try to keep their drinking a secret from others. They deceive others but not themselves. Other alcoholics display their alcoholism publicly but develop immunities to comprehending social feedback intended to challenge their self-conception that they have no drinking problem. They deceive themselves but not others.

So real selves are fictive. But they are less fictive than fictional selves because they are more answerable to the facts. The second way in which the idea that one's self is a fiction can be misleading is if it leads one to think that the self plays no functional role in mental life. In fact, it plays a pivotal role in giving organization and meaning to a life that will last on average three-quarters of a century. But the question haunts: In what sense can a fiction organize or guide anything? And how can a fiction give real meaning to a life?

The answer is that a person's narrative self is one of the many models contained in his brain. Once acquired and in operation, this model is part of the recurrent brain network causally responsible for the life a person lives and how he thinks and feels. This is true whether a person's model of his self is in touch or out of touch with who he is and what he is really like, and it is true whether a person's self contains worthwhile or worthless aims and ideals. Self-representation, even massively deceived self-representation, is causally efficacious—it causes the person to say wildly false things about himself. This is inexplicable unless the self-deceived thoughts that (sometimes) precede and prompt false self-descriptions are realized in the brain. Even though the self model is not *the* control center of the mind—the mind may well have no single control center—in setting out plans, aspirations, and ideals, it plays an important causal role in a person's overall psychological economy.

The self model changes, evolves, and grows. It displays a certain continuity, and its home is the brain—a brain actively embedded in the world. The fact that my higher-order conception of my self is a model housed in my brain explains the first-person feel I have for my self (but not for your self), and it explains my special concern that my story go as I plan. If things go awry, if my plans don't materialize, if great pain befalls me, it will happen to this subject of experience, to the individual wrapped in this particular narrative. It is not surprising that I care so deeply that the story go the way in which I intend. It's me, myself, and I that we're talking about, after all.

The upshot is that the self can be a construct or model, a "center of narrative gravity," a way of self-representing, without being a fiction in the problematic sense. Biographies and autobiographies are constructs. But if they are good biographies or autobiographies, they are nonfictional or only semifictional.

Who Writes the Dreams?

To be a whole person involves possessing or enacting narrative connectedness over time, connectedness caused in part by the authorial work of the agent. When we dream, fantasize, or dissociate we may to varying degrees lose this connection by deliberately or unconsciously ceasing our authorial work and the weaving of the narrative strands together into a whole. Patients with MPD, multiple personality disorder (now DID, dissociative identity disorder), fail altogether in this project. Their narratives do not systematically permeate each other in the way the narratives of normal individuals with profoundly complex and complicated lives do. The puzzle with dreams is whether authorial work, the sort of work that goes into genuine self-expression, for example, is off-line or whether it continues, as I believe it does, to operate to some degree while we dream. If authorial work is operative sometimes in dreams, then dreams are to some degree self-expressive. And if self-expression is identity constitutive and grist for the mill of self-knowledge and self-transformation, then dreams are to some extent self-expressive, identity constitutive, and sources for self-knowledge and personal growth all at once.

The dreaming associated with, indeed caused by, sleeping, is not an adaptation in the biological sense. The question remains: Does dreaming serve a function? If it does, it is a derivative psychological function constructed via mechanisms of individual and cultural imagination. And indeed dreams do—or at least can—serve such a function. Just as we have learned to use the noise our hearts make in the project of assessing well-being, we have sometimes put dreams to good use. We were able to do this because dreams, despite not serving a direct psychobiological function, are not totally meaningless; thus dreams can be used to shed light on mental life, on well-being, and on identity.

The mind-brain's day job, one of its important jobs at any rate, is to make sense out of experience so that we can negotiate the world successfully. For a highly intelligent animal like *Homo sapiens*, capable of adapting to most earthly environments, a well-designed mind should, and indeed does, have the following features: the capacity to comprehend how the world works in multifarious locales, as well as what oneself is like, what one sensibly wants given available resources, what capacities one has to achieve what one wants, and so on. It is precisely such labor that the mind-brain engages in during the day and that doesn't cease altogether during sleep. Thinking comes in handy while awake; and, apparently, the costs of doing so while asleep are not harmful from the point of view of biological fitness.

The logically perseverative thoughts that occur during NREM sleep often display knowledge of both oneself and the world. Take my sports jacket dream discussed earlier. Sometimes one gets very attached to a particular piece of clothing, in my case, my brown washed-silk sports jacket. One tries to take care of things one is attached to, so it makes sense that one might want his jacket to be hung up rather than thrown in a heap. Clothing thrown down in a heap is prone to getting wrinkled, sat on or stepped on, used by the dog for a nap, and other bad fates. Especially if one knows that one might throw a piece of clothing in a heap—that is, if one knows that one tends to be careless with one's clothing—it is not unreasonable to wonder whether one did in fact hang up the beloved jacket. When awake and struck by such a worry, one goes and looks to see where the jacket is. When dreaming and struck by the worry, one tends to play it over and over in one's head.

Wakeful worrying and wondering and problem-solving are less likely than their NREM kin to get caught in perseverative ruts or involve running around in circles. It is this rutlike quality of NREM dreams that leads us to describe them as illogical, or unrealistic, or unproductive. It is not that the laws of logic or physics are standardly violated in NREM dreams, as they are sometimes in REM dreams. It is just that during NREM dreaming the nature of what we think, wonder, or worry about is often unworthy of attention. Furthermore we don't respond in an efficient manner to whatever it is—silly or not—that concerns us.

The feature I want to key in on and emphasize now is how much knowledge about the self and the world dreams typically display. We express ourselves, what's on our minds, what we know and fear even during the unproductive NREM dreams. We worry about the fate of our clothing, our exam, our job, our car. The same is true with REM mentation. Phenomenologically, REM dreaming lies closer to psychosis or delirium than to any other type of mental state. Still, the cortex takes what it gets during REM sleep and tries to fit it into the narrative, scriptlike structures it has in place about who I am—a philosopher, a parent, a teacher; about how my life goes—for example, about the everyday structure of my job, the important personal gains and losses that have occurred in my life; and about how ordinary situations that we all (in our own ways) engage in go, for example, dining out, visits to amusement parks, trips to the beach, the fate of our sports jackets, and so on.

The brain does not always succeed in producing REM dreams that make sense, yield interesting interpretations, and are worthy of attention—at least it does not always produce dreams that have all three of these features. Other times, the brain produces dreams that make sense, that are interpretable in virtue of having narrative structure and in virtue of being in some sense self-expressive—they are about me as opposed to just thoughts I have—and important. Some recent dreams I've had fit this bill. Here are three:

1. *I was a passenger in a car that skidded on black ice until it was halfway off a bridge, dangling above a river far below. After escaping, we—there were three of us—walked to a nearby baseball field to watch a Little League game.*

2. *Two friends were shopping for cheese at an open air market in France. I saw them doing this and wanted to warn them about the latest reports about the Hong Kong chicken flu. But I was not anywhere near them. A beautiful naked woman climbed on top of me, kissed me, and then explained that she had mistaken me for someone else and left.*

3. *I was with a man and a woman who had huge bulging eyes. Various friends of theirs appeared looking very much like monstrous variations of Humpty-Dumpty and Mr. Potato Head—they moved mostly by rolling around the ground. I became frightened as more and more of these odd-balls joined. One of the creatures draped a colorful sheet over me, and I was required to join in a dance. After the dance, the man with the bulging eyes explained that he and his kin had all been sent over from Italy by relatives who thought them strange.*

I can easily imagine circumstances—one's life is really slipping off a precipice, one is having trouble attracting women, one thinks one is a freak, or belongs with freaks—in which these dreams or segments of these dreams might be given the relevant interpretations. To the best of my knowledge, not all these things are true of me at the moment. Some are.

On the other hand, even if none of these dreams applied to me in some transparent way now, these are themes I am personally familiar with. They have been issues for me at certain times over the last thirty years—just not recently.

Remembering and interpreting these dreams reminds me of my past and rekindles a feeling of my own vulnerability to certain kinds of problems. I feel more in touch with myself and as if I have benefited from having been reminded of issues that I face, have faced, and may face again. It isn't as if I think some part of me—"my personal dream-maker"—thought I needed this jolt of reminiscence and realism. The best explanation is that these are three good stories that my cortex—containing my self model—put together from the serendipitous activation created by PGO waves. My brain was able to construct these particular dreams out of memories and experiences stored in my mind. In so doing, it does me some good without intending to.

In addition to displaying themes, such as living on the edge, that are common currency (the great writer Vladimir Nabokov noted that we pin our life stories on the ways that stories are told in the magazines and books we read, the TV shows and movies we watch) these three plots display knowledge that I possess (not just personal issues I have or have had) about the dangers of driving on ice, about the Hong Kong flu, about Humpty-Dumpty and Mr. Potato Head. And they contain scenes involving things I like—baseball, beautiful women, French open-air markets, as well as things that I don't like or that make me uneasy—being seduced only to be rejected, passing time with freaks, and especially dancing with them. This is to be expected. Remember, for each of us when we dream, it is our individual mind-brain, with a unique history, and possessed of a unique self-conception, where all the action is taking place. The construction of the narrative works, as best it can, with emotions, desires, thoughts, and memories stored in our mind-brain and cast in a way that is affected by our ways of telling stories, by culturally available genres of storytelling, as well as by whatever spin our self-conception contributes to the structure and trajectory of the narrative.

Dream Interpretation

Some, possibly many, dreams are noise; some dreams, at least, are meaningful, interpretable, and self-expressive. Consider this dream I had the week before Christmas 1997.

> December 19th: *A teenage boy read aloud from the newspaper that sick people had only until May 20th to touch or be touched by other people, after which time they would be put into bubbles that isolated them from everyone. I reassured him that this was not true, and certainly did not apply to J.'s case. Then I was on a bus where they were having trouble stuffing a human-filled bubble through the door and down the aisle. The passengers were getting angry about the inconvenience and I was*

*angry at them and embarrassed to somehow be involved with the lady in
the bubble. Next I was in Texas, very nervous about the job talk I was
about to give. Just before the talk was to begin an unknown man told me
that there had been a big mistake. I had already turned down the job for
which I was being interviewed and it had been offered instead to a colleague. I was very upset and embarrassed. I gave the talk, now no longer
a job talk, in a Hawaiian shirt. A dean from Duke was in the audience.
But we were suddenly back in North Carolina, where he angrily
explained to me that my outfit and the fact that I showed the wrong
slides prevented me from receiving the prestigious offer in Texas. I was
very upset and embarrassed. I threatened to quit and join the I.R.A.
unless he fired a colleague with whom I was very angry and whom I
described as a "loose cannon."*

What does this dream mean? I know more about what it means
than I wish to say. But here are some relevant facts. On the evening of
the 18th, several hours before the dream occurred, I heard that an
old friend had a recurrence of her cancer. When I think of this
women I think of her teenage sons, now in their mid-twenties, whom
I often watched play high-school soccer a decade ago and whom I
have not seen since. On the 13th, I was asked to toast and roast a dear
friend at his sixtieth birthday celebration which I did to good effect
on the 14th. For some reason this request from his wife had made me
feel unusually nervous before the celebration, and that unfamiliar
feeling returned before the "job talk" in the dream. Regarding the
confused job situation, I did have an offer from another university
that I took seriously but turned down a couple of years ago. I had discussed the job with the chair of that department on one occasion in
which I wore a Hawaiian shirt. The job was not in Texas, but Texas
had been in the news the previous few days for stealing away the University of North Carolina's football coach. Finally, on the 17th, I had
an unpleasant exchange with a colleague and smarted for several
days from the unpleasantness. Thus, the dream.

Here is another dream, a dream Sigmund Freud had several years
before he wrote *The Interpretation of Dreams*. Frank Sulloway, a promi-
nent historian of evolutionary theory and psychology, provides a
useful account and analysis of Freud's famous dream of "Irma's
Injection."

The immediate circumstances associated with this famous

dream were as follows. Irma, a young woman who was on very friendly terms with Freud and his family, had been receiving psychoanalytic treatment from Freud in the summer of 1895. After several months of therapy, the patient was only partially cured, and Freud had become unsure whether he should keep her on. He had therefore proposed a solution to her, but she was not inclined to accept it. The day before the dream, Freud was visited by his friend "Otto" (Oskar Rie), who had been staying with the patient's family at a summer resort. Otto reproved Freud for his failure to cure Irma of all her symptoms. That evening Freud wrote out Irma's case history so that he might present it to "Dr. M." (Josef Breuer) in order to justify his treatment of the case. Later that night Freud dreamt that he met Irma at a large party and said to her, "If you still get pains, it's really only your fault." Irma looked "pale and puffy," and Freud wondered if she might not have an organic disease after all. He therefore examined his patient and detected white patches and scabs in her mouth. Otto and Dr. M., who were also present in the dream, then examined the patient for themselves; it was agreed by all that Irma had contracted "an infection." The three physicians further determined that the infection had originated from an injection previously given to the patient by Otto, who had apparently used a dirty syringe.

Sulloway then writes: "Upon interpretation the next morning, Freud's dream revealed the fulfillment of at least two unconscious wishes. First, the dream had excused him of responsibility for Irma's pains by blaming them on Otto (Oskar Rie). Simultaneously the dream had exercised revenge upon Otto for his annoying remarks about Freud's unsuccessful therapy." This is what Freud himself thought the dream meant. And it seems entirely plausible as an interpretation.

But notice the interpretation requires none of the psychoanalytic apparatus: no orthodox manifest-latent content distinction, no repressive "dream work," and certainly no symbols requiring Lamarckian transmission. This dream presupposes the following: a life, an unfolding history, a sense of self, fairly normal insecurities about whether one is doing one's job well, various defensive strategies. What it does not require is "two unconscious wishes." Freud knew before his head hit the pillow that he was upset and angry. To be sure the dream is not a simple read. What is? But neither the vengeful thoughts against Otto nor the self-absolution for Irma's woes expressed in the dream fit the description of "unconscious wishes" in the sense Freud came to believe were ubiquitous soon after the "Irma Dream." The Irma dream, as dreams go, is in need of interpretation. But it is hardly difficult to interpret.

The Dream Team and the Narrative Structure and Content of Dreams

There are some data, objective data, as they say, about dreams. J. Allan Hobson at Harvard has assembled a remarkable dream team, a team that has been gathering phenomenological reports and coordinating them with psychophysical data for the last two decades, and lately with neurophysiological data. Here are some interesting findings about dreams discovered—in some cases rediscovered—by Hobson's dream team.

- *Children's dreams are populated more than adult dreams by family members and close friends.* The simplest explanation is that everyone's dreams are populated with people one knows, has seen, or combinations thereof. Freud held the not-so-simple view that thanks to the work of dream-disguise, adult dreams of strangers and nameless people are in fact dreams of "people very near to one."
- *Children are as present in their dreams as adults.* This finding is something of a surprise. Jean Piaget, the great developmental psychologist, thought that because children have a less-well-developed sense of self than adults, their dreams would be more like watching a film than like being in a play. However, both children and adults are usually "there," at the scene of the dream, participating, in some way, in the action.
- *Children's dreams are often bizarre, but they are less often bizarre than adult dreams.* Freud, recall, took the frequent nonbizarreness of children's dreams as evidence for the theory that dreams express wishes. In the *Introductory Lectures* of 1917, Freud writes that children's dreams "are short, clear, coherent, easy to understand, and unambiguous. The dream produces a direct, undisguised fulfillment of a wish." According to orthodox psychoanalysis, adult dreams are more bizarre in virtue of being

more complexly disguised than children's dreams. Greater bizarreness is confirmed by the data assembled by dream researchers. We need an explanation for this difference. One possibility is that because there are more memories on the adult mind than in a child's mind to be activated during REM sleep, the work of making narrative sense is more complicated and produces thereby a more complex story for the adult than for the child.

Imagine that the case of memories works this way. The dream-narrator has a tough job that gets worse the more the organism knows. If I have two memories then there are just two ways I can order them (first-second/second-first), but if I have three memories then there are six ways I can order them, and if I have four there are twenty-four different orderings. For five, there are 120. For ten, there are 36,628,800, and for twelve distinct memories, the possible different series sequences are 4,835,001,600, almost five billion. You get the idea; combinations explode.

The function is simple: for any n the number of uniquely ordered series is n!, n-factorial, so if $n = 5$, then the number of possibilities are $5 \times 4 \times 3 \times 2 \times 1 = 120$.[1] Supposing, as I think it is, that the analogy from numerical strings to mental strings is relevant. Then the point is that the number of memories or thoughts available matter hugely to what can be thought or how it can be thought. Size of the memory store matters when one is putting memories together. There is a combinatorial explosion of possible stories one can tell as the number of memories grows. It is amazing that we ever put our ideas together in coherent form by the light of day. It is even more amazing that the brain can make sense of things at night—unless, as I think, the brain is acting on principle, to a point.

Flanagan's First Law of Dream Science is this: Bizarreness will increase the more control mechanisms are turned down and the more you have on your mind. Quantity impacts quality. No crew of psychoanalytic dream disguisers need be posited to account for the bizarre character of adult dreams. Flanagan's Second Law of Dream Science is a corollary of the first: While awake we attend better than we do in sleep, and we apply more efficiently and reliably while awake than asleep criteria of relevance and common sense in taking the measure of things as they are presented, and in representing what is presented.

- *Children's dreams and adult dreams, insofar as they are bizarre, display approximately the same ratio of types of bizarreness.* This is expected if Flanagan's First Law is true. Grown-ups have more bizarre dreams in part because they have more memories. Bizarreness can be measured according to a scale that plots *incongruities, uncertainties,* and *discontinuities.* For simplicity call the scale that measures dream bizarreness the *IUD* scale. Incongruity (I) refers to mismatches—the blue Caribbean waters viewed from the restaurant in Montreal; Socrates in a business suit. Uncertainty (U) refers to actual persons, things, and events that are not specified in a dream, one's geographical location, the person herself—maybe Beth or maybe Jane. Discontinuity (D) refers to an abnormal shift in person, place, or action—Clinton becomes Reagan; I am in New Jersey one second and I am with the same people in Paris the next.

The IUD scale is a way of measuring dream bizarreness, and it reflects the relative order of bizarre elements. The ratio of Incongruity to Uncertainty to Discontinuity is approximately 5:3:2. Uncertainty or vagueness is more common than plot, person, or scene discontinuity; but incongruities—mismatches of various sorts—dominate the bizarreness scale, accounting for about half of the bizarre elements in dreams.

- *Dream emotions and dream events track each other about as well as they do while we are awake.* Mom dies, you are sad. Hitler dies, you are happy. Awake and asleep, you feel the same. Mismatches of feelings and thoughts are a kind of incongruity. But they are a relatively rare type of incongruity in dreams.
- *Emotions and moods experienced in dreams involve in almost equal proportion: anxiety-fear, on the one hand and joy, happiness, elation, on the other.* Almost 60 percent of dreams involve these strong emotions.
- *Overall, more than two-thirds of the emotions experienced in dreams are negative—involving anxiety, fear, sadness, guilt.* "Sweet dreams!" Not likely.
- *Dream affect goes downhill.* A sad dream gets sadder. A happy dream rarely gets happier.
- *Female and male dreams do not differ in terms of emotions experienced.*

Figure 5.1   Discontinuity in dreams. © Creators Syndicate 1998. Used by permission.

- *Erotic feelings are relatively uncommon in dreams, after adolescence.* Sexual acts are also uncommon. As few as 6 percent of adult dreams involve feelings of eroticism or sexual activity.

Dreams and Narrative

All these facts matter. But how they matter is not entirely clear. If dreams are self-expressive, do they reveal that we are sad more than happy, generally? Do they reveal that life is not only less filled with sex, but also less filled with sexual thoughts than we sometimes think or pretend? Do dreams, just as Freud thought, matter more than we think they do? Many dreams, I have been insisting, are storylike. Dreams have narrative structure. Is this an illusion? Is narrative structure imposed after the fact, an artifact of trying to recount to oneself or others some strange phantasms that occurred during sleep? I think not.

In his 1994 book, *The Chemistry of Conscious States,* Allan Hobson acknowledges that he believed in the narrative structure of dreams until the technique of "dream splicing"—cutting dreams at scene shifts and mixing and matching—turned out to be undetectable by third parties. Initial studies indicated that third parties could not tell mixed and matched dream reports from intact reports. This led Hobson, contrary to his initial leanings, to conclude that "although each subplot may be a storylike unit, there is no story line connecting one subject to the next. Dream coherence may be in the eye of the beholder, but it is not in the text of the reports."

Hobson has changed his mind, in part because his dream team has amassed recently evidence that dreams really do involve weaving meaningful, emotionally complex stories into complex narrative structures—structures that are, in fact, detectable by third parties. Hobson's group is now studying the underlying grammar of dream mentation, and the evidence is fascinating. *Settings* and *scenes* are fairly unconstrained, *plot* is intermediate, and *characters* and *objects* tend to be transformed in the most gradual ways. So one's true love might be in Japan one second and in France the next. There will be some work to make the plot coherent, which will be hard, so what she's doing in Japan and France might involve an odd plot shift but not a completely incoherent one. But you may also find that she has turned into an old true love, but probably not into a sofa, in the transcontinental scene shift. These findings about the structure, the syntax, the grammar of dreams add detail to the IUD scale. Furthermore, they are to be expected if the mind-brain imposes, as best it can, the structure of ordinary life onto dreamy-thoughts.

Splitting the scene and changing the topic are easy. Changing the essence of a person or an object is harder. It is not surprising therefore that character transformation is fairly constrained, so that characters do not transform into inanimate objects, nor do inanimate objects transform into characters. Eggs do change texture in dreams, just as they do in life. But people don't become chairs or chairs people in dreams. People do, however, sometimes become plants, and plants people—still not all that often.

As I said earlier, mentation about one's current true love and one's old true love might be informative about what is on your mind, or it might be uninformative, just the best story line the brain can construct given the material it has to work with. But the latter could be true, and such a dream could still be a good starting point in therapy if your love life is going badly, or if you are suffering from a psychosocial problem. This may be because the content itself is revealing—remember, there is a top-down/bottom-up struggle going on between the noise from below and the cortex that is trying to interpret the noise in terms of narrative structures, scripts, and self-models it utilizes in making sense of things while awake. It could be that the dream is uninterpretable, or is meaningless as a narrative construct, or that it has nothing like the meaning we are inclined to assign, but is nonetheless a good conversation starter for someone trying to figure out the shape of his or her life.

Dream Themes

How is the narrative structure created? One possibility is that the dreamer sets out a plot outline to which the dream then conforms— like a ninth grader outlining a paper and then following her outline. According to Hobson's dream team, some such view is behind the Freudian line about unconscious plot preparation as well as dream long and sometimes all night long thematic continuity among dreams. This idea, however, seems unlikely since the dreamer does not have any idea—and only minimal control over—what noise the PGO waves are going to activate during a particular REM period. A more credible hypothesis is that the dreaming mind takes the random noise produced and attempts to generate a narrative bit by bit by trying to produce sense in terms of what it just made sense of. Of course, this is compatible with the idea that certain things are on one's mind and activated, and that my self model is there ready to make sense of things. It is also possible that the self is out of the loop. How could that be?

To convey the out-of-the-loop idea to my students I sometimes play a game in which we produce a "dream" as a class. I start by saying whatever comes to mind: "She rode in on a big white horse." Then we proceed around the room, extending the narrative piece by piece and ending up with a funny and crazy narrative in under a minute— usually very sexual (these are young adults raised on Freud after all).

Daniel Dennett has a more diabolical dream-production game that also yields a "dream" without a real dream-maker. I have played this game at Dennett's home and also tried it with great success on my own students. A volunteer—ideally someone who thinks he is good at dream interpretation—is asked to leave the room so that someone can report to the remaining group a recent dream. His job will be to get at the dream, interpret it, and identify the dreamer. Once the stooge has left, the host explains the rules: Upon reentry the stooge will be allowed to ask only questions about the dream that admit of "yes" or "no" answers. If the question ends in a letter from *a* through *l* anyone or everyone in the group (they all have allegedly heard the dream) answers "yes." If the question ends in *m* through *z*, the answer is "no" (the only exception is if following the rule would make a later answer contradict an earlier answer, in which case the earlier answer is trump). The stooge is invited back in the room and within several minutes he has detected an elaborate, richly symbolic, invariably sexual dream, plus identified the dreamer—only to be told by the assembled group, most of whom are rolling on the floor with laughter, that there was no dream, only this thing he invented by his questions!

In order to resolve whether dreams are created piece by piece as in these games, or are produced in a more coherent preoutlined manner by a single author who is *really* in charge, the dream team attempted to pit the "adjacency" hypothesis proposed by Marty Seligman and Amy Yellen against its alleged psychoanalytic rival. According to the principle of adjacency, dream segments are logically connected to those immediately preceding them and following them, but there is no overarching, coherent, or preplanned plot that spans the length of a dream.

To test these two hypotheses the dream team took actual dream reports and either cut them in half, recombining them with their nonmates to form spliced reports, or left them intact. The idea is that asking subjects to identify spliced versus intact reports as such will help determine the presence or absence of thematic continuity in ordinary (intact) dream reports. If judges can determine the presence of thematic continuity in dreams, they should equally be able to detect the absence of such continuity when no such continuity exists. The extent to which judges find more continuity in intact dreams than in spliced dreams is quantifiable and serves as a measure of the amount of perceptible continuity in the intact dream reports relative to the spliced reports.

Two sets of experiments were conducted using this technique, one involving sets of complete dream reports and the other involving sets of abridged reports. By analyzing these results and comparing the results of the first experiment with those of the other, the aim was to: 1) measure the amount of perceptible continuity in intact dream reports; 2) determine whether such thematic continuity extends across entire dreams; and 3) study the nature of this thematic continuity.

In the first experiment, five judges were each presented eleven intact reports and eleven spliced reports and asked to distinguish spliced from unspliced reports. The reports that were used were characterized by two common features: they were complete, and they contained no (detectable) scene and plot discontinuities. The results obtained show that out of 110 scores of dream reports, ninety were correct (82 percent). Judges were effective at correctly identifying both the spliced and unspliced reports in the sample, since out of the ninety correct scores, forty-eight were of intact reports and forty-two of spliced reports. Individual judges' accuracies were also significantly better than chance, ranging from 77 percent to 91 percent. Moreover, closer examinations of the scores of individual reports show that thirteen of the twenty-two reports were correctly scored by all five judges while no reports were misscored by more than three judges.

In the second set of experiments, a similar procedure was conducted but with abridged spliced and unspliced dream reports—both with the midsection missing. Seven judges produced 126 scores of dream reports. Of these 126 scores, seventy-three (58 percent) were accurately scored. More precisely, there were thirty-eight correct scores of unspliced reports and thirty-five of spliced reports, a rate only marginally better than chance. However, individual judges' accuracies ranged from 42 percent to 72 percent. Furthermore, closer examination of individual dream scores did show that three of the eighteen dream reports were scored correctly by all the judges, while fewer than one in one hundred would be expected by chance. In addition, three of the eighteen reports were correctly identified by six of the seven judges, while only one such scoring would be expected by chance.

While the first set of tests clearly indicates that dream reports are characterized by a perceptible thematic continuity (judges in the first set of experiments excelled at determining which of the reports were spliced), the second set of experiments suggested to the dream team that this thematic continuity does not extend across entire dreams—at least not in a way reliably discernible to individuals who did not themselves have the dream. The judges' inability to distinguish between spliced and unspliced reports in the case of abridged reports (in contrast to their excellent ability to distinguish between spliced and unspliced reports in the case of unabridged reports) suggests that perceptible thematic continuity of dreams does not extend across entire dreams.

What do these experimental results show? They show that dreams, even from a third-person perspective, make some sort of sense, play some sort of tune—they are not straightforward cases of "unmusical fingers wandering over the keys of the piano." The dream team thinks they show something more, namely that there is no overarching coherent plot in dreams, and thus no evidence for an inner dream master that designs dreams prior to their actual production. This directly contradicts Freud, while lending support to Seligman and Yellen's principle of adjacency hypothesis.

This is overstated. First, the studies show that, in fact, dreams often possess a detectable plot that spans their length. Second, Freud, to the best of my knowledge, never claimed that the plot of a dream would be easy to detect, or that coherence and thematic continuity would be worn on the sleeve of even an intact unabridged report. Indeed, by drawing a distinction between how a dream seems or is remembered (manifest content) and what is intended or meant by the dreamer (latent content), psychoanalysis protects itself from attributing any significance to judgments of thematic continuity or discontinuity in dream reports by non-experts.[2] Third, the dream team tests for the ability to detect thematic continuity of dream reports detached from particular persons, indeed, without any knowledge of the dreamer. But detection of continuity is just some sort of detection of meaning, and no one has ever thought that the meaning—if there is any—of dream reports, even of fragmented reports, could be detected in any consistent way without knowing facts about the dreamer. Fourth, and relatedly, we need some sort of control—a way of comparing the relative coherence and decipherability of spliced and unspliced, abridged and unabridged awake thinking reports with dream reports and possibly these with short stories, postmodern novels, theater of the absurd dramas, and poems—as well as the thematic coherence of, say, twentieth century free verse poems and classical sonnets. Do these modes of thought, these media, operate with some stronger form of plot construction and coherence than adjacency and, if they do, are their themes, their meanings, their narrative connections, reliably detectable in intact and tampered with forms by individuals who are not their authors? If not, there is much ado about nothing. Let me explain.

Poetic Devices

Consider sonnet splitting. Suppose I wonder whether Shakespeare's sonnets will be detectable according to the methods of the dream splicing experiments. Imagine therefore that I take two Shakespearean sonnets unabridged, possibly rejoined to themselves, possibly mismatched; and then two split sonnets with missing midsections which again are rejoined either to the poem to which they belong or not. The reader's job is to detect which is which.

Here are the two unabridged target sonnets.

> Being your slave, what should I do but tend
> Upon the hours and times of your desire?
> I have no precious time at all to spend,
> Nor services to do, till you require.
> Nor dare I chide the world-without-end hour,
> Whilst I, my sovereign, watch the clock for you,
> Nor think the bitterness of absence sour,
> Without accusing you of injury.
> Be where you list; your charter is so strong,
> That you yourself may privilege your time:
> Do what you will, to you it doth belong
> Yourself to pardon of self-doing crime.
> I am to wait, though waiting so be hell;
> Not blame your pleasure, be it ill or well.

> That God forbid, that made me first your slave,
> I should in thought control your times of pleasure,
> Or at your hand the account of hours to crave,
> Being your vassal, bound to stay your leisure!
> O, let me suffer (being at your beck)
> The imprison'd absence of your liberty,
> And patience, tame to sufferance, bide each check
> When you have bid your servant once adieu;
> Nor dare I question with my jealous thought
> Where you may be, or your affairs suppose,
> But, like a sad slave, stay and think of nought,
> Save, where you are now happy you make those:
> So true a fool is love, that in your will
> (Though you do anything) he thinks no ill.

Since I've spliced these poems at midpoint and either rejoined them to themselves using just two poems, I've provided a simple analog of the dream splicing experiments, since either both sonnets are intact or both are not. In the dream-splicing case, the mixes and matches come from an unspecified number of original reports. So make a judgment now: matched or mismatched? The answer is in a note, but don't look yet. First, try these two abridged sonnets. The conditions are the same as before, both beginnings meet their end, or neither does.

> Let me not to the marriage of true minds
> Admit impediments. Love is not love
> Which alters when it alteration finds,
>
>   * * *
>
> This I do vow, and this shall ever be,
> I will be true, despite thy scythe and thee.

> No, Time, thou shalt not boast that I do change:
> Thy pyramids built up with newer might
> To me are nothing novel, nothing strange
>
>   * * *
>
> If this be error, and upon me prov'd,
> I never writ, nor no man ever lov'd.

And the answers are—*fanfare*—as I said, in this note.[3] You may now check your answers.

Okay, be honest. How did you do on the sonnet exercise? Even if you did perfectly, face facts. Unless you know Shakespeare well, you were lucky. Tenuous thematic threads led you down the right road. It is hard, really hard to follow even a great poem from its beginning to its end, abridged or unabridged. Nonetheless, trying to detect short-lived logically coherent sequences—adjacency—as well as some sort of long-lived logical coherence—overall thematic unity—is a plausible strategy in the poetic detection case, as well as in the dream cases. Such a strategy will work if anything will.

However, use of the principle of adjacency in interpreting or, what is different, in constructing dream narratives may not distinguish the case of dreams from other media or genres. Adjacency seems to operate in awake thought, in conversation, in lectures, and in literary creations in a way that differs only in degree, rather than in kind, from the way it operates in dreams. To be sure, it seems likely that much more preplanning goes into writing a poem or contemplating the shape of one's day over breakfast than operates in dream construction. But surely in both poetic construction and getting through the day most of the details are unspecified by the overall theme or plan. Plus, things come up, new ideas, interruptions, and we adjust bit by bit, word by word, line by line, moment to moment, hour by hour, to make the poem or day work out as best we can. So, the first point is that adjacency principles may well play an important role across many, even most, forms of thinking and living, and not be specially indicative of, or unique to, dream consciousness, construction, or interpretation.

The second point is that the experiments are too crude to provide decisive grounds for choosing between Freudian and non-Freudian views of dream coherence and the process(es) of dream construction.[4] We are told that these experiments measure a difference between overarching thematic coherence that is produced in accordance with a master plan and, assuming they are coherent at all, a one-thing-next-to-the other sort of coherence that is produced piecemeal. This is not obvious, in part because the issue of how a dream is constructed and the issue of the kind of coherence it displays are run together in the experiments, whereas they are, in fact, distinct matters. This is easy to see. The practice of free association, where a person agrees to say whatever comes to mind over, say, a half-hour period, is the possibility proof that we can set ourselves to and then abide by a plan to produce a text that will lack (or be perceived to lack) discernible coherence. That is, we can preplan the construction of a text, using a method such as free association, that will lack, or at least appear to lack, the storylike unity that a typical short story or newspaper article possesses. Or, as is the case with both Dennett's and my dream games, a party host or a teacher can establish in advance rules for the construction of an alleged dream report that uses as its construction device a principled but silly alphabetical rule (as in Dennett's game) or that requires adherence to the principle of adjacency (as in my game) that will seem to a third party to be a thematically coherent and interpretable, albeit weird, narrative. Thus the fact that a dream report, or any other text for that matter, appears to have, or even in fact has, a strange, even an incoherent thematic structure, does not tell anything clear about the manner in which the dream or text was produced. The problem is that we are told the experiments pit the psychoanalytic theory of dream construction against the hypothesis that dreams are constructed piecemeal, according to the principle of adjacency. But the points just made show that the two hypotheses do not necessarily yield incompatible predictions about the outcome of the experiments; that is, both hypotheses about how dreams are constructed are compatible with third-party judgments that dream reports are thematically disjointed. Furthermore, it is not the case that there are only two contending hypotheses for how dreams are constructed, the Freudian view and the adjacency view. The view I have sketched provides a third possibility. Roughly, the hypothesis is this: The brain is designed to make sense of things by the light of day, and this ability or disposition does not turn off while we sleep. Further, we hold in our mind a self-model, a storehouse of memories, including memories for how standard events, for example, dinner parties or visits to amusement parks, go. When we enter NREM, things that are actively on our mind continue to reverberate and are activated, so we worry about the upcoming exam. But since we are asleep and not awake, we do not study for the exam. As the brain works on its restorative tasks (cell repair, refilling the adrenals with cortisol, replenishing gonadatrophic hormones, and the like), it can also activate the mind in more random ways, producing NREM dreams, which are more weird than those that involve continued reverberations of things already on our mind. The cortex tries to rein these thoughts in and provide them as best it can with some sort of sensible shape. So we find ourself happy to be driving to the airport to pick up Socrates but also worried that he may be arriving at Newark and not LaGuardia (all this, if it is an NREM dream, will not involve visual imagery). When we enter REM sleep, the brain is activated in a more chaotic fashion by the PGO waves, and thus the material, the thoughts including visual images that are activated, are less likely candidates for a smooth and sensible story than those activated or allowed to continue to reverberate during more quiescent NREM sleep. Still, the self-model is in place, the cortical disposition to make sense of things has not turned off, emotions are aroused, and the brain, possibly the whole brain, works to weave a narrative as best it can from the odd materials it is offered. It is extremely unlikely that there is preplanning of the dream, since the PGO waves that initiate entry into REM and that are designed in the first instance to get the brain to refill the serotonin and norepinephrine tanks so we awake alert and attentive, as well as to set the brain awash with acetylcholine, which works to fix memories, are chaotic and not designed to be concerned with what thoughts they activate while doing these jobs. Still, the brain, disposed to make sense of things, does its best and produces REM dreams, which, as we know, typically are bizarre but not altogether incoherent.

This picture of dream construction provides a third, intermediate hypothesis to the dreams-are-preplanned and the dreams-are-pro-duced-piecemeal hypotheses. The idea is that the self-model that is already in place works with the cortical disposition to make sense of input it receives. During sleep this is almost entirely internally gener-ated input involving activation of neural nets that contain both single thoughts—"there is an exam tomorrow"—and more extended script or scene or episode like structures. Our brains do not store memo-ries in single neurons but in networks—thus the expression "neural nets." When a node of a net receives a hit the entire net is activated. Suppose a picture of a beach cottage is activated. In all likelihood, a set of memories and associations are also activated—beach scenes, memories of relatives or acquaintances one has spent time with at the beach, beach balls, fried clams. Since the executive centers of the brain are less active and thus less vigilant to keep thought on track than they are while we are awake, subsequent associations may be somewhat odd, but not completely unprincipled. Remember the executive centers, although operating less efficiently than they do when we are awake, are not turned off altogether. If the beach ball network is activated, then the round thing network may be activated, and I may find myself, as I have, playing on the rings of Saturn. Aunt Mame, who died in the mid-sixties, was often at the beach with us when I was a boy, so she may be along for the ride. Perhaps I will then eat lobster (lobster being in the same net as clams) with my nephew Jessie, with whom I have never been to the beach, but who is a rela-tive. Jessie was born in Guatemala, which might get me thinking about driving a German-made car in Costa Rica (also in Central America), where I have visited and where I once drove in a Toyota with some German acquaintances. That sort of thing.

The intermediate hypothesis is that dreams are not preplanned (the view allegedly held by Freud) but nonetheless involve activation of memories and associations, including emotional associations, already in place. Many of these memories and associations possess complex, albeit often short span, narrative structure. Insofar as adja-cency rules are involved (this, to me, is an open question), they con-nect units larger than single thoughts (or sentences, as in my dream construction game). In addition, because my self-model is in play, and because these are my memories, thoughts, and feelings that are being activated, the dream produced is to some degree identity expressive and may contain a length-long interpretable theme. The dream may insofar as it can be interpreted be interpretable by the dreamer himself or by a savvy acquaintance or therapist, possibly both. Sometimes the dream will lack any interesting meaning and not be worth exploring. When this occurs we can explain why. The activation of the associative networks is sometimes so chaotic that the brain is not able—despite its best efforts—to rein them into a thematically stable or meaningful narrative.

I don't intend to be giving any solace to the Freudian by the remarks I have just made. Indeed, my proposal is to reject the view of dream construction attributed by Hobson's dream team to Freud, as well as the view that dreams-are-deep thought for reasons I have stated just now as well as throughout this book. At the same time, I want to be clear that in all likelihood the construction of dreams involves more than a process of one-after-another linking of short snatches of thoughts or images according to a principle of adjacency—as does my dream construction game.

My reason for preferring the view I have just sketched of dream construction and dream meaning is not that I am in a kind and gentle mood and seek some compromise position between the two contending hypotheses that will keep each side somewhat happy. The reason is that it is the best account of dream structure and meaning available, given everything we now know about what the brain is doing while we are awake and what it is doing at different points in the sleep cycle.

My Dreams, My Self

I want to be clear that dreams are more bizarre—indeed, some make no sense at all—than most sane awake thought and conversation. This is revealed in the data on disorientation—on the relatively high degree of incongruity, uncertainty, and discontinuity that occurs in dreams relative to awake thought. Furthermore, both the disorientation of dreams and the lack of preplanning can be given a unified explanation: the frontal cortex, which is responsible both for keeping us oriented and for hatching plans, is relatively quiescent during sleep.

Nonetheless a self-model is kept as a complex dispositional structure in the brain, and is involved (and continually updated) to some extent in all thinking. So what I think about myself helps constitute who I am, and what I think is constructed within various systems of constraints as I go along. Dreams both reflect and participate in the project of self-creation. In all probability, however, dreams have less overall causal importance to how my life goes and seems than awake thinking. This is so for several reasons: Dreams are less sensitive to the external world than awake thought as well as less reliable at coordinating emotion and reality tracking than are dreams; the noise-to-signal ratio is much higher in dreaming than in awake cognition, which means that the cortex must make more effort and in all likelihood achieve less success in reining in the endogenously generated, somewhat chaotic input it receives.

Dreams sometimes express important things about oneself. But not always. When they do, and when they don't, they can be used as grist for the interpretative mill or as meaningless stimuli for further thought. Read your diary or look at a dot on the wall. It is not obvious which leads or would normally lead to better self-exploration or deeper self-knowledge. But surely, and this is perhaps the main point: thinking (awake, REM, NREM) often is identity expressive, and this is true even when what is thought is pretty much nonsensical. My thinking is processed by and through me, this organism, this thinking thing. This thing with a history, a life—a life whose shape and content and contours I know something about.

In the end, it should come as no surprise that I, this thinking thing, should express in its thoughts its nature; should express itself. There is something that it is like to be me, and I can sometimes experience, even on occasion say, what it is like. In this way I express who I am, what matters to me, and where I locate meaning, significance, and worth. I express who I am when I am awake and, in all likelihood, to some lesser extent when I dream.

Neuroscience allows that much. This seems like enough to me, enough for thinking that I am a person with a unique identity for whom the project of seeking self-knowledge is worthwhile, but whose achievement is no simple task. This picture locates grist for the mill of self-knowledge in both awake thought and in dreams. On this view, dreams are neither meaningless noise, nor are they a privileged mode of thought behind or beneath which lies something like our deepest, essential, or true self.

Notes

1. If one allows repetitions so that you are allowed to think of two identical memories moments apart, for example, *AA, BB,* as well as *AB, BA,* then the function is N^n and the numbers are even more frightening than they are when the function is n! with no repetitions allowed.

2. Starting with Sir Karl Popper and continuing in recent work by the philosophers Adolf Grünbaum and Patricia Kitcher, Freud has been taken to task for making his theory untestable except from the point of view of true believers, who when they "test" the theory simply "see" that it is true. I think this criticism is right on target. Here I am simply pointing out why, because of the way the theory protects itself, it is not clear how the present studies would be viewed by an orthodox Freudian, who believes that the meaning, theme, and continuity of a dream is not only not revealed in a dream report, it is concealed in such reports.

3. The two unabridged sonnets are, respectively, No. 57 and No. 58; the two abridged sonnets are, again respectively, No. 116 and No. 123. All four cases are mismatches. Now anyone who has read Shakespeare should be primed to guess correctly. I have so far had only two cooperative subjects perform this task, one a head of a psychiatry division at Johns Hopkins, the other a neurobiologist at Duke. Both scored zero. I hardly claim to have constructed a good experiment, let alone, God forbid, performed one. In fact, I cheated some since I searched the sonnets for ones I thought would be very hard to detect using these methods.

4. One problem with the experiments is that the Freudian can easily protect his theory from any damage. This is because an orthodox Freudian need not predict, indeed he will not predict, that dream reports will have discernible coherence in the eye of the uninitiated. Even when they do, what is being detected is not what the dream really means or is about. Meaning, theme, coherence all lie beneath the surface. That is, the Freudian can easily protect his theory of dreams-as-deep-thought by pointing out that whatever odd features dreams or dream reports are discovered to have is expectable since a dream report, a remembered dream, is by its very nature disguised. And it is disguised because it is constructed in a code that will release repressed, socially unacceptable wishes, without the conscious mind being able to see through the disguise.

6

Philosophical Perplexities

The work of a philosopher consists in assembling
reminders for a particular purpose.
There is not *a* philosophical method, though there
are indeed methods, like different therapies.

—*Ludwig Wittgenstein*, Philosophical
Investigations, *127; 133*

Three Philosophical Problems

I proposed at the start to delay treatment of the traditional philosophical problems about dreams until my neurophilosophical theory was in place. The plan was to see how these problems looked from the perspective of a theory of dreams informed by contemporary mind science. That theory is now in place, so the time has come to play some good old-fashioned philosophy. As we know, there are three classical problems about dreams:[1]

- Whether it is possible *to know for certain* that one is awake and not dreaming and vice versa.
- Whether dreams are *experiences* we have while sleeping or fabrications that we make up after we awake.
- Whether we can be *immoral* in dreams.

Treating the problems in this order involves taking them out of their actual historical order, since the third problem is older than the second. But it has the advantage of putting together the two epistemological problems, the problems that have to do with distinguishing dreams from reality and with the reliability of dream reports, and separating these from the ethical question of whether we are morally accountable for our dreams.

The First Problem

Most nonphilosopher friends think the problem of distinguishing dreams from reality is a purely philosophical problem if ever there was one. This is not intended as a compliment, as in "Gee, you sure are lucky to get to work on such an interesting and important problem."

In fact, this is not a purely philosophical problem. There are actual neuropsychological patients with various types of lesions who have trouble on a day-to-day basis distinguishing dreams from reality. To meet ten of them, read the twentieth chapter of Mark Solms's wonderful book, *The Neuropsychology of Dreams*.

In any case, the grip of the first problem, insofar as one who is not impaired as these patients are can find it gripping, comes from the twin facts that everyone dreams and everyone is familiar with the experience of dreams that seem, while they are occurring, to be perfectly real, to be tracking events that are really happening, but which in fact did not really happen. Descartes put the familiar observation this way: "The same thoughts we have when we are awake can also come to us when we are asleep, without any of the latter thoughts being true." This observation led Descartes to the conclusion that we possess "no definite marks" to distinguish sleep from wakefulness, a verdict Plato came to two thousand years before, and which Bertrand Russell came to three hundred years later.

Russell reports a dream in which he sees a ruined church and comments that the experience of seeing a ruined church in what we call a dream is "intrinsically indistinguishable" from seeing a ruined church during times we deem ourselves wide awake. Russell writes, "It is obviously possible that what we call waking life may only be an unusually persistent and recurrent nightmare."

Relative to a standard of absolute certainty, Descartes was right to say that there are "no definite [certain] marks" to distinguish sleep from wakefulness. However, his considered opinion is that there are reliable signs to tell that one *is* awake when one *is* awake, and there are reliable signs to tell that one *was* dreaming when one *was* dreaming. Our judgments about wakefulness when we are awake are highly reliable, as are our judgments that we were asleep after we wake up.

One advantage of this reading of Descartes is that the features he thinks we deploy to reliably distinguish our dreams from awake experiences are in fact the ones our best contemporary theories claim we use.

One Night, Three Dreams

For many years now I have been recording my dreams. Here are three dreams I had on the night of November 10th when I was twenty-three years old:

1. *I was assailed by weird creatures, a ghostly mob, then a tornado spun me around and I could not stand upright. I made it to the college campus and attempted to reach the chapel, but the wind thwarted my forward movement. My right side felt so weak I could barely stand, and I crossed to the left side of the street. A friend approached bringing news of a gift—a piece of fruit, a melon, I think it was, from some foreign land.* I woke up frightened.

2. *I heard a loud thunderclap, sparks were everywhere.* I woke up terrified, the room filled with fading afterimages of fiery sparks.

3. *I found a dictionary on the table as well as a book filled with ancient poems, one of which began "What road in life shall I follow?" A man appeared and told me of another poem whose first line was "It is and is not."* Then I awoke.

The first point is that while I was having these dreams, they seemed completely real to me, as real as any awake experiences, "intrinsically indistinguishable" from the very same events taking place while I was awake—completely different from watching the same scenes unfold on a stage where, no matter how great my absorption in the drama, I would never be so absorbed that I would be deceived into thinking that I was actually *in* the play rather than *in* the audience. That said, I knew these were dreams when I awoke, but not while I was having them.

These dreams also seemed very meaningful, and I quickly came to my own interpretations. But not trusting completely my own techniques of dream interpretation, I sent a copy of the November 10th dreams to a renowned psychoanalyst in London asking for his assistance. He wrote back explaining that he did not interpret dreams without knowing the analysand and his or her situation. Nor did he do pro bono work.

However, in his rejection letter—one I thought to border on the passive-aggressive—the analyst did offer two tantalizing insights based purely on the symbolism contained in the first dream: Going from the right side of the road to the left suggests unconscious feelings of sexual deviance or at least some sort of generalized guilt over some real or imagined sins, crimes, or misdemeanors. The appearance of the melon, as a symbol of "the larger hemispheres of the female body" but also sometimes a symbol of male testicles, was suggestive that my feelings of sinfulness were due to certain inappropriate sexual desires, probably heterosexual, but possibly homosexual.

Puzzled and troubled by this first pass explanation, I provided the analyst with more information about myself. I explained that I was a college graduate, mathematically talented, but something of a solitary soul. Needing to travel after college before settling into a real job or continuing my education, I was hiking in Germany in the second week of November when an early winter storm hit. I spent the day of the dreams indoors sitting by the stove as snowy winds howled around my cottage, contemplating my future, a future I had somewhat idealistically and narcissistically resolved the year before would be dedicated only to believing what is true beyond all shadow of doubt.[2] I explained to the analyst that I was greatly agitated by nightfall about both my future and the meaning of my resolution. But eventually I fell asleep, only to have the dreams I then recorded in my diary.

My own interpretation, I explained, was this. The first two dreams are dreams of fear, dreams of being deflected by powerful forces outside or inside me (the winds, the gifts), and then punished (the firestorm) for straying from the straight road, or for not being able to muster the strength to move forward against the forces of evil and illusion. The last dream took the warnings contained in the first two dreams seriously and pointed me back to the right track. A divine voice spoke to me and posed the question, "What road shall I follow in life?," and answered as cryptically as the Buddha, "It is and is not." My mission, my life's work as revealed in the last dream, I surmised was to be a philosopher—to find the way to the true and the good, the path to what is, and to avoid the path to the false and the bad, the path to what is not. So certain was I that these dreams were messages from the divine that I entitled the series *Olympica*, my Olympian dreams.

The analyst, exhausted by age and illness and impatient with unsolicited and unremunerated letters such as mine, but sensing no doubt my fragile state of mind, politely wrote back that his initial interpretation was based on relatively transparent dream symbolism in the first of my three dreams. These aspects come from the unconscious or preconscious and are elements, as it were, "from below." My interpretation that I feared being led astray by internal or external desires was compatible with his interpretation about the sorts of desires I am particularly, and rightfully, concerned about—my deviant heterosexual or homosexual desires.

That said, the new information I had provided about my life, my passions, my circumstances, and my thinking, and especially my mood on the day of the dreams, allowed a more complete interpretation.

The analyst wrote that my dreams "are what we call 'dreams from above,' that is, formations of ideas that could have been created as well during the waking state as during the sleeping state." My dreams were not messages from God but messages from me to myself, ever so thinly disguised rehearsals of exactly what I had been thinking about all day, and possibly for several years. Some dreams are like that. More therapy might help me understand my compulsion for the neat and clean, the certain, my troubles with authority, and the rest. The famous psychiatrist would offer recommendations for a top-notch analyst if I felt the need to continue with my dream work once I had settled in a real city.

The Hoax and The Truth

What I have just been saying is completely staged. It is all false. But it is also all true. The truth is that the young man who had the dreams on November 10th had them on November 10, 1619. His name was René Descartes. Although the *Olympica* itself was lost, most everyone treats the transcription from Adrien Baillet's *La Vie de Monsieur Des-Cartes* published in 1691 to be accurate. Furthermore, Descartes interpreted the dreams just as I have said I (that is, he) did.

As there were no psychoanalysts in 1619, René Descartes couldn't have sent his diary transcripts to an analyst, let alone a famous one. However, in 1928 Maxime Leroy, a distinguished French social theorist, asked for help from the old and infirm, but most distinguished analyst ever, Sigmund Freud himself. And over the course of several missives Freud interpreted Descartes's Olympian dreams just as I have said. Now I am speaking only the truth.

So Descartes had these three dreams, and he and Freud interpreted them in the ways I have said.

This Is Philosophy We Are Playing, Not Biography

What, you might ask, is the purpose when dealing with the "deep"— full-throat is important here—philosophical problem of distinguishing dreams from wakefulness of telling you about Descartes' dreams, how he interpreted them, and what Freud made of them three hundred ten years after the fact? Our topic, after all, is philosophical, not biographical. The personal facts are irrelevant.

I don't think they are irrelevant in this case. Indeed, there is a remarkable consistency in the marks the young Descartes used to identify the Olympian dreams as dreams, and the marks he argues we reliably deploy, and rightly trust, in telling dreams from wakefulness at the end of his philosophical treatise, the *Meditations*.

It is perhaps unsurprising that Freud took Descartes' dreams seriously as dreams, as grist for his interpretive mill. It is much more surprising for those—almost everyone—who read Descartes as the most famous and articulate proponent of the claim that there is no certain way to distinguish dreaming from wakefulness, nor wakefulness from dreaming, that he had no doubt that these dreams of his were dreams. He did not know these dreams were dreams while he was dreaming, but he knew it each time he found himself waking up.

How did Descartes know that the Olympian dreams were dreams? First, waking up is a reliable indicator, especially if one remembers dozing off in a bed, that one has been asleep, and that any recent mentation was dreamed. Indeed, Descartes describes waking up after each of the first two dreams and struggling for a time with their meaning and with his agitated mood before falling asleep again. The third dream may have been a semi-lucid dream, since according to Baillet, Descartes reports working to interpret it while it was going on and as being somewhat confused about whether he was dreaming or meditating. However, once he found himself waking up, he judged the third dream to be a dream.

The second mark that the Olympian dreams were dreams comes from the fact that the events and the relations among the events in the dreams can be seen from the perspective of wakefulness to be abnormal relative to the sort of connections that obtain among events of ordinary life—ghosts, a person appearing out of nowhere, news of a gift rather than the gift itself.

Third, for reasons Freud noted, these dreams fall into the class of "dreams from above," continuations of recent obsessions that were easy for Descartes to understand as significant from the point of view of his identity—revealing his divine mission according to his own self-understanding, *or* re-revealing and solidifying the project he was already committed to, according to Freud. Whichever it is, the dreams were seen correctly by both interpreters to be, in some important sense, identity expressive.

Not all dreams are like this; some are mostly noise. Indeed, the second dream, of fireworks, from which Descartes immediately awoke with visual afterimages of sparks in his room, may not have been a real dream with narrative structure at all, but either a hypnopompic hallucination of the sort common while a person is waking up but not quite awake, or a hypnagogic hallucination of the sort one has while one is falling asleep but not quite asleep.

This issue to the side, the fact remains that mental episodes that occur during sleep, that contain abnormal story lines, and that connect up with things on a particular individual's mind are typically dreams, as are mental episodes that occur during sleep that are noisy, nonsensical, and not worthy of the effort of interpretation (although Freud famously denied this latter possibility).

Judging that mentation occurred during sleep is a necessary condition for judging a dream a dream; various disconnects and irregularities as perceived from the point of view of wakefulness secure the judgment.

Descartes was able to identify the Olympian dreams as dreams using precisely these marks, that is, recalling falling asleep, finding himself waking up in bed on three occasions while recalling unusual thoughts, odd plot lines, and strange occurrences relative to the sorts of regularities he expected from awake life.

Confidence Regained

Okay, you say, supposing Descartes used these marks to identify his Olympian dreams as dreams, this speaks not one bit to the issue of his or anyone else's *justification* for picking out these or any other particular mental episodes as dreams.

My reply draws on the consilience between the autobiographical work and Descartes' strictly philosophical writings. Famously and familiarly in the *Discourse on Method* of 1637 and the *Meditations* of 1641, Descartes undertakes the project of setting knowledge on firm foundations. The First Meditation is entitled "Concerning Those Things That Can be Called into Doubt." The aim is to see what, if anything, remains that cannot be doubted after everything that can be doubted is set (temporarily) to one side. I will not rehearse the familiar details of the process of undoing and redoing knowledge. I simply want to emphasize that the worry about there being no "certain [definite] marks" to distinguish dreaming from being awake works rhetorically, and successfully, to move along the process of doubting whatever can be doubted.[3]

At the end of the *Meditations*, Descartes believes himself to have regained a basis for trusting many of the things he believed before he engaged in the exercise. He exists for sure; God exists; and God will not allow him to be deceived about what he perceives with clarity and distinctness, for example, that the soul is distinct from the body. We are also reassured that the external world exists, that the laws of nature are discoverable, and that dreams can be distinguished from awake thought. The Sixth Meditation concludes with Descartes describing his "methodic doubt," particularly as applied to the dream-awake distinction, as "hyperbolic" and "laughable," as not worthy of real doubt, of real ongoing concern.

On what basis did Descartes regain confidence in his ability to tell wakefulness from dreaming? God's goodness plays a crucial role. It follows from the existence of an all-powerful and all-good God that I cannot be wrong about my most well-examined general beliefs such as that there is an external physical world and that there is a distinction I can reliably detect between dreams and wakefulness. An all powerful, good, and loving God could not by the logic of his nature allow me to be *that* confused.[4] Still, being a willful finite creature, I will make all sorts of specific mistakes. I might think that the sun really is small, and I might easily be confused about whether I told my student Anne that she had philosophical talent or merely dreamed that I had done so.

Confidence in Connectedness

Once Descartes is reassured that he is not under the spell of constant illusion, he reminds us of a mark we reasonably and reliably use to distinguish dreams from wakefulness that harkens back to one of the marks he used to tell that the Olympian dreams were dreams. It is one that the theist or the naturalist will agree we in fact deploy.

> For now I notice that a very great difference exists between dreaming consciousness and wakeful consciousness. Dreams are never joined with all the other actions of life by the memory, as is the case with actions that occur when one is awake. For surely, if someone, while I am awake, suddenly appears to me, then immediately disappears, as happens in dreams, so that I see neither where he came from or where he went, it is not without reason that I would judge him to be a phantom conjured up in my brain, rather than a true man. But when things happen which I notice distinctly where they came from, where they are now, and when they happened, I connect them without interruption to the rest of my life, obviously I am certain that these perceptions have occurred not in sleep but in a waking state.

Being There

If the analysis so far is on the right track, then the marks Descartes used to know that his Olympian dreams were dreams receive articulation, elaboration, and justification in his explicitly philosophical writings. There are four marks.

1. *Being in bed.* One set of regularities that people come to deploy in telling whether or not some mental episode is a dream is simple and straightforward, but underestimated. It is this: Experiencing oneself coming to in bed (or with the newspaper on one's face, or one's head on one's chest and one's book on the floor) is reliably connected to just having been asleep, which is reliably connected to the likelihood that any very recent mentation was a dream, especially if the mentation involved was bizarre or perseverative.

2. *Being bizarre.* Descartes's point in the quoted passages is that we use sensible standards of rational connectedness, of lawlikeness to distinguish dreams from wakeful mentation. Allan Hobson's group has refined Descartes' basic insight and shown that there are three main kinds of disconnections that are reliable intra- and interpersonal indicators that some mental episode is a dream.

As described previously, what Hobson's group calls bizarreness can be measured according to a scale that plots incongruities, uncertainties, and discontinuities—the IUD scale, which reflects the relative order of bizarre elements that occur in a ratio of 5:3:2.

Incongruity refers to mismatches or disconnects—watching aliens eating grass in St. Stephen's Square, Dublin, from the courtyard of my favorite restaurant in Union Square, Manhattan; finding Mao Tse Tung chairing a faculty meeting; Madonna dating the Pope.

Uncertainty refers to actual persons, things, and events that are not specified in a dream. I am with a dear old friend, but which dear old friend it is, is uncertain, and this despite the fact that she has the familiar face of Jane, but doesn't seem to be Jane in the dream. Uncertainty refers to what seems vague in a dream, not to what seems vague upon awakening.

Discontinuity refers to an abnormal shift in person, place or action—my mother becomes my daughter; I am in Paris having lunch and an instant later I am with an overlapping but nonidentical luncheon party finishing the meal in Melbourne; I am riding a dolphin in the Aegean and then in a 747 over the ocean.

3. *Being metacognitive.* Lucid dreams aside, most dreams do not involve meta-awareness, awareness that one is dreaming while one is dreaming. Wakefulness, on the other hand often, possibly typically, involves meta-awareness, or at least a powerful disposition to express confidence if queried that one is awake and thinking or doing whatever it is one is thinking or doing. This is a regularity, a difference, that is widely noted, and thus it is the kind of regularity that would allow a claim to the effect that typically wakefulness is metacognitively richer than is sleep. Is there any evidence—nonphenomenological evidence—that this seeming difference exists, that it is a real difference?

Yes. Recent brain-imagery studies show that the executive centers in frontal cortex that are important for self-awareness, for forming action plans, and for carrying out voluntary actions are relatively quiescent during REM sleep.

The point about metacognition is important in another way. The usual way of framing the first dream problem assumes that there are two perfectly symmetrical problems: we cannot know that we are awake and not dreaming in the same way we cannot know we are dreaming and not awake. But in fact the problems are *not* symmetrical—we know we are awake when we are. What we don't normally know is that we are dreaming while we are dreaming. The difference in metacognitive activation in the two conditions helps explain why. Furthermore, the metacognitive difference helps explain why the consensus about how we reliably discern which state we are in— awake or dreaming—involves contemporaneous judgments in the case of wakefulness but after the fact judgments in the case of dreams.

4. *Being vivacious.* Another way in which dreams differ from wakefulness is this. Many philosophers, thinking they follow Descartes— take for example, Russell's claim that the awake and dreamed thoughts of the ruined church are "intrinsically indistinguishable" from each other—think that the fact that often we cannot tell we are dreaming when we are dreaming is because dreams seem as real as real can seem. One reason dreams seem so real is related to the point just made: Our metacognitive powers are typically turned way down in dreams and thus so are our judgmental capacities to perceive incongruities, uncertainties, and discontinuities as odd while they are occurring. Perceiving that such things are odd is hard, since perceiving them as odd requires layering thoughts, for example, having the thought that one is flying while also having the thought that people can't fly. We understand from a neurophysiological perspective why we are better able to think metacognitively when we are awake than asleep. But in any case, the fact that dreams seem so real while we are dreaming that we can't tell that we are not awake does not imply that dream mentation is just like awake mentation in terms, say, of vivacity or along other phenomenological dimensions.

Ask people whether the imagery in dreams—just take the visual imagery—is as vivid as an actual visual experience. If most people say, as I suspect they will, that such imagery does not have the vivacity of awake experiences, then Russell is wrong. The dreamed scene of the ruined church is not "intrinsically indistinguishable" from seeing the real church. It is not indistinguishable, all things considered.

Furthermore, if one challenges this point on the grounds that I am depending on occurrent versus remembered thoughts, then let both the actual and dreamed experience of the ruined church be remembered. I predict that most people will say that the remembered actual experience is more vivid than the remembered dream experience. The claim is that so far as the experiences themselves tell us, seeing a ruined church or remembering seeing one has greater vivacity than dreaming about the ruined church or remembering that one has dreamed about the ruined church.[5]

To sum up, the answer to the first dream problem is this: There are no *certain* phenomenological marks to distinguish episodes of wakefulness from dreaming. We can, however, thanks to God's goodness, or nature's wise engineering, trust that there is a general distinction between the two mental state types, and we can rest assured that we are not systematically mistaking dreams for wakefulness or vice versa, especially if we conscientiously apply our reason, our memory, and our senses. So much for the first dream problem. Certain theological props to the side, Descartes got both the problem and the solution right.

Morning Stories: The Second Skeptical Problem

The second problem, recall, is whether dreams are *experiences* we have while sleeping or fabrications that we make up after we awake.

In dealing with the first dream problem I took it for granted, as Descartes and most everyone else did and does, that dreams are experiences that take place during sleep. This is the "received view." The first problem is concerned with whether we can reliably discern the location of our experiences in sleep or wakefulness. The second problem questions our basic assumptions about location and timing. Why think that there are *any* experiences at all that occur during sleep? What actual or possible evidence could there be for this idea?

When I first wrote a paper in which I cited the distinguished philosophers Norman Malcolm and Daniel Dennett as pushing this question, and in which I suggested taking the problem seriously, several students as well as one major dream researcher wondered whether the entire philosophical community might be suffering from some ancestral form of mad cow disease. Just the other day, one of my best graduate students couldn't resist telling me that this was a silly problem if ever he had heard one.

But it isn't. One does not need to have lost one's senses to wonder about the extent to which dreams are mental events that occur while we sleep or are morning stories. Many have thought that the length of dreams and the plot of dreams are greatly exaggerated when dreams are reported. Kant, Leibniz, and my mother thought this.

Further, most everyone thinks we humans are great confabulators. Recent studies of memories of long periods of physical or sexual abuse, often at the hands of loved ones—memories with powerful conviction that what is remembered happened as it seems to have happened—have shown that some percentage of such memories, perhaps a very high percentage, are false, degree of conviction notwithstanding.

Usual responses to both the first and the second dream problems depend on the reliability of memory. I wake up and tell you about experiences I remember happening, experiences I seem, often dimly, to recall happening. If the reliability of memory is all that the belief that dreams are experiences that take place during sleep is based on, we have reason to take the second dream problem seriously. This is true, Daniel Dennett points out, even if one brings lucid dreams into the debate, for the evidence for lucid dreams, simultaneous experiences of dreams as dreams while they are occurring, are themselves morning stories, stories about what people believe themselves to have experienced while asleep.

Here are some further curious facts which might make one worry about the received view that dreams are experiences that take place during sleep.

- Many people claim never to remember dreaming. Some think they don't dream at all.
- Many people claim to remember that they have dreamed, but confess to no ability to recall what they dreamed about.
- Among those who claim to remember their dreams there are no comforting modes of confirming the reports since dream experiences (if there are such things) are completely private. It is unclear in the case of alleged dream experiences that or how we could gain the confidence about what was actually experienced during sleep similar, say, to the sort of confidence an optometrist has about the experiences of a person reading an eye chart in her office.

Imagine that a man awakes from sleep as in Figure 6.1 and sincerely reports, "I dreamed of Jeannie with the light brown hair." How can we know that he in fact dreamed of Jeannie, as opposed to an armadillo, or even nothing at all?

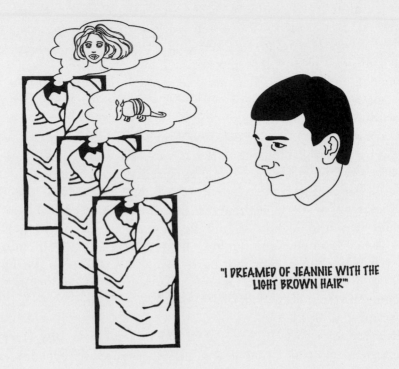

"I DREAMED OF JEANNIE WITH THE LIGHT BROWN HAIR"

Figure 6.1 When I report a dream, am I accurately reporting a conscious episode that happened while I was sleeping, am I misreporting such an event, or could it be that there was no such event at all?

Is the "Received View" Testable?

As I mentioned earlier, REM sleep was discovered by Aserinsky and Kleitman in 1953, the same year Watson and Crick discovered the double helix structure of DNA. Norman Malcolm's book *Dreaming* was completed in 1958 in the early years of scientific dream research. Malcolm was influenced by a certain brand of positivism, one guided by a very strong verification principle. Hilary Putnam writes: "Malcolm's is the sharpest statement of Verificationism in the 1950's . . . [i]n Malcolm's view it is impossible to refer to a thing (or kind of thing) if in no case do we have better than *indications* of its presence or absence."

Malcolm's argument proceeds as follows:

1. "The received view" is that dreams are experiences that take place while we are asleep.

2. Our only evidence that this is so comes from reports awake people give.
3. An awake report gives at most an *indication* that a dream occurred during sleep.
4. It follows according to the principle of verification, which says that it is impossible to refer to a thing (or kind of thing) if in no case do we have better than *indications* of its presence or absence, that we are not referring to anything, that is, we are speaking senselessly, or unintelligibly when we speak of dreams as experiences that occur during sleep.[6]

One plausible response to this argument is to point out that we have more *indications* than just morning stories. For example, there are correlations of REM-period durations with dreams of roughly the right length. There are reports of greater visual imagery during periods of REM than during NREM. Furthermore, in the forty-five years of research since the discovery of REM, we have developed many imaging techniques that allow us to correlate reports of visual or auditory experiences with observations of visual or auditory processing areas. This can be done for awake subjects or for asleep subjects who are then awakened when, for example, visual areas light up to see if they report having just had visual experiences.[7]

Malcolm sees this response coming and points out that all such data will ever add up to—imagine the correlations piling up endlessly as high as Everest—are additional *indications*. And indications as numerous as all the tea in China or piled as high as Everest do not warrant sensibly referring to dreams as experiences that take place while we are asleep.

The quick way out of this second dream problem involves locating the error in an impossible demand for more than *indications*. This problem was understood by the earliest positivists. What the positivists called "protocol sentences," sentences like "I see red, here, now," were attempts to speak the truth while depending as little as possible on memory. But still, since there is a time lag between the presentation of a red stimulus, the experience of red, and the report of "seeing red, here, now," there is still *some* dependence on memory. Thus running Malcolm's criterion for distinguishing sense from nonsense on a virtually simultaneous sensory report would result in saying that the report of seeing red was simply an *indication* of seeing red and since no indication can secure reference to an experience of red, we are speaking unintelligibly, talking nonsensically, when we take a report of seeing red to refer to an experience of seeing red. It looks as if every report is merely an *indication* of an experience and thus that there is no possible evidence that there are any experiences, any mental events at all! In philosophy—at least the way I do it—when one gets a result like this, one gets rid of the criterion that yielded the result.

Once we get rid of the verification criterion as formulated, the second dream problem begins to yield in exactly the way discussed earlier. There is reasonable and growing inductive support, theoretical consilience, coming from phenomenological reports, physiological studies, and neurobiological data of both awake and asleep subjects, that experiences are occurring during sleep.

The fact that the best explanation for the morning stories is that people had certain experiences while asleep does not imply much at all about the accuracy of the reports, whether, that is, such reports are accurate as representations of the preceding experiences. But even here one can see windows of opportunity. Suppose, for example, that we come to think that we have fairly well isolated the neural activity that typically accompanies seeing a red ball in an awake person. Then suppose the same activity is seen in the brain of a sleeping person, who then reports a dream in which a red ball appears. This sort of consilience would justifiably increase our confidence that in addition to dreams being experiences we have while sleeping, we sometimes accurately remember their content. There is also the possibility that reports of lucid dreams might be set more convincingly within a theory that lends more than only subjective support to the claim that lucid dream reports are reports of lucid dream experiences. There is evidence from research by Stephen LaBerge, a psychologist at Stanford, that we can learn to be lucid dreamers and can also learn to give reports of lucid dreams while they are occurring, by raising an index finger, for example.

It is this sort of evidence, not Malcolm's impossible evidence, that Daniel Dennett was asking for when he declared in 1976 that the question of whether dreams are experiences that take place during sleep is open, pending the development of a well-confirmed theory of dreams. My claim is that we now possess enough of a well-confirmed theory of dreams to be confident, if not absolutely positive, that the received view of dreams is true.

So goes the second dream problem, and it goes in roughly the same way the first dream problem went. Skeptical doubts wane—sometimes they can be abandoned altogether—"when," as Descartes puts it, " after having called upon all my senses, my memory, and my understanding, nothing is brought forth by any one of them that is repugnant to what is set forth by the others."

Sinful Dreams

We come finally to the third dream problem. In his *Confessions*, Augustine recalls registering this complaint with God about his dreams after his transformation, in his early thirties, from philanderer to ascetic. The quote is worth repeating:

> You commanded me not to commit fornication. . . . But when I dream [thoughts of fornication] not only give me pleasure but are very much like acquiescence to the act. . . . Yet the difference between waking and sleeping is so great [that] I return to a clear conscience when I wake and realize that, because of this difference, I am not responsible for the act, although I am sorry that by some means or other it happened in me.

It is important to stress that the issue of whether one can express oneself morally or immorally in dreams is not just a quirky idea that surfaced among Christians. There was a schism among early Buddhist sects in the fifth century C.E. over whether nocturnal emissions displayed a lack of moral self-control. And to this day, the Cunas Indians, living on islands off the coast of Panama, believe that when dreams reveal unworthy desires, the dreamer must work to rid himself of these desires. Furthermore, this is not just private work at moral improvement. If a person dreams four times of sex with an individual to whom he or she is not married, the person is obliged to confess to a dream doctor, who assists the dreamer in the project of gaining release from the inappropriate desire (interestingly, by eye-cleansing), but who also informs the object of sexual desire to exercise caution in the presence of the dreamer.

In any case, Augustine proposed a theory for how dreams might contain sinful content (in his case thoughts of fornication) without being sins. His proposal, in modern terms, is that dreams are happenings, not actions. Whereas one is responsible for what one does or chooses to think about, one is not responsible for thoughts that involuntarily occur in one's mind.[8] This is, I think, the received view regarding the third dream problem, but, like the received view on the first two dream problems, it could be wrong.

One way, and a different way from Augustine's, to solve or dissolve the problem would be to claim that only behavior, real actions in the world, can count as immoral. According to this idea, mental episodes occur only in the head and thus are not subject to moral evaluation. On this view, the issue would not turn on whether some thought, say murdering my business partner, just popped into my head involuntarily or was deliberately conjured up and pleasurably entertained by me, so long as I didn't commit the murder.

The advantage of this view is that it avoids excessive moralism. A disadvantage is that extending immunity from moral evaluation to all mental states, even all the passions, may be too lax.

Take the feelings of envy and avarice that might lead to thoughts of killing my business partner. I should presumably work to modify myself so as to be less prone to the envy and avarice that cause these thoughts to occur to me. Why? First, because it will be better for me; I will gain peace of mind and have as it were an improved character. Second, no matter how powerful we think the will is when it comes to stopping thoughts, passions, or emotions from being acted out, everyone thinks, and thinks truly, that there is some probabilistic relation between wanting powerfully to do something and doing it.

So, the view that we cannot be immoral in dreams could be wrong if:

- dreams are (sometimes) actions; that is, if dreams are sometimes voluntary mental acts;
- no mental states, be they voluntary or involuntary, are altogether immune from moral evaluation;
- dreams express aspects of my personality or character that I helped form or could have worked to dissolve, moderate, or otherwise transform, and for whose nature I thereby am somewhat responsible.

I discuss each possibility as it pertains to the third dream problem. First, could a dream be voluntary? The answer is "yes." It is common to attempt to continue an unfinished good dream or discontinue a bad dream from which one is awakened. Sometimes the effort pays off; sometimes it doesn't. I once woke up in the middle of a very good dream involving Marilyn Monroe. I succeeded in returning to the aborted dream, as I wished. I will not say what happened. But

I was pleased. This dream has two relevant properties: It involved some voluntary effort, and it involved effort to commit notional adultery. Is that bad? I'm not sure.[9]

This Marilyn Monroe dream involved antecedent effort to have it go, or continue to go, in a certain direction. Work on lucid dreaming suggests not only that certain people can antecedently plan their dreams, but can actually work on plot revisions as the dream occurs, as the action unfolds. If this is true, then the dreams of lucid dreamers are robustly voluntary.

It looks, therefore, as if some dreams have voluntary components. If voluntariness is a mark of moral accountability or justifies moral evaluation, then it appears that the answer to the third dream problem is "yes, we can be immoral in dreams."

Second, could it be that no mental states, be they voluntary or involuntary, are immune from moral assessment? Yes. The Yale University philosopher Robert Adams claims that "the thesis that we are ethically accountable only for our voluntary actions and omissions must be rejected. There are involuntary sins." Adams argues that there are "morally objectionable states of mind," hatred, jealousy, misanthropic feelings, pride, and the like. Suppose I am angry out of all proportion with you, but refrain from hurting you. My self-restraint is good; my anger, however, remains a moral fault. Adams writes:

> Our desires and emotions, though not voluntary, are responses of ours, and affect the moral significance of our lives, not only by influencing our voluntary actions, but also just by being what they are, and by manifesting themselves involuntarily. Who we are morally depends on a complex and incompletely integrated fabric that includes desires and feelings as well as deliberations and choices.

The general view is that even if states of mind are not directly under voluntary control, they are often indirectly controllable. For example, meditative work, work at self-examination and at self-transformation, can yield changes in how we feel and think, and in how we experience ourselves and the world.

The application to dreams is straightforward. If one has dreams in which one entertains and takes pleasure in thoughts one ought not to want to have, then one should work to change what one dreams about.

There is of course one big complication with this idea. Namely, if the Freudian view is right, then it is good that I dream about sex and aggression, relish cruelty, break promises, and tell lies in dreams since otherwise I would do these things in the world or, if I didn't do them in the world, would suffer neuroses and personal and moral disequilibrium. If all my dreams were sweet ones, I might be awful or, if not awful, awfully messed up. If, and it is a big if, the Freudian view is correct we might want to grant dreams a special immunity from moral evaluation or from being good targets for transformative work.

Another possibility is that the Freudian view is largely false but that sometimes working out certain wishes, say homicidal ones, in the head is a good way of releasing or working through the issues that produce such impulses. If this is true, and if there is no other better way to work out such issues, then having these fantasies is better than any alternative. Sad, but true. Bad, but true.

Under these and related scenarios, the idea of involuntary sins retains its coherence and thereby keeps open the possibility that we can be immoral in dreams. Even the view that holds that impure dreams are inevitable, possibly necessary for mental health, and not worth censoring, can hold that such dreams involve entertaining and taking pleasure in bad things, and thus are immoral.

The third issue is related to the second: If dreams express aspects of my personality or character that I helped form or could have worked to transform, then don't I bear some responsibility for my dreams? I think the answer is "yes." Some dreams are highly self-expressive, possibly even identity constituting. If what is expressed is ugly, or reveals problems I am not dealing honestly with, or speaks of personal relations that I allow to remain in disrepair, they reveal something about me, about my identity and my life. And thus they are grist for the mill of self-examination, self-transformation, and for locating where in my character or circumstances I am making a contribution to the state of things as revealed in my dreams.

Some dreams are mostly noise created by work the brain does on the night shift. But even these noisy dreams activate one's own memories, things that are on one's mind. The brain may fail utterly to put the noise into a richly revealing narrative. Still, seeing what is on one's mind, if only bits and snatches, especially if certain images, feelings, thoughts, or memories appear with any regularity, may warrant attention to who one is, what one has been like and done, and what in one's character is worth reshaping.

It is time to stop. The answer to the third dream problem, Can I be immoral in dreams?, is not "no"; it is "maybe" or "yes."

Notice that all three philosophical problems have more or less affirmative answers. We can distinguish dreams from wakefulness reliably. Dreams are experiences we have during sleep. And we can be immoral in dreams. Why do I give these answers? Philosophy and science tell me so.

Notes

1. Many would add this fourth problem to the list: Whether my self disappears when I go to sleep. If personal identity or selfhood is necessarily linked to continuity of consciousness, and if sleep involves periods of unconsciousness, the answer seems to be yes. I think that our self never disappears while we are alive, and have suggested some reasons why throughout the book. But I'll leave a more complete discussion of this fourth classical dream problem to another time and place. I gave a version of this chapter as the Royal Irish Academy Lecture in Dublin in the summer of 1998.

2. My actual diary entry reads "to seek no knowledge other than that which could be found in myself or in the great book of the world."

3. Indeed, dreams are so powerful a tool for getting skeptical doubt going that they might have alone been sufficient to get Descartes to the *cogito* had it not been for the fact that Descartes notices, and notices correctly, I think, that whereas natural laws are violated all the time in dreams, mathematical truths aren't. There are dreams in which I am the lead goose in a flock of migrating geese, but there are no dreams in which $2+2=5$, or the circle is squared, or in which the Pythagorean theorem is false. My own dream phenomenology as well as spot checks among dream researchers indicate that Descartes was right about the immunity of mathematical judgments to dreams' mayhem.

4. Although I won't go into it here, a naturalist will need to give some account of how natural and cultural evolution equip him with reliable knowledge yielding mechanisms and principles and thereby do something like the work God does for Descartes.

5. Actually, I may be cheating a bit here by reading the claim about vivacity into Descartes. David Hume famously makes this point by arguing that vivacity decreases in some relation to the immediacy/recency of a stimulus's presentation, so perhaps I am reading Descartes through that lens. But in support of the truth of the idea that we use degree of vivacity to tell dreams from reality (whether the attribution of the germ of

this idea goes to Descartes or Hume), the neuropsychologist Mark Solms hypothesizes that the patients who have trouble making the dream-reality distinction have dreams that are too vivid.

6. Malcolm is clear, and correct, to point out that his view would do no harm to the practice of psychoanalytic dream interpretation since insofar as this (these) practice(s) make sense, they proceed exclusively from morning stories and free association to these stories in the company of the analyst.

7. In saying this sort of experiment can be done, I don't mean to imply that it has been done. I am not sure, one way or the other.

8. Descartes took something like this tactic in discussing the passions, states such as wonder, love, hatred, desire, joy, and sadness. The experience of excessive anger is not something for which I can be judged immoral. I am passive with respect to its overcoming me. However, if I act on this anger that is an altogether different matter, since I can control where a passion takes me.

9. According to Gareth Matthews, this would be a sinful dream for Augustine. The first appearances of Marilyn just happened to me. But then I consented to these appearances, worked to make them continue, and was pleased at the content of my dream and my success in bringing it to completion.

Here Comes the Sun

I dreamed towards break of day,
The cold brown spray in my nostril.
But she that beside me lay
Had watched in bitterer sleep
The marvellous stag of Arthur,
That lofty white stag, leap
From mountain steep to steep.

—*William Butler Yeats, "Towards Break of Day"*

I CLOSE WITH THREE BRIEF MEDI-
tations, comments really, on matters of importance that I have mentioned several times. First, there is the issue of dreams and creativity;
then the issue of what can be salvaged from psychoanalysis if my theory of dreams is on the right track; and finally the question of the
implications of what I have said in these pages for questions about
the nature, function, and evolution of the conscious mind. We have
been together for a long time now, so I'll be brief.

Creativity in Dreams

Many people have told me that they are inspired by dreams. This is
not surprising in itself, since dreaming is a kind of thinking and certain thoughts, at least, are inspiring. But then it is added that many
of the greatest poems, novels, and paintings were first hatched in
dreams. This is not entirely false if the point is that we produce or
develop certain ideas in our sleep which we then take back into the
world and do something with by the light of day. Here is a nonartistic
example of what I have in mind.

In July of 1998, I had a dream, probably an NREM dream, in which I rehearsed the actual events that occurred at a conference the previous week. A professional colleague arrived in Squaw Valley, California, for a conference that we both were attending and received the news that his ninety-one-year-old mother had died. We had lunch, at which time he told me of his loss and explained that he needed to leave for Seattle in a couple of hours. In my dream, several of the conferees, myself included, argued over who should drive our friend to the airport in Reno in the Volkswagen bug we somehow had available to us. Except for the part about taking him to the airport and there being a Volkswagen bug, the rest of the dream was pretty much a reenactment of the events as they had occurred.

But I awoke from this dream in a state different from the one I was in when I had finished the actual lunch with my motherless colleague. I had, at lunch, sincerely expressed my condolences. But it was only after the dream reenacting the lunch that I could really feel myself feeling things—feeling sorrow and not just sorry for my friend, and experiencing the painful emotions that well up when I allow myself to reexperience, and not deflect, the memories of the losses of loved ones of my own. So I awoke from this dream inspired, prepared to think and feel things that I probably would not have been so open to think and feel had my limbic system and my memory not been allowed the space of free play that dreams permit. Furthermore, I think I was personally enriched by having this dream, and by taking it as well as the thoughts and feelings it evoked into waking life with me.

The trouble is that those who insist that dreams are inspiring, that they are wellsprings for creative forces, usually have more in mind than this fairly commonplace way dreams can inspire us, deepen us emotionally and enhance self-understanding. They think that many, possibly most, great thoughts are fully hatched in dreams. Some even think that creativity is *the* function of dreams, *the* reason dreams exist.

I try to be as polite as I can be to friends, students, and acquaintances who try this line on me. I have taken to asking for examples. The top two examples in my experience are both literary. There is Samuel Taylor Coleridge's dream in which the poem "Kubla Khan" came to him, and Mary Shelley's production of what came to be, once she found time to write it down, the famous novel *Frankenstein*.

Now for the facts. First, regarding Coleridge, he writes in his "Preliminary Note" to the poem that he "continued for about three hours in a profound sleep . . . during which time I had the most vivid confidence, that I could not have composed less than from two to three hundred lines. . . . On awakening I . . . instantly and eagerly wrote down the lines that are here preserved. At this moment I was unfortunately called out by a person on business from Porlock."

We know from his notebooks and from his poems that Coleridge largely suffered his dreams. He was a victim of nightmares from his youth and abused opium to ward off bad dreams and provide himself with peaceful sleep (opium, in case you wonder, is not good for this). In Part V of "The Rime of the Ancient Mariner," Coleridge writes of the sort of dream he must have wished for, but rarely had. At this point in the poem, many days have passed in which there is: "Water, water everywhere, / Nor any drop to drink" and "The very deep did rot: O Christ! / That ever this should be! / Yea slimy things did crawl with legs / Upon the slimy sea." Then Part V begins this way:

> 'O sleep! it is a gentle thing,
> Beloved from pole to pole!
> To Mary Queen the praise be given!
> She sent the gentle sleep from Heaven,
> That slid into my soul.
>
> The silly buckets on the deck,
> That had so long remain'd
> I dreamt that they were filled with dew;
> And when I awoke it rained.

So there is no question that Coleridge had a rich, often painful, dream life; he understood the relief that pleasant dreams can bring; and he rightly understood that dreams were often self-expressive and worth the project of interpretation. Still, what about "Kubla Kahn"? Was it really composed in a dream on one night? The actual poem is fifty-four lines long. According to Coleridge, the dreamed poem was two to three hundred lines long. We would have had the whole poem had Coleridge not been interrupted by the person calling him "out on business."

It is wonderful to imagine this happening—a great poem of several hundred lines full born in a three-hour dream. But did it happen that way? Could it have happened that way? No. First, there is no evidence that any continuous dream lasts three hours. Second, the

poem we have is pretty perfect. It is hard to imagine a better beginning than

> In Xanadu did Kubla Kahn
> A stately pleasure-dome decree:
> Where Alph, the sacred river, ran
> Through caverns measureless to man
> Down to a sunless sea.

And a better ending than

> Weave a circle round him thrice,
> And close your eyes with holy dread,
> For he on honey-dew hath fed,
> And drunk the milk of Paradise.

If Coleridge had another hundred fifty to two hundred fifty lines in
him, we are lucky that he was interrupted on business. Third,
Coleridge in commenting on the dream in the "Preliminary Note" to
the poem says this immediately after he writes that he composed a
poem of two to three hundred lines: "if that indeed can be called
composition in which all the images rose up before him as *things.*"
This indicates that Coleridge himself had doubts that he had actually composed the lines of a poem in his dream, as opposed to having
dreamed about the scene eventually depicted in the poem. Fourth,
and most tellingly, there exist many earlier versions of the poem in
Coleridge's own pen. Coleridge could not have conceived and given
birth to "Kubla Kahn" on the night of the dream, since the poem was
already in progress. The dream might have been about the poem,
and it may have inspired Coleridge to finish it. But it is simply false
that the poem came to him in the dream. So much for the first case.

What about Mary Shelley and *Frankenstein?* The novel was originally published in 1818 when Mary Shelley was nineteen years old. In
the revised 1831 edition, the author provides a preface in which she
recounts the origins of the novel in a dream. In the dream, she perceives with "acute mental vision—the pale student of unhallowed arts
kneeling beside the man he had put together," the "hideous corpse"
who comes to life, stirring from its inanimate state "with an uneasy
half-vital motion," eventually "intruding on its maker . . . looking on
him with yellow, watery, but speculative eyes."

There is no question that this dream, which Mary Shelley wrote down immediately upon awakening contains the thematic germ for the novel she eventually produced. But it hardly constitutes the novel. She did not wake up with even the whole plot fully formed in her head.

In fact, the circumstances of the dream are telling. Mary Shelley spent the evening of the night in which the dream occurred conversing with Lord Byron, a doctor friend, and her lover, Percy Bysshe Shelley. At the time, she was still Mary Wollstonecraft Godwin, since despite her having eloped with the still married Percy when she was sixteen, and having had two children with him, they did not marry until his wife Harriet committed suicide four months after Mary began writing *Frankenstein*. In any case, on the fateful evening, the "noble author" Lord Byron proposed that each "write a ghost story." The assembled group agreed and retired to bed, and Mary dreamed the dream she reported in the 1831 preface, realizing upon awakening that it could be used to meet Byron's challenge. She began composing the novel immediately thereafter in June of 1816, completing in sometime in 1817 and publishing it in 1818.

Nothing more needs to be said, I take it, to dissolve any notion that *Frankenstein* sprang fully formed from Mary Shelley's dream. The dream played a role of course in the complex mix that included being to the manner born, incredibly well educated, spending time with other great minds (including her parents), and having a desire to meet Byron's challenge.

I want to be clear that nothing I have said involves denying that dreams can be sources of inspiration. Indeed, I take it that dreams were exactly that in both the Coleridge and Shelley cases. I simply want to deny the strong, and surprisingly widely held view, that dreams are a unique and privileged place where creative juices flow. Dreaming is part of living and as such contributes in varied and sundry ways to who we are, what we do, and what we make. But making art takes work, invariably work by the light of day.

One final point: The case for mathematical, scientific, or philosophical insight arising fully formed in dreams is even less plausible than it is for the arts, and this for the simple reason that these forms of thinking despite often involving beautiful insight, also require logical rigor, something dreams are noticeably lacking in. The most famous alleged example of hatching a scientific idea, indeed of great scientific insight, is that of August Kekule's discovery of the structure of the benzene molecule in 1854. The facts, as reported by Kekule, are these. He dozed off in a chair by his fireplace and "dreamed" of atoms flitting before his eyes; the atoms then formed themselves into a twisted snakelike structure with one snake taking hold of its own tail and then whirling in a circular fashion. He awoke "as if by a flash of lightning."

There are four points. First, the chemical structure of benzene was already known to be C_6H_6, what was not known was its shape and the exact configuration of the carbon and hydrogen atoms. Second, Kekule had been working on this problem for many years, including on the very day he dozed off. Third, Kekule reports that after he came to he set to work out the details of his visual hallucination: "Let us dream gentleman, but let us also beware publishing our dreams until they have been examined by the wakened mind." Fourth, it is unusual to doze off in a chair and enter REM sleep. It seems more likely that Kekule was going to sleep, but not quite asleep, and thus not even in NREM sleep, and thus that the snake image was a hypno-gogic hallucination of the sort common when one is falling asleep but not quite yet asleep. In any case, the evidence hardly supports the claim that the benzene problem was solved in a dream.

I conclude that in dreams we often think about what we are already thinking about. But dreams are hardly a reliable or regular source of artistry or of scientific discovery.

Freud, Again

The question inevitably returns: What of the work on dreams of Sigmund Freud? Don't we already have a first-rate theory of the nature and function of dreams? Referring specifically to his theory of dreams, published in 1899/1900 as *The Interpretation of Dreams*, Freud wrote, "insight such as this comes only once in a lifetime," and he claimed that dreams were "the royal road to the unconscious mind." Why do we need a new theory when we have Freud's theory? Let me begin my reply with an example, one that I think neatly identifies some of the main reasons to prefer my theory of dreams to Freud's.

I began the book with a dream I had in 1955 when I was five years old in which I was chased by wolves. Call me "the wolf boy." One of Freud's most famous patients was "the wolf man." The wolf man suffered from a severe anxiety disorder, animal phobia, and religious obsession. The key to his problems, according to Freud, was an overwhelming fear of his father, represented in this dream by wolves. The wolf man was four years old at the time of this dream.

> *I dreamt that it was night and that I was lying in my bed. (My bed stood with its foot towards the window; in front of the window there was a row of old walnut trees. I know it was winter when I had the dream, and night-time.) Suddenly the window opened of its own accord, and I was terrified to see that some white wolves were sitting on the big walnut tree in front of the window. There were six or seven of them. The wolves were quite white, and looked more like foxes or sheep-dogs, for they had big tails like foxes and they had their ears pricked like dogs when they pay attention to something. In great terror, evidently of being eaten up by the wolves, I screamed* and woke up.

Freud interprets this dream as follows. The wolf man, just like me, the wolf boy, had been exposed to the usual fairy tales that teach that wolves are animals to be feared (indeed, his older sister had done her best to scare him witless with these tales). The theory of dream symbolism implies, however, that wolves in dreams do not stand for wolves. They stand for some other creature to be feared, in this case the wolf man's father. Why fear one's father? Well, one's father is powerful and can harm you. If he had reason to think you were a sexual rival for your mother (his wife) he could, for example, castrate you. Furthermore, severe neuroses and very memorable dreams are linked to each other in that long remembered dreams typically express the cause of the neurosis which typically has its source in "a real occurrence—dating from an early period."

The key to Freud's interpretation of this dream had to do with certain biographical facts or surmises. As a baby (one and one-half years old), the wolf man suffered malaria. One afternoon he awoke with fever and was brought to his parents' bed to sleep. There he observed his parents having intercourse three times, with his father entering his mother from behind on each occasion. The evidence for this interpretation, including the exact number of penetrations, was established by the wolf man's free associations in light of the assumptions that dreams have hidden meaning, express a wish (in this case for mother's sexual affection), and relate to real life occurrences. There is also the assumption that a one-and-one-half-year-old child could perceive and comprehend what his parents were doing, so that the events could be symbolically rerepresented in a dream several years later.

Implausibility abounds here. First, starting with the last assumption, experimental work in child development casts doubt on the idea that a one-and-one-half-year-old child could perceive, assess, and store an episode such as the one the wolf man allegedly remembers. Second, it is standard in science to seek the simplest possible explanation compatible with the evidence. This rule can be overridden when there are strong theoretical reasons to do so. But each theoretical strand used by Freud to motivate his nonsimple explanation—the theory of symbolism, the latent-manifest content distinction, the postulation of unconscious psychic causes for all neuroses, the theory of universal sexual rivalry between children and their same sex parent for the opposite sex parent—have not, despite being on the table for over a century, been remotely vindicated.

It is not as if Freud's theory of dreams has been disproved—indeed, it is not clear that his theory makes scientifically testable claims. Freud's theory of dreams and dream interpretation has simply not proved to be a productive and progressive theory of dreams and dream interpretation. My claim is that the rival theory I have proposed here is testable and already shown signs of being progressive, productive, plausible, and subject to refinement in accordance with the canons of science.

According to the neurophilosophical view I recommend, most dreams do not express wishes. Most dreams do not conceal their content. Most dreams do not involve sex or aggression, neither on the surface nor deep-down inside, neither manifestly nor latently. Most dreams do not have deep meaning—not sexual or aggressive deep meaning, nor even deep spiritual meaning. Dreams sometimes don't mean much of anything, and they certainly don't, as a matter of policy, mean any one kind of thing. It is predictable from the fact that dreams originate in chaotic activity in the brain stem that most are "bungled," as Nietzsche put it, or that "things fall apart" because "the center cannot hold," as Yeats put it. Indeed, sometimes a thematic center cannot even be found or, if found, cannot be maintained in the internal chaos in which dreams are hatched.

However, for interesting psychobiological reasons, dreams do sometimes, possibly often, involve self-expression, sometimes expression of wishes, hopes, fears, and anxieties that are kept at bay during the day. The brain areas responsible for keeping such thoughts at bay, for keeping one's defenses up, for assisting in the project of keeping one's eye on practical success are simply less active during dreaming sleep than they are during wakefulness.

Freud was certainly right that we sometimes, possibly often, defend ourselves and thereby preserve the integrity of, and the spin on, the narratives we tell ourselves and others by mechanisms akin to repression and suppression. The way the brain works during sleep involves relatively greater activation of emotional areas and relatively less activation of areas responsible for attention, planning, and management of the ordinary tasks of living than it does while awake. So it is true that the cognitive mechanisms we use to screen off and censor thoughts that might get in the way of attending to matters at hand are turned off, or at least turned down, while we are asleep. In this way, dreams are not only self-expressive, but self-revealing. But this is not the only reason dreams are self-revealing. Even more important than the fact that thought runs free and defenses are down during sleep is the fact that the thoughts, images, and memories activated while we are asleep are *our* thoughts, images, and memories, and they are given narrative shape by *us* as we sleep. Still, this structure is typically narratively degraded, due again to the neurobiological facts about how dreams are produced.

The Evolution of Consciousness

The brain is a massively parallel information processing system that operates to guide the body that houses it to successfully negotiate reality. It is not clear why the executive system in the brain that tracks reality and guides action is conscious as opposed to unconscious, as are, for example, the executive systems in computers. But both conscious and unconscious systems do share this important feature: Normally, only the information the system needs to know, only the information that the system needs to successfully track reality and guide action, becomes positioned to yield knowledge and guide action. A serial, streamlike, one-thing-at-a-time information processing system seems to be an excellent solution strategy (but probably not the only strategy) for tracking reality and for guiding action in both conscious and nonconscious systems, and this despite the fact that down below what Dennett calls a "parallel pandemonium" is taking place.

Mother Nature did, in fact, settle on the solution strategy of building a conscious serial processing system, rather than a nonconscious one for most medium- to large-sized earthly animals. It will be good to have better theories of why Nature settled on conscious information processing as her favored solution strategy. One plausible suggestion is that a general purpose conscious information-processing system is a better solution strategy than a nonconscious one (let alone a conscious or nonconscious pandemonium model where every bit of information processed sees "the light of day") for enabling mobile creatures with multiple modes of sensory pickup that live in changing environment to be reproductively successful.

It seems pretty clear that consciousness is adaptive. This does not settle by itself the question of whether consciousness is an adaptation. But it seems likely that it is an adaptation, in particular, that there were selection pressures operating over evolutionary time to build and refine a system that, at a minimum, would bring the five senses into a coordinated interplay that would lead to the sort of reality tracking and action guidance that would confer the capacities needed for reproductive success. Consciousness allows us to track external reality as well as our own mental states; it enables us to recall and assess past behavior, to anticipate what lies ahead, to plan, and to coordinate thought and action. Conscious creatures are reproductively successful and appear to be so—at least to some significant degree—in virtue of being guided by consciousness.

But what about dream consciousness? Earlier I discussed an argument that went like this: Consciousness is an adaptation. Dreaming is a type of consciousness. Therefore, dream consciousness is an adaptation.

It will be useful to explain why the argument is fallacious in a slightly different way than I did earlier. Consider this analogy: The possession of hard bones, a rigid skeletal structure, is an adaptation. The off-white color of bones is a feature of our skeletal structure. Therefore, the color of bones is an adaptation.

The arguments have the same form and fall prey to the same fallacy, a version of what logicians call a fallacy of composition. Parts do not necessarily have the properties of wholes, nor vice versa. Sports teams can be excellent while lacking even one excellent player. Princeton basketball teams are typically like this. Other teams have excellent players but are not excellent themselves—the Red Sox, for example. Similarly, not all realizations of some capacity possess all the properties of the capacity they depend on. The capacities to walk and to run are adaptations, but my capacity to tango, despite its being in some sense a type of walking and running is not an adaptation.

The off-white color of bones is a by-product of living in a calcium rich environment, but Mother Nature cared not one bit about the color of bones. Similarly, dream consciousness is a type of consciousness, but Mother Nature cared not one bit about selecting for it. Dreaming is what you get from a conscious system designed to serve the functions consciousness serves while we are awake and from a system that autostimulates itself in order to perform the functions that sleep and sleep-cycling were selected for. Awake consciousness is an adaptation, as are sleep and sleep-cycling. But dream consciousness is not, and this despite the fact that dreaming is realized by and in a brain designed to be conscious.

The upshot is this. Philosophers, psychologists, cognitive neuroscientists, psychiatrists, and evolutionary biologists need to stop assuming that every mental capacity we possess, even universal ones, must have an adaptationist explanation. Dreams are universal. But dreaming is not an adaptation.

The final point is that the denial that dream consciousness is an adaptation, the denial that dreaming was selected for because it served some fitness-enhancing role, is not to demean dreams. Dreams, I have insisted, are not just noise. Some dreams are self-expressive and worth attention in the project of gaining, enhancing, and refining self-knowledge. We are dreaming souls. And the brain is the seat of our soul whether we are asleep or awake.

This is as good a place as any to stop. It leaves us as we are—as complex conscious animals with mutifarious mental capacities, some of which Mother Nature directly selected for, some of which are products of cultural invention, and some of which just come for free. This is not bad news: Some of the best things in life are free.

Selected Bibliography

Books

Allen, Colin, Marc Bekoff, and George Lauder, eds. *Nature's Purposes: Analyses of Function and Design in Biology*. Cambridge, Mass.: MIT Press, 1998.

Barkow, Jerome H., Leda Cosmides, and John Tooby. *The Adapted Mind: Evolutionary Psychology and the Generation of Culture*. New York: Oxford University Press, 1992.

Brandon, Robert. *Adaptation and Environment*. Princeton: Princeton University Press, 1990.

Churchland, Patricia Smith. *Neurophilosophy: Toward a Unified Science of the Mind/Brain*. Cambridge, Mass.: MIT Press, 1986.

Churchland, Paul M. *The Engine of Reason, the Seat of the Soul: A Philosophical Journey into the Brain*. Cambridge, Mass.: MIT Press, 1995.

Cole, John R. *The Olympian Dreams and Youthful Rebellion of René Descartes*. Chicago: University of Illinois Press, 1992.

Conze, Edward. *Buddhism: Its Essence and Development*. 3rd ed. Oxford: Bruno Cassirer, 1957.

Cottingham, John. *Descartes*. Cambridge, Mass.: Blackwell, 1986.

Damasio, Antonio R. *Descartes' Error: Emotion, Reason, and the Human Brain*. New York: G. P. Putnam's Sons, 1994.

Dement, William C. *Some Must Watch While Some Must Sleep: Exploring the World of Sleep*. New York: W. W. Norton, 1972.

Dennett, Daniel C. *Consciousness Explained*. Boston: Little, Brown, 1991.

———. *Darwin's Dangerous Idea: Evolution and the Meanings of Life*. New York: Simon & Schuster, 1995.

Descartes, René. *Discourse on Method and Meditations on First Philosophy*. Trans. Donald A. Cress. Indianapolis: Hackett Publishing Co., 1980.

Finger, Stanley. *Origins of Neuroscience: A History of Explorations into Brain Function*. New York: Oxford University Press, 1994.

Freud, Sigmund. *The Interpretation of Dreams*. Trans. and ed. James Strachey. New York: Basic Books, 1965.

——. *Introductory Lectures on Psychoanalysis.* Trans. and ed. James Strachey. New York: W. W. Norton, 1966.

——. *Three Case Histories.* Ed. Philip Rieff. New York: Macmillan, 1963.

Hobson, J. Allan. *The Chemistry of Conscious States: Toward a Unified Model of the Brain and the Mind.* Boston: Little, Brown, 1994.

——. *The Dreaming Brain.* New York: Basic Books, 1988.

——. *Sleep.* New York: Scientific American Library, 1989.

Huxley, T. H. *Methods and Results.* New York: Appleton Co., 1910.

Keller, Evelyn Fox, and Elisabeth A. Lloyd, eds. *Keywords in Evolutionary Biology.* Cambridge, Mass.: Harvard University Press, 1992.

Kitcher, Patricia. *Freud's Dream: A Complete Interdisciplinary Science of Mind.* Cambridge, Mass.: MIT Press, 1992.

Lavie, Peretz. *The Enchanted World of Sleep.* Trans. Anthony Berris. New Haven: Yale University Press, 1996.

LeDoux, Joseph E. *The Emotional Brain.* New York: Simon & Schuster, 1996.

MacIntyre, A. C. *The Unconscious: A Conceptual Analysis.* London: Routledge & Kegan Paul, 1958.

Malcolm, Norman. *Dreaming.* London: Routledge & Kegan Paul, 1959.

Pinker, Steven. *The Language Instinct.* New York: William Morrow, 1994.

Solms, Mark. *The Neuropsychology of Dreams: A Clinico-Anatomical Study.* Mahwah, N. J.: L. Erlbaum Associates, 1997.

Sulloway, Frank J. *Freud, Biologist of the Mind: Beyond the Psychoanalytic Legend.* New York: Basic Books, 1979.

Van de Castle, Robert L. *Our Dreaming Mind.* New York: Random House, 1994.

Williams, George C. *Adaptation and Natural Selection: A Critique of Some Current Evolutionary Thought.* Princeton: Princeton University Press, 1966.

Wilson, Margaret Dauler. *Descartes.* New York: Routledge, 1978.

Articles

Adams, Robert Merrihew. "Involuntary Sins." *Philosophical Review* 94, no. 1 (1985): 3–31.

Adolphs, Ralph, Hanna Damasio, and Antonio R. Damasio. "Cortical Systems for the Recognition of Emotion in Facial Expressions." *Journal of Neuroscience* 16, no. 23 (1996): 7678–87.

Antrobus, John. "Cortical Hemisphere Asymmetry and Sleep Mentation." *Psychological Review* 94, no. 3 (1987): 359–68.

——. "Dreaming: Cognitive Processes During Cortical Activation and High Afferent Thresholds." *Psychological Review* 98, no. 1 (1991): 96–121.

Aserinsky, E., and N. Kleitman. "Regularly Occurring Periods of Ocular Motility and Concomitant Phenomena During Sleep." *Science* 118 (1953): 273–74.

Barinaga, Marcia. "New Imaging Methods Provide a Better View Into the Brain." *Science* 276 (1997): 1974–76.

Braun, Allen R., Thomas J. Balkin, Nancy J. Wesensten, Fuad Gwadry, Richard E. Carson, Mary Varga, Paul Baldwin, Gregory Belenky, and Peter Herscovitch. "Dissociated Pattern of Activity in Visual Cortices and Their Projections During Human Rapid Eye Movement Sleep." *Science*, 279 (1998): 91–95.

Braun, Allen R., Thomas J. Balkin, Nancy J. Wesensten, Richard E. Carson, Mary Varga, Paul Baldwin, S. Selbie, Gregory Belenky, and Peter Herscovitch. "Regional Cerebral Blood Flow Throughout the Sleep-Wake Cycle." *Brain* 120 (1997): 1173–97.

Burian, Richard M. "Adaptation: Historical Perspectives." In *Keywords in Evolutionary Biology*, ed. Evelyn Fox Keller and Elisabeth A. Lloyd, 7–12. Cambridge, Mass.: Harvard University Press, 1992.

Cowey, Alan, and Petra Stoerig. "The Neurobiology of Blindsight." *Trends in NeuroScience* 14, No. 4 (1991): 140–45.

Crick, Francis, and Christof Koch. "Are We Aware of Neural Activity in Primary Visual Cortex?" *Nature*, May 11, 1995, 121–23.

——. and Graeme Michison. "The Function of Dream Sleep." *Nature* 304 (1983), 111–14.

——. and Graeme Michison. "REM Sleep and Neural Nets." *Behavioural Brain Research* 69 (1995): 145–55.

Dennett, Daniel C. "Are Dreams Experiences?" In *Brainstorms: Philosophical Essays on Mind and Psychology*, Montgomery, Vt.: Bradford Books, 1978.

——. "The Onus Re Experiences." *Philosophical Studies* 35 (1979): 315–18.

Ebisch, Robert. "Life in the Twilight Zone." *Sky*, October, 1997, 121–25.

Emmett, Kathleen. "Oneiric Experiences." *Philosophical Studies* 34 (1978): 445–50.

Feinberg, Irwin, and Jonathan D. March. "Observations on Delta Homeostasis, the One-Stimulus Model of NREM-REM Alternation and the Neurobiologic Implications of Experimental Dream Studies." *Behavioural Brain Research* 69 (1995): 97–108.

Flanagan, Owen. "Deconstructing Dreams: The Spandrels of Sleep." *Journal of Philosophy* 92, no. 1 (1995): 5–27.

Foulkes, David. "Dream Research: 1953–1993." *Sleep* 19, no. 8 (1994): 609–24.

Giora, Zvi. "The Function of the Dream: A Reappraisal." *American Journal of Psychiatry* 128, no. 9 (1972): 57–63.

——, and Zohar Elam. "What a Dream Is." *British Journal of Medical Psychology* 47 (1974): 283–289.

Godfrey-Smith, Peter. "A Modern History Theory of Functions." In *Nature's Purposes: Analyses of Function and Design in Biology*, ed. Colin Allen, et. al., 453–78. Cambridge, Mass.: MIT Press, 1998.

Gould, Stephen Jay. "Darwinian Fundamentalism." *New York Review,* June 12, 1997, 34–41.

———. "Evolution: The Pleasures of Pluralism." *New York Review,* June 26, 1997, 47–52.

———. "Evolutionary Psychology: An Exchange" (letter). *New York Review,* October 9, 1997, 56–58.

———. "Exaptation: A Crucial Tool for an Evolutionary Psychology." *Journal of Social Issues* 47, no. 3 (1991): 43–65.

———, and Elisabeth S. Vrba. "Exaptation: A Missing Term in the Science of Form." *Paleobiology* 8, no. 1 (1982): 4–15.

Gould, Stephen Jay, and Richard C. Lewontin. "The Spandrels of San Marco and the Panglossian Paradigm: A Critique of the Adaptationist Programme." *Proceedings of the Royal Society of London* 205 (1978): 581–98.

Greenberg, Mark S., and Martha J. Farah. "The Laterality of Dreaming." *Brain and Cognition* 5 (1986): 307–21.

Greenwood, Pamela, Donald H. Wilson, and M. S. Gazzaniga. "Dream Report Following Commissurotomy." *Cortex* 13 (1977): 311–16.

Hobson, J. Allan. "Dreaming as Delirium: A Mental Status Analysis of our Nightly Madness." *Seminars in Neurology* 17, no. 2 (1997): 121–28.

———. "Sleep and Dreaming." *Journal of Neuroscience* 10, no. 2 (1990): 371–82.

———. "The Sleep-Dream Cycle: A Neurobiological Rhythm." *Pathobiology Annual* 5 (1975): 369–403.

———, and Robert Stickgold. "Dreaming: A Neurocognitive Approach." *Consciousness and Cognition* 3 (March 1994): 1–15.

Hobson, J. Allan, Edward Pace-Schott, and Robert Stickgold. "Dreaming and the Brain: Toward a Cognitive Neuroscience of Conscious States." submitted.

———. "The Neuropsychology of REM Sleep Dreaming." *NeuroReport* 9, no. 3 (1998): R1–R14..

———, and David Kahn. "To Dream or Not to Dream? Relevant Data from New Neuroimaging and Electrophysiological Studies." *Current Opinion in Neurobiology,* 8, no. 2 (1998): 239–244..

Hobson, J. Allan, and Robert W. McCarley. "The Brain as a Dream State Generator: An Activation-Synthesis Hypothesis of the Dream Process." *American Journal of Psychiatry* 134, no. 12 (1977): 1335–48.

Joliot, M., U. Ribary, R. Llinás. "Human Oscillatory Brain Activity near 40 Hz Coexists with Cognitive Temporal Binding." *Proceedings of the National Academy of Science,* USA 91 (1994): 11,748–51.

Kahan, Tracey L., and Stephen LaBerge. "Lucid Dreaming as Metacognition: Implications for Cognitive Science." *Consciousness and Cognition* 3 (June 1994): 246–64.

Kahn, D., E. F. Pace-Schott, and J. A. Hobson. "Consciousness in Waking and Dreaming: The Roles of Neuronal Oscillation and Neuromodulation in

Determining Similarities and Differences." *Neuroscience* 78, no. 1 (1997): 13–38.

Kingsolver, J. G., and M. A. R. Koehl. "Aerodynamics, Thermoregulation, and the Evolution of Insect Wings." *Evolution* 39 (1985): 488–504.

Kitcher, Philip. "Function and Design." In *Nature's Purposes: Analyses of Function and Design in Biology*, ed. Colin Allen, et. al., 479–504. Cambridge, Mass.: MIT Press, 1998.

Labruzza, Anthony L. "The Activation-Synthesis Hypothesis of Dreams: A Theoretical Note." *American Journal of Psychiatry* 135, no. 12 (1978): 1536–38.

Lapierre, O., and J. Montplaisir. "Les Parasomnies." *L'Encéphale* 18 (1992): 353–60.

Lavie, Peretz, and J. Allan Hobson. "Origin of Dreams: Anticipation of Modern Theories in the Philosophy and Physiology of the Eighteenth and Nineteenth Centuries." *Psychological Bulletin* 100, no. 2 (1986): 229–40.

Llinás, R., U. Ribary, M. Joliot, and X.-J. Wang. "Content and Context in Temporal Thalamocortical Binding." In *Temporal Coding in the Brain*, ed. G. Buzsáki, et al., 251–72. Heidelberg: Springer-Verlag, 1994.

Llinás, R. R., and D. Paré. "Of Dreaming and Wakefulness." *Neuroscience* 44, no. 3 (1991): 521–35.

Llinás, Rodolfo, and Urs Ribary. "Coherent 40-Hz Oscillation Characterizes Dream State in Humans." *Proceedings of the National Academy of Science, USA* 90 (1993): 2078–81.

Mahon, James. "Descartes on Dreaming and the Essential Self." Unpublished manuscript.

Mancia, Mauro. "One Possible Function of Sleep: To Produce Dreams." *Behavioural Brain Research* 69 (1995): 203–6.

Maquet, Pierre. "Positron Emission Tomography Studies of Sleep and Sleep Disorders." *Journal of Neurology* 244, Suppl. 1 (1997): S23–S28.

———, and Georges Franck. "REM Sleep and the Amygdala." *Molecular Psychiatry* 2 (1997): 195–96.

———, Christian Degueldre, Guy Delfiore, Joël Aerts, Jean-Marie Péters, André Luxen, and Georges Franck. "Functional Neuroanatomy of Human Slow Wave Sleep." *Journal of Neuroscience* 17 (1997): 2807–12.

———, Jean-Marie Péters, Joël Aerts, Guy Delfiore, Christian Degueldre, André Luxen, and Georges Franck. "Functional Neuroanatomy of Human Rapid-Eye-Movement Sleep and Dreaming." *Nature*, September 12, 1996, 163–166.

Matthews, Gareth B. "On Being Immoral in a Dream." *Philosophy* 56, no. 215 (1981): 47–54.

Merritt, Jane M., Robert Stickgold, Edward Pace-Schott, Julie Williams, and J. Allan Hobson. "Emotion Profiles in the Dreams of Men and Women." *Consciousness and Cognition* 3 (March 1994): 46–60.

Miller, Laurence. "On the Neuropsychology of Dreams." *Psychoanalytic Review* 76, no. 3 (1989): 375–401.

Nofzinger, E. A., M. A. Mintun, M. B. Wiseman, D. J. Kupfer, and R. Y. Moore. "Forebrain Activation in REM Sleep: An FDG PET Study." *Brain Research* 770 (1997): 192–201.

Parker, Sue Taylor. "A General Model for the Adaptive Function of Self-Knowledge in Animals and Humans." *Consciousness and Cognition* 6 (March 1997): 75–86.

Putnam, Hilary. "Dreaming and 'Depth Grammar'." In *Mind, Language and Reality, Philosophical Papers, Volume* 2, 304–24. Cambridge: Cambridge University Press, 1975.

Resnick, Jody, Robert Stickgold, Cynthia D. Rittenhouse, and J. Allan Hobson. "Self-Representation and Bizarreness in Children's Dream Reports Collected in the Home Setting." *Consciousness and Cognition* 3 (March 1994): 30–45.

Revonsuo, Antti. "Consciousness, Dreams, and Virtual Realities." *Philosophical Psychology* 8 (1995): 35–58.

Ribary, U., A. A. Ioannides, K. D. Singh, R. Hasson, J. P. R. Bolton, F. Lado, A. Mogilner, and R. Llinás. "Magnetic Field Tomography of Coherent Thalamocortical 40-Hz Oscillations in Humans." *Proceedings of the National Academy of Science, USA* 88 (1991): 11,037–41.

Rittenhouse, Cynthia D., Robert Stickgold, and J. Allan Hobson. "Constraint on the Transformation of Characters, Objects, and Settings in Dream Reports," *Consciousness and Cognition* 3 (March 1994): 100–13.

Shepard, Roger N. "Ecological Constraints on Internal Representation: Resonant Kinematics of Perceiving, Imagining, Thinking, and Dreaming." *Psychological Review* 91, no. 4 (1984): 417–47.

Smith, Carlyle. "Sleep States, Memory Processes and Synaptic Plasticity." *Behavioral Brain Research* 78 (1996): 49–56.

Stephens, G. Lynn, and George Graham. "Psychopathology, Freedom, and the Experience of Externality." *Philosophical Topics* 24, no. 2 (1996): 159–82.

Stickgold, Robert, Edward Pace-Schott, and J. Allan Hobson. "A New Paradigm for Dream Research: Mentation Reports Following Spontaneous Arousal from REM and NREM Sleep Recorded in a Home Setting." *Consciousness and Cognition* 3 (March 1994): 16–29.

——, Cynthia D. Rittenhouse, and J. Allan Hobson. "Dream Splicing: A New Technique for Assessing Thematic Coherence in Subjective Reports of Mental Activity." *Consciousness and Cognition* 3 (March 1994): 114–28.

Sutton, Jeffrey P., Cynthia D. Rittenhouse, Edward Pace-Schott, Robert Stickgold, and J. Allan Hobson. "A New Approach to Dream Bizarreness: Graphing Continuity and Discontinuity of Visual Attention in Narrative Reports." *Consciousness and Cognition* 3 (March 1994): 61–88.

Sutton, Jeffrey P., Cynthia D. Rittenhouse, Edward Pace-Schott, Jane M. Merritt, Robert Stickgold, and J. Allan Hobson. "Emotion and Visual Imagery in Dream Reports: A Narrative Graphing Approach." *Consciousness and Cognition* 3 (March 1994): 89–99.

van den Daele, Leland. "Direct Interpretation of Dreams: Neuropsychology." *American Journal of Psychoanalysis* 56, no. 3 (1996): 253–68.

Vogel, Gerald W. "An Alternative View of the Neurobiology of Dreaming." *American Journal of Psychiatry* 135, no. 12 (1978): 1531–35.

Webb, Wilse B., and Rosalind D. Cartwright. "Sleep and Dreams." *Annual Review of Psychology* 29 (1978): 223–52.

West-Eberhard, Mary Jane. "Adaptation: Current Usages." In *Keywords in Evolutionary Biology*, ed. Evelyn Fox Keller and Elisabeth A. Lloyd, 13–18. Cambridge, Mass.: Harvard University Press, 1992.

Williamson, P. C., A. Csima, H. Galin, and M. Mamelak. "Spectral EEG Correlates of Dream Recall." *Biological Psychiatry* 21 (1986): 717–23.

Wilson, M. A., and B. L. McNaughton. "Reactivation of Hippocampal Ensemble Memories During Sleep." *Science* 265 (1994): 676–79.

———. "Dynamics of the Hippocampal Ensemble Code for Space." *Science* 261 (1993): 1055–58.

Index

acetylcholine, 78–80, 89–91, 118
  memory fixation, 90
Adams, R.
  on involuntary sins, 181–182
adaptation (biological), 8, 20–21,
    25, 37–38, 101–102, 109–113,
    140
  adaptedness, 97–100
  nonadaptations, 107, 122–124,
    194–195
  preadaptationism, 107
adjacency, principle of, 152–160
Adler, A., 42, 44
  on inferiority complex, 44
adrenalin, 13
  adrenal glands, 88, 158
adult dreams, 12, 16, 146–148
AIM model, 78–81
  See also sleep
amines
  See norepinephrine, serotonin
amygdala
  and emotions, 13, 28
animal dreams, 10, 86–87
animal sleep, 84–87
Aristotle, 35–36, 38–40, 49, 67,
    86–87
  Parva Naturalia, 35–36
Aserinsky, E., 62, 176
astrology, 5
Augustine, 18, 19, 130, 179–183

awake cognition, function of, 49,
    140
  as adaptation, 112, 193–195
  See also dream consciousness

Baillet, A., 167
blind persons
  dreams, 83–84
  sleep disorders, 88
blindsight, 122
blood, color of, 106, 108, 116
bones, color of, 5, 116, 195
brainstem, 13, 49, 78, 127
  pontine, 40, 81
  See also PGO waves
Brandon, R., 106, 108–109, 115
  epiphenomenal traits, 106–107
  gene linkage, 106–107
  pleiotropic connections,
    106–107, 117
  ideal adaptation explanations,
    113–117

Cebes, 2
children's dreams, 12, 16, 146–148
cholinergic neurons
  See acetylcholine
Churchland, P. S.
  on "co-evolutionary strategy," 14
Churchland, P. M., 36, 38
Cicero, 18